The Altruistic Species

D0161056

The Altruistic Species

SCIENTIFIC, PHILOSOPHICAL, AND RELIGIOUS
PERSPECTIVES OF HUMAN BENEVOLENCE

Andrew Michael Flescher
and Daniel L. Worthen

TEMPLETON FOUNDATION PRESS
PHILADELPHIA AND LONDON

Templeton Foundation Press
300 Conshohocken State Road, Suite 670
West Conshohocken, PA 19428
www.templetonpress.org

Templeton Foundation Press helps intellectual leaders and others learn about science research on aspects of realities, invisible and intangible. Spiritual realities include unlimited love, accelerating creativity, worship, and the benefits of purpose in persons and in the cosmos.

Library of Congress Cataloging-in-Publication Data
Flescher, Andrew Michael, 1969-
  The altruistic species : scientific, philosophical, and religious perspectives of human benevolence / by Andrew Michael Flescher and Daniel L. Worthen.
     p. cm.
  Includes bibliographical references and index.
  ISBN-13: 978-1-59947-122-8 (pbk. : alk. paper)
  ISBN-10: 1-59947-122-1 (pbk. : alk. paper) 1. Altruism. I. Worthen, Daniel L. II. Title.
  BJ1474.F54 2007
  171'.8—dc22
                                                              2007009545

Designed and typeset by Gopa & Ted2, Inc.
Printed in the United States of America
07   08   09   10   11   12   10 9 8 7 6 5 4 3 2 1

Contents

Preface

AT CALIFORNIA STATE UNIVERSITY, Chico, we have a fine tradition of offering to our honors students upper-division general education courses that, in addition to being exceptionally rigorous, are distinctive in that they are explicitly interdisciplinary and often team-taught. One of these courses was conceived through discussions between the two of us, one a psychologist and the other an ethicist, devoted respectively to understanding the way we are and elucidating the way we ought to be. At the intersection of our interests, we found the phenomenon of altruism. We immediately recognized that altruism could provide the basis for a stimulating interdisciplinary course. We certainly did not imagine at the time just how inspiring the course would turn out to be, for both our students and ourselves. The inspiration arises, in part, from the collision of different disciplinary approaches and the synergistic formation of new perspectives that emerge from that collision. This book is our attempt to impart the outlook we have gained through teaching this course.

Altruism is interesting to psychologists because its existence—if, that is, it really does exist—challenges certain long-held beliefs about human nature and the motives underlying our behavior. To ask "Does altruism really exist?" is to ask something important about our very nature as human beings. Many have assumed that true altruism does not exist, that what seems on the surface to be other-regarding in fact always reflects an underlying self-interested motive (a position called psychological egoism). Is it really our nature to be selfish? If so, can we overcome that essence of our being and become selfless in spite of ourselves? How? Or is selflessness already part of human nature? And if so, how prominent a feature of our psychology is it? Is it merely vestigial or incipient, requiring great energy or unusual circumstances to harness? Is it a rare characteristic possessed only by a remarkable few? Or is it ubiquitous in our species?

The possibility of altruism is intrinsically interesting to ethicists because it presses us to reflect on the core of all moral consideration: the issue of how we treat others. The long history of the field of ethics has been governed until only very recently by an approach that seeks to specify the conditions under which the self is free to pursue its own aims and interests. That is, ethics is traditionally associated in our society with the preservation of liberties and the avoidance of wrongdoing, altruism representing a happy exception to the rule, but not part of the "rules" society must obey in order to remain civil and intact. What if this model turned out not to be appropriate for the sorts of beings we are because it misjudged our inherent connectedness to one another, or at least overstated the dichotomy between self-regard and other-regard? Ethics would then proceed from proactive rather than reactive premises. Helping others would take center stage, and what we should do would become a greater moral concern for us than what we should not do. In turn, altruism would become the paradigmatic moral event, justified not because of a reclarification of what our duties to others are, but because it would in this case become tantamount to human flourishing. Ethics is not studied in a vacuum. The insights it provides are at best thin if divulged from the aloof vantage point of "armchair philosophy." Ethicists must listen to biological and social scientists, whose research importantly bears on properly understanding their subject: human beings. It follows that as we learn more about ourselves, it is ethically honest to adjust our moral expectations accordingly.

One of our purposes in writing this book is to provide readers with multiple entry points into the academic debates concerning altruism. (Different chapters introduce different disciplinary perspectives, ranging from biology and psychology to philosophy and religion.) At the same time, however, we have attempted to sew a single thread through the material, tying together disparate perspectives and their respective methods into a coherent whole. In so doing, we not only review much of the literature from these various disciplines but also attempt to synthesize it in a way that is our own, arriving, in the process, at some basic conclusions. Among these: (1) Altruism exists. It is not merely an illusion that reveals itself, upon close examination, to be disguised self-interest. (2) Altruism is, however, compatible with some forms of self-interested motivation. (3) Altruism is, to a degree at least, explicable. However, no single disciplinary perspective has the market cornered when it comes to explaining altruism and drawing out its implications. We suggest here that the best understanding is arrived at through making connections across the disciplines. (4) Altruism is a capacity that can be nourished through various means that human beings have at their disposal.

We are not born altruistic and we do not divide into "altruists" and "non-altruists." More likely, each of us falls somewhere on a spectrum, although we have the capacity to move within this spectrum in one direction or another. Our nature determines the spectrum's range, while where we, individually, are to be found on it depends on the various ways in which nature is nurtured in our own case. What this means is that how altruistic human beings will be, in contrast to the rest of the animal kingdom, is largely within their control. This presents a challenge both to the psychologist and to the ethicist. As human beings, we distinctively have the ability to adjust our normative expectations and (consequently) our conduct in light of who we discover ourselves to be. In this book, we address this challenge by simultaneously suggesting a more psychologically realistic and a more morally demanding approach to ethics than the one to which our society has become accustomed, one that places the phenomenon of altruism right in the center of the fields of psychology and ethics.

No comprehensive scholarly work of this nature sees the light of day without the selfless critical input of others. We would like to call particular attention to Stephen Post, who graciously discussed our project with us from its inception to its completion and consistently urged us to head in more fruitful directions. The seeds for many of the organizational and substantive decisions we made were planted during a conference that took place at Claremont School of Theology in April of 2005, organized by Stephen Post and Thomas Oord. In addition to these two, we would like thank Craig Boyd, Stephen Pope, Shelley Kilpatrick, Thomas Phillips, Wolfgang Achtner, Kevin Reimer, Nancy Howell, Ron Wright, James Smith, F. LeRon Shults, Patricia Bruininks, Jay McDaniel, Jeffrey Schloss, Warren Brown, and John Cobb for enriching our outlook by offering their unique perspectives during the discussions that took place at that conference. Letha Dunn read the entire manuscript at the last minute and alerted us to remaining ambiguities and areas that warranted further emphasis. For providing perpetual intellectual stimulation and eager engagement with our topic we would also like to thank Jock Reeder, Stephen Pope, Robert Burton, Daniel Veidlinger, Bruce Grelle, Joel Zimbelman, Eddie Vela, Margaret Bierly, Andy Bane, Paul Villegas, Joel Minden, Amy Quarré, Shawna Brewer, and Jeff Steinberg. For providing us with financial assistance during the formative stages of this project, we are grateful to the Institute for Research on Unlimited Love, and particularly its director, Stephen Post.

The impetus for writing this book, our course ("What Motivates Altruism?"), could not have happened without the support of our colleagues

Andrea Lerner, Dennis Rothermel, Joel Zimbelman, Paul Spear, Scott McNall, Manuel Esteban, and Barbara Brautigam, who provided us with the opportunity, encouragement, and financial resources to take on what some might have felt was a risky venture. We are fortunate to be at a university that welcomes, supports, and even facilitates creative, entrepreneurial endeavors undertaken by the faculty. Our course would have been much less than it was had it lacked the contributions of the members of our community engaged in social advocacy, welfare, and service, who met with and mentored our students for five hours a week over a fifteen-week semester: Judy Sitton, Dick Stein, Greg Higgins, Kathy Halloran, Jim Jessee, Kirk Monfort, Tami Ritter, Ed McLaughlin, Nancy Fox, Jack Fox, Jay Coughlin, Katy Thoma, Matt Jackson, Ed Kimball, Darrel Stevens, Kay Stevens, Barbara Kopicki, Cathy Augros, Ryan Bonea, Farshad Azad, Melanie Bassett, Justine Lehman, Marg Smith, Tom Lando, Trish Dunlap, Philip Larios, Scott Chalmers, Bill Such, Ruthie Robertson, Gary Manwill, Bob Michels, JoAna Brooks, Faelin Klein, and Bob Hennigan. They demonstrated altruism in action to our students and, as people who act altruistically are prone to do, exceeded our already high expectations of them. We cannot say enough about the quality of the honors students from whom we were fortunate enough to learn over the few years that we have been teaching this course. Many of their searching and perceptive observations have made their way into these pages.

For patiently enduring our neglect while we wrote this book and for sustaining us with their nurture throughout the process, we want to thank our families: Robert and Joyce Flescher, Ellen, Ethan, Benjamin, and Samuel Foxman, Sharon Flescher, Lynn Worthen, Paul and Carol Worthen, and David Worthen. We dedicate this book to them.

The Altruistic Species

Introduction
Selfishness and Selflessness

ON OCTOBER 28, 2005, forty-five police officers and six staff members were fired from the New Orleans police department for desertion. At the time of this writing, another sixty have since resigned after being placed under investigation for suspicion of abandonment or as a result of personal reasons directly related to the inconvenience of continuing their jobs in the wake of Hurricane Katrina. Such civic negligence, unprecedented in our nation in modern times, understandably represents cause for serious concern. Yet it might be rash to cite this occurrence as an example of the kind of irresponsibility for which the neglectful agents are deemed morally blameworthy. This is because these 105 officers who defaulted on their duties to a citizenry depending on them did so facing some unusual burdens. We can recall with unpleasant ease the widespread devastation, mass hysteria, graphic displays of suffering and death, and unruly, sometimes dangerous, masses precipitated by the crisis. After the fact, some of the police officers who had been dismissed said that to be expected to enforce the law under such circumstances was, in effect, to be asked to perform a suicide mission, and at the very least to show inappropriately little concern for their own welfare and that of their families.[1] While this response does not dispute the justifiable causal link between their desertion and subsequent firing, it does imply a defense against the charge of moral failure. The defense rests on an appeal to the majority view that not inconsiderable weight ought to be given to self-interest in ethical decision making. Although considered a good thing, helping others is not something our society expects of us. It is understood that our instinct to survive and to safeguard our own happiness is primarily what governs our actions, even in a crisis.

This judgment, callous though it may seem to some, is supported by commonsense morality. According to commonsense morality, we should not be expected to endure especially high costs in order to provide aid and assistance to others in need, even when such costs are entailed by our job descriptions.[2] Most of us consider altruism to be an exception to the rule, and while we are happy and ready to praise people for being altruistic, we do not want to live in a society in which altruism is morally required of us. We would rather regard altruism as a morally special kind of activity, appropriate for morally special kinds of people. In this respect, commonsense morality caters to the masses. Its virtue is its ability to explain the normal procedures sensible people follow when making ethical decisions.[3] Within the commonsense framework, it is possible to identify who displays morally culpable or commendable conduct based on noticeable departures from the norm. With respect to the case currently under examination, according to commonsense morality it is not excusable but nor is it irrelevant that 105, and not merely a few law enforcement personnel, abandoned their posts. In defense of the disgraced officers, there is something unfair and even a little self-righteous about a holding them in judgment for acting in a way that, statistically speaking, a sizable portion of the general public would have acted. That those officers in New Orleans who did bravely continue to perform their duties amid the crisis were dubbed "heroes" for doing so calls into further question the assumption that deserters acted egregiously outside of norms or expectations.

And yet, the heroes of Hurricane Katrina, we and the media seem eager to acknowledge, were *also* ordinary men and women, regular sorts of people in whom the best had been awakened as a result of the crisis. They consisted of normal college kids foregoing their fall semester to travel to New Orleans to work with the Red Cross, families in distant parts of the United States inviting orphaned children into their homes for an indefinite period, and fellow victims from New Orleans, who shared their limited resources with others who needed them more. Enormous amounts of blood and money were donated by hundreds of thousands of citizens living across the country.

When we consider what factors might have come to separate the selfishly inclined from the selflessly inclined in the wake of this crisis, we are left shrugging our shoulders. *Both* kinds of people come from every conceivable demographic category. While more of us did not respond to the crisis than did, and while commonsense morality backs our decision not to do so if that is what we decide, the question remains: why do some of us act one way and others act the opposite? This question leads to two others, both of which are central to the aim of this book. How essential is the phenomenon of altruism to the human experience? Does it have the potential to become a ubiquitous phenomenon?

We open with the disturbing case of the desertion of New Orleans law enforcement officials not to defend commonsense morality—indeed, one of us has elsewhere presented a sustained argument *against* commonsense morality in favor of a more demanding moral framework[4]—but rather as a way of emphasizing a truism that can be tempting to overlook when we hold others in judgment, namely, that the vast majority of people are complicated, neither wholly good nor bad, and responsive in their conduct to a variety of motivations. Most of us are selfless *and* selfish. Nature endows us with the propensity to be givers and takers. The vast majority of us will, throughout the course of our lives, pine in both directions at one time or another. There is not only something disturbingly "ordinary" about the 105 that cowered from responsibility under duress, but also something refreshingly "ordinary" about the courageous ones who fulfilled their obligations under the same circumstances. That someone should behave altruistically rather than selfishly is therefore genuinely a subject of interest. In this book, through reference to several disciplinary perspectives, we hope to explain not only how it is that someone can be altruistic instead of selfish, but also whether it is possible through the course of our lives to control how altruistic we can be.

A proper investigation into the nature of these questions, we will see, depends in large part on our animal nature and in particular on our special place within the animal kingdom. Our biology, at the level of our DNA, furnishes us with the raw material that enables us to be altruistic. Insofar as this much is true, we are no different from several other species. Vampire bats have been known to regurgitate blood they have consumed to replenish their famished peers. Belding's ground squirrels, at great risk to themselves individually, frequently issue alarm chirps to help other squirrels avoid approaching coyotes and other terrestrial predators. In these two cases, and many others, the degree to which individuals go out of their way for others in the group is a function of genetically determined dispositions and can be explained by the theories of kin selection, reciprocal altruism, and group selection. Animal altruism, in other words, is for the most part predictable. It can be calculated through reference to the cost-benefit analyses that yield recommendations for when it makes "evolutionary sense" for individual organisms to act selflessly for the sake of the long-run perpetuation of the genes they contain. This does not mean that animals are necessarily aware of the altruistic deeds they perform—that they have deliberately formed altruistic intentions of some sort—but only that they have evolved to behave in an other-regarding manner based on genetic dispositions that have, over time, maximized their survival.

Likewise, human beings display similar tendencies, as when, for example, a mother sacrifices herself for her baby or when participants in a complex competition temporarily ally themselves with one another to defeat an enemy they have in common. In both of these cases the decision to act may take place without apparent conscious deliberation and, as is true for the vampire bats and Belding's squirrels, can be explained nicely by the theories of reciprocal altruism and kin selection. However, in the case of human beings (and perhaps other sophisticated mammals), these instances of altruistic conduct do not constitute the *whole* story. As we suggest in our title, human beings are the "altruistic" species. We can avail ourselves of resources particular to human thought and experience that allow us to expand the genetically predictable scope and degree of concern for others with which we are naturally endowed. How this occurs, we hope to show, involves thinking about how the fields of evolutionary biology, economic game theory, psychology, philosophy, and religion interrelate to explain a special human phenomenon.

Some Proposed Definitions of Altruism

How selfish or selfless particular human beings are, then, is a variable, not a constant. It remains contingent on a series of events that occur after birth, although practically everyone is endowed at birth with the limited genetic capacity to be altruistic. This explains divergent perceptions of which good deeds ought to be considered morally required and which ought to be deemed "above and beyond." In terms of human conduct that we reasonably have a right to expect from one another, is altruism the exception or the rule? The answer depends on whom you ask. From the commonsense perspective, altruism is most often regarded as extraordinary behavior, achievable only by a small, virtuous minority. Many courses in ethics make a point of including inspirational figures such as Gandhi, Martin Luther King Jr., and Mother Teresa because of the depth of their sacrifice for, and unusual devotion to, humanity. Throughout their lives, these three figures distinguished themselves by defying the conventional wisdom about how much any prospective giver should be required to bestow upon a recipient. They stood in harm's way so that others would not be harmed, foregoing in the process the instinctual pull of survival and material replenishment. On the other hand, not only do the most everyday sorts of people engage in altruistic behavior,[5] but altruists themselves declare with unwavering conviction that what they do is nothing special. Gandhi routinely stated that "whatever is possible for me is also possible for a child." The differing perceptions of what is possible for us to do for others are rendered sensible through reference to our divergent upbringing, education, and life experiences, each equipping us differently, over the course of our lives, to alter the limitations nature imposes on us.

The lack of consensus about the normative expectedness of altruistic behavior in human conduct extends to the competing views of human nature held by theologians and philosophers, evolutionary biologists, economists, psychologists, and other social scientists. Process theologians, for example, maintain that at any moment a human being remains susceptible to a loving impulse, the realization of which will, from that moment forth, govern all future spurs to action. On this account, altruism need not be considered the exception to the rule; it is a realizable norm. Augustinians, by contrast, emphasize our fall from grace, resultant moral ineptitude, and utter dependence on God to deliver us from sin; without God, altruism remains a virtual impossibility. Thoroughgoing utilitarians maintain that we are not only able to but must always act to produce the greatest good for the greatest number of people, regardless of how many sacrifices we have to endure to do so. Meanwhile, many economists and psychologists subscribe to a version of "rational actor theory" according to which the deliberate performance of any action necessarily depends on the maximization of self-regarding preferences. The implication of this theory is that we should *never* expect individuals to engage in truly altruistic behaviors.[6] Many philosophers and, notably, some biologists and psychologists demur, contending that just because a selfless act happens also to increase an individual's evolutionary fitness and survival (as determined over time in the process of natural selection), it does not follow that that act is not also authentically altruistic, for the *consequence* of such an act is that one individual is helped by another. Some social scientists think that we can become altruistic through "social norming," which involves the deliberate structuring of our intentions through the internalization of certain societal values. Social psychologist C. Daniel Batson, while accepting the biologist's contention that our limited capacity for altruism is a given of human nature, focuses on intention, defining altruism as "a motivational state with the ultimate goal of increasing another's welfare."[7] Through the repetitive enforcement of values through the medium of culture, we have the capacity to convert selfish dispositions into altruistic ones, so that self-interest need not be the dominant impulse on which we act, even if it is one with which we are also naturally endowed. Auguste Comte, who coined the term in the early nineteenth century, described "altruism" as social behavior that reflects an unselfish "desire to live for others."[8] Thus, Comte's understanding of altruism as an unselfish desire of the self called into question—at the inception of the term—the supposed dichotomy between altruism and self-regard that would come to represent the dominant understanding in later years.

Even a cursory consideration of these options reveals that a plethora of views have been advanced by various fields and disciplines not only about what altruism is, but also about the extent to which it is reducible to self-interest, if at all. Any adopted definition of altruism depends on the prior methodological commitments underlying it. For example, Kantians, interested in ascertaining the purity of an agent's motives, are much more likely to require that intentions count more than consequences in identifying altruistic behavior. Evolutionary biologists, by contrast, are concerned with the effects of someone's actions on an individual or organism in need of help; motives are beside the point and perhaps cannot even be assessed. Methodology also determines assessments about the conceptual possibility of altruism in the first place, i.e., is it an authentic category? Psychological egoists, for whom all behavior is a reflection of self-interest at some level, deny that altruism really exists, while other representatives from disciplines as diverse as the biological sciences, the social sciences, and the humanities allow that other-regard can coincide with genuine interests of the self (which is not necessarily the same as "self-interest").

In chapter one we will discuss in detail the relevant criteria that have been proposed for inclusion in any definition of altruism, after which we will proffer our own definition that comprehensively takes into account each of these various contributions. We intend the definition we introduce to be broad enough to accommodate the insights of several disciplines in the academy, yet not so broad that we will be unable to distinguish altruistic conduct from other behaviors. For now, we wish merely to point out the importance of the relationship between methodology and content. The phenomenon of altruism can be examined from many disciplinary angles, each of which colors our understanding according to its distinctive methodological assumptions. By restricting our investigation into the topic to any one of these, at the expense of others, we would likely miss out on some conceptually relevant features of the phenomenon. This consideration leads to an important clarification of our approach to understanding altruism as contrasted with two others that have been more dominantly employed in the literature.

Unlike scholars who give primacy to a particular discipline in their analyses, and unlike others who find wanting any theoretical explanation that does not rely exclusively on the firsthand testimony of altruists themselves, we see the various disciplines as pieces of a larger puzzle that can each appreciate, and then make sense of, descriptive accounts of altruistic conduct. Thus, our approach, which is methodologically diverse in orientation, is neither reductive nor one that insists on the irreducibility of altruism to any theoretical explanation. It respects a theorist's right to offer explanatory hypotheses about phenomena he or she studies without letting any one of these hypotheses monopolize the investigation. Furthermore, it insists on the distinction between description and explanation, not simply accepting what altruists themselves have to say about their actions as the final word on the topic but, at the same time, making a concerted effort to incorporate their testimony into any proffered theory.[9]

It may be helpful to give some examples of thinkers from whom we distinguish ourselves. First, we may consider theories that regard altruism as a calculated outcome that ultimately advances the "altruistic" agent's self-interest. Three classic cases we will reflect on in part II are Thomas Hobbes' *Leviathan*, Robert Axelrod's *The Evolution of Cooperation*, and Richard Dawkins' *The Selfish Gene*. From the perspectives of psychological egoism, economics, and evolutionary biology, respectively, these three thinkers reduce altruism to something more obviously expressive of our (selfish) human nature. For Hobbes, pity and sympathy are interpreted either as the result of our desire not to be placed in proximity to the abject sufferer or as our instinctive response to imagining ourselves in a similar situation at some future date.[10] When we perform good deeds, Axelrod argues, we do so in response to prior similar gestures because such a "tit-for-tat" strategy of cooperation maximizes our long-term success.[11] Finally, Richard Dawkins' distinction between genes and their survival machines leads him to the conclusion that individuals are capable of unselfish behavior only because such activity has, for certain organisms at certain times, led through the process of evolution to the best outcome for the genes that inhabit them.[12] In each of these cases, and others we will look at too, the actor's perception of his or her actions is not necessary for interpreting them. Rather, altruism is explained to serve the theoretical discipline in which it is being examined, altruists' remarks on the impetus for and significance of their own conduct notwithstanding.

At the other end of the spectrum lie those interpretations of altruism that resist attempts to apply an explanatory framework to altruists' self-understandings of their own conduct. Kristen Monroe, for example, insists in *The Heart of Altruism* that "canonical expectations" of altruists—their most fundamental assumptions about the world—dispose them to see no distinction between their own welfare and that of others.[13] Altruists' first-order testimony about the urgency and immediacy of their obligation to help the one in need serves, in Monroe's account, to trump competing psychological, economic, sociological, and biological explanations for the phenomenon, including explanations in which the actors themselves may not necessarily be fully aware of their motivations. Referring to them as "John Donne's people" ("No man is an island . . .") to signify their superior and exceptional way of looking at the world,[14] Monroe systematically refutes attempts by noninsiders to penetrate the altruist's mindset. In similar fashion, the postmodern ethicist and hagiographer Edith Wyschogrod rejects the notion that motives for action based on either reason or emotion are sufficient to fuel saintly conduct, altruism par excellence. Rather, saints see someone in need, and the loving deed required of them is performed. According to Wyschogrod, attempts to think or feel one's way to other-regard take too long and do not in any case reflect what an altruist is doing when acting altruistically. A saintly "ethics of excess," according to which one divests oneself of one's entire being for the sake of the person helped, is, she asserts, "anti-theoretical"; i.e., it issues forth entirely from the need of the other as a command to which the actor has no (moral) choice but to respond.[15] Saints are "saintly" because they realize what is true of all of us: that we are creatures born "in the red,"[16] ever indebted to those worse off than we are. As such, nonsaints do not have the conceptual resources to contest what saints aver, that whether we realize it or not, we are already altruistic beings (in our essence) and therefore should be (existentially). Although Monroe's and Wyschogrod's approaches are rhetorically powerful, neither sufficiently emphasizes the fact that humans are complex beings, born as animals with certain biological constraints and proclivities, which slowly enable them, through recourse to the cultural, moral, and religious traditions to which they can appeal throughout the course of their lives, to expand upon their innate endowment.

To be persuaded by the first group of theorists is to see altruism as something exceptional and even puzzling, until, that is, it is construed as the odd species of the larger genus of behaviors already predicted by the theory under consideration. Those who defer entirely to the insider testimony of altruists themselves, on the other hand, regard altruism as normatively to be expected of everyone by virtue of our constitution as human beings qua human beings, even if this responsibility is embraced only by a "saintly" few. Between these two extremes, we hope to provide a way of understanding the phenomenon of altruism that on the one hand takes seriously the insider testimony of altruists themselves but on the other hand manages to incorporate explanatory theories from several disciplines into a comprehensive account.

In this book, we explore arguments for the existence of genuine altruism from several perspectives. For example, we try to demonstrate that there are important kernels of truth in biological, psychological, and finally philosophical and religious theories for accounting for selflessness. While the phenomenon of altruism is not reducible to any single one of these methodological approaches, we argue that they are not mutually exclusive, as some have suggested. To the contrary, we believe that the various methodologies available to the scholar interested in learning about altruism can be synthesized to contribute to a coherent, comprehensive, and truly interdisciplinary account of the phenomenon. Thus, in our book, we not only aspire to introduce students and general readers to the major theories from different fields that have been advanced to explain the mystery of altruistic conduct, but also to propose an equally accessible argument of our own that integrates these classic approaches in a new way.

How can disparate disciplines be tied together to shed light on a single phenomenon? Can a methodologically diverse approach to explaining altruism yield a definition that is broad enough to incorporate insights from traditionally competing approaches, and yet narrow enough to make headway in our understanding of what altruism is? Finally, if altruism is indeed something more than self-interest in disguise, how do we account for its presence in human behavior in the first place? That is, what *motivates* altruism, which we would seem not ever to expect from human beings whose desires seem so often governed by sheer prudential impulse? These questions become more pressing when we consider the frequency with which exemplary altruists themselves insist—against commonsensical observation—that they in fact do nothing out of the ordinary. What seems very difficult for most of us is not only possible but normal for them. Somehow, those who perform acts of altruism with unusual frequency are naturally endowed with or have come to cultivate the ability to act for the sake of others even though doing so often does not coincide with the pulls of self-preservation and self-inter-est. Moreover, they do this within and not above the human context. Indeed, it is their understanding of "humanity" itself that, according to their testi-mony, spurs them to act altruistically.

Correspondingly, in this book we call attention to the *human* resources in "nature" and through "nurture" that combine to sustain altruistic behavior. "[G]race does not repudiate nature, but brings it to its completion," Stephen Pope remarks upon introducing his interpretation of Christian love from within his own religious tradition, Catholicism.[17] Grace, to be sure, repre-sents but one form of "nurture," one which we will examine in our chapter on altruism and religion. But Pope's general point is relevant here. Nature and nurture are not only compatible with but dependent upon each other. One of the most distinctive things about human altruism, we argue, is that it neither can be discussed apart from nor is predetermined by the con-straints of human nature. Indeed, to restate a point made earlier in a differ-ent way, the frequency of altruistic conduct is not a constant, but rather a variable that is dependent on the degree to which we come to avail ourselves of those human resources over which we do have control. To be sure, it may turn out that while altruists hyperbolize when they suggest that they are no different from anyone else, they accurately hypothesize that nonaltruists have the potential to "expand their own circles" of concern to include not only others close to them, but also complete strangers.

If this is so, then selflessness in the animal kingdom—which plausibly can be explained by exclusive reference to the theories of kin selection and recip-rocal altruism from the field of evolutionary biology—is an occurrence that becomes significantly more complex in the human situation. Indeed, in the human case distinctively, it may turn out that "nurture" works from the limits of "nature," limits that more obviously constrain the possibility for altruistic conduct in the animal kingdom. Our decision to adopt an inter-disciplinary approach to understanding human altruism is thus not moti-vated by an egalitarian desire to be ecumenical in our outlook, but rather by a genuine conviction that one discipline cannot do all the explanatory work required for grasping this particular phenomenon.

ALTRUISM UNDERSTOOD IN THE DISCIPLINES

We hope that in addition to offering an independent argument for combin-ing the disciplines to account for the phenomenon of human altruism, our book will provide the reader with a clear, basic understanding of both the issues and the general approaches that traditionally have been applied to the study of altruism. To this end, we intend to cover important distinctions that have been proffered to clarify what altruism is, as well as provide the reader with a conceptual apparatus for appreciating foundational concepts in the fields of biology, psychology, philosophy, and religion. As such, some of these chapters stand well on their own as entry points into a particular method of inquiry. For this reason, it may be helpful at the outset for us to provide a general outline of the book as well as preview some of the specific objectives of each chapter.

The book divides into three parts. Part I contains one chapter (chapter one), which is devoted to laying out the key issues surrounding the construction of any prospective definition of altruism. Part II (chapters two through six) addresses the central question of the book, "What motivates human altruism?" from the perspective of several disciplines, both presenting the arguments for and raising criticisms against these viewpoints. Finally, part III (chapter seven) attempts to arrive at a coherent theoretical account of altruism that integrates the various approaches scrutinized in part II. Rather than committing ourselves to the adoption of a single perspective or dismissing theories because they are incomplete, we will here try to show that altruism is in fact an explicable human behavior once we avail ourselves of the insights from a confluence of disparate fields of inquiry.

The aim of chapter one is to clarify some of the disputes over what constitute the relevant features of altruism. What is meant by "altruism"? Is it other-regard? If so, does this make it the opposite of self-interest? Can altruism and self-regard ever coincide? Is there necessarily a self-sacrificial component to altruism? Must the altruist endure a cost for the deed to be considered truly altruistic? Are the intentions of the altruistic deed more indicative than the consequences of it? Who is more altruistic, the refugee who shares his meal with a starving countryman, or Bill Gates, who in 2003 individually gave unprecedented amounts of money to improving health care abroad? Must the altruist be aware of his or her actions for them to be considered altruistic? Who is the quintessential recipient of altruistic conduct? Is giving most authentic when those geographically remote—strangers—receive, or are family and friends, the near and the dear, the proper objects of altruistic conduct? Are altruistic acts supererogatory, above and beyond the call of duty, or are some altruistic acts also rightly considered morally required? Finally, is the ability to act altruistically a special talent possessed only by a few, or is the degree to which we may act altruistically throughout our lives more akin to a skill, one that can be honed and harnessed through training? Each of these questions speaks to the relevant features of altruism. By answering them definitively, one commits oneself to an understanding of the phenomenon that includes some concepts and marginalizes others. Our purpose in chapter one is simply to lay out the various debates, identifying what sorts of scholars might be likely to defend which sides. By the chapter's close, we will offer our own provisional definition of altruism, which, while hopefully widely applicable, will at the same time be discriminating enough to enable one to distinguish the conduct of the exemplary practitioner of altruism from the conduct of the rest of us.

Part II, which constitutes the bulk of the book, provides focused explanations of the phenomenon of altruism from five different disciplinary perspectives. We begin chapter two, which examines theories of egoism, by advancing arguments that treat altruism as a phenomenon that logically must be reducible to self-interest. In this chapter, we seek to analyze some of the classic arguments that have been forwarded to suggest that altruism does not exist, that it is really only the *appearance* of selfless conduct, or egoism in disguise. After presenting these arguments in their most convincing forms, we will then offer rebuttals of those arguments by showing that they are based on circular reasoning, that they often beg the question, and that they invoke mistaken assumptions about human nature and psychology. The remainder of the book will, in some sense, be an elaboration of these rebuttals.

Chapter three addresses the serious attempts that biologists have made to reckon with altruism. We will begin with a rudimentary review of some of the basics of genetics and evolutionary biology—just enough to provide the relevant context for the ensuing discussion. We then attempt to weigh in on the debate over whether altruism is a natural function of biological organisms or rather something that we have to summon "artificially," as it were, in order to overcome our otherwise selfish tendencies. It might seem that natural selection should preclude the possibility of selfless behavior, since any behavior that is less than optimal for the actor should be targeted by natural selection for elimination. But biologists have shown that the genes possessed by individuals may replicate at relatively higher rates in those who display altruistic tendencies. In this chapter, we describe the conventional examples of kin selection, reciprocal altruism, and group selection. In our analysis of these processes, we consider the possibility that the ruthlessly selfish process of natural selection plays an indispensable role in crafting the psychological states that themselves constitute *genuine* other-regard. In this chapter, we consider briefly cost-benefit analyses and game-theoretic models.

Chapter four considers the psychological manifestations of the dispositions furnished by our evolutionary history and the manner in which our individual experiential histories interact with those biological tendencies. Certain emotional responses, such as sympathy, pity, compassion, gratitude, and guilt, are explicable in terms of the evolutionary dynamics described in chapter three. We will argue that evidence from experimental social psychology supports our contention that people may in fact be motivated by regard for the interests and welfare of others, and that it is therefore misplaced cynicism to consider self-interest the common denominator of all motivation. The situations in which altruistic emotional responses are elicited and the behavior thereby produced vary greatly among individuals, however, and in this chapter we will consider developmental and situational determinants of altruistic behavior, which, to some extent, might operate independently of biologically provided dispositions. We will also draw on the work of those who have examined exemplars of extraordinary altruism, and we will attempt to paint a picture of the phenomenology of the remarkable people for whom altruism is not a rare curiosity but a way of life.

Chapter five takes a philosophical turn by assessing systematically the competing major theories that have been forwarded to explain altruism in normative ethics, in particular Kantian, utilitarian, and Aristotelian models of moral action. Besides elucidating key notions within these models (e.g., the "categorical imperative"; "greatest good for greatest number"; "eudaimonia"), the chapter also raises some basic questions about the interface between philosophy and morality: Can universal norms about what we should do for others be grounded in rational discourse? Does helping others constitute a central facet of human flourishing? Is altruism something to which we can reason our way in the first place, or does the impulse for altruism somehow precede reason and theory? That is, if we seek to be moral beings, how far can reason alone take us? Chapter five dovetails nicely with the preceding two in that we continue our argument for the combination of different perspectives to account fully for the phenomenon of altruism. In this chapter, we examine the limits of the will, rationality, and the habituation of virtue for bringing about a loving self, while remaining open to the idea that these qualities can be harnessed to take the self beyond the level of benevolence inculcated by genes or upbringing. In this chapter, then, we look at the efficacy of traditional philosophical approaches as an expansion of the discussions about nurture and nature undertaken in the preceding two chapters.

Chapter six examines the phenomenon of altruism from the perspective of religious practitioners. Here, we delve into a theological and a nontheistic account of benevolence. In the Christian tradition, the believer derives his or her good-samaritanism from foundational scriptural narratives that contain, in one form or other, the commandment to love the neighbor. In the Buddhist tradition, altruism is the natural upshot of taking seriously the Anatta ("no-self") doctrine, which every Buddhist practitioner at every stage of advancement toward enlightenment is enjoined to do. After comparing these two traditions on the question of altruism, we take a look at the nature of some personages who have been proposed as world "saints," for example, Gandhi, Martin Luther King Jr., and Dorothy Day, each of whom has a great deal to say about human nature. The saintliness of these figures is their very vocation; it is woven into the narrative of their daily lives. As such, saintliness, or extreme altruism, might seem excessive from the perspective of common sense. How do we, as ordinary persons, relate to the saints? Are they exemplars to admire from afar or examples to emulate in our own lives? If the latter—if saints are to be emulated—must we take the same "leap of faith" they themselves have taken? From a religious perspective, how accessible is altruism to the ordinary, struggling soul?

In part III, we do our best to make sense of the perspectives addressed in this book and consider some of the commonalities among them. We attempt, additionally, to make the connection between what motivates altruism and practical understandings of the way in which altruism actually works. In chapter seven we move from theoretical models advanced by other thinkers to a synthesis that is our own. As stated previously, between the position that altruism is reducible to the account from a particular disciplinary perspective and the competing view that none of the perspectives considered can do justice to the phenomenon of altruism as seen from the insider's (i.e., the altruist's own) perspective, we attempt to carve out a third alternative: that altruism is indeed a real phenomenon with which to reckon but one precipitated by a *series* of underlying motivations operating at both the unconscious and the conscious level. A comprehensive view best accounts for evidence of different kinds of altruism, as well as for the presence of a wide variety of altruists themselves. In chapter seven we consider the value of interdisciplinary work generally and make an implicit argument for methodological diversity in teaching and research.

ALTRUISM AND OUR DAILY ROUTINE

This book is primarily descriptive in its scope, intended to explain to our readers the different ways in which various disciplines approach a common human phenomenon and, in the process, bring further clarity to a concept that is today still not clearly defined. This central descriptive objective, however, does lead up to a related normative one: in these pages we wish also to enjoin our readers to engage in the introspective enterprise of looking at themselves critically with two questions in mind: Can I be more altruistic than I have been up to this point in my life? If so, should I be?

For the last three years, we have been exploring these two questions with our students in a hands-on, real-world manner. In our co-taught class on altruism we have arranged to have our students shadow persons who live in Chico, California, and are directly engaged in social advocacy, welfare, and service. These students, serving as "participant observers," have been charged with the task of following their "altruists" for a minimum of five hours a week over a fifteen-week semester. In that time, our students have kept journals and have reflected on the overlap and/or disconnect between the theories to which they were exposed in the classroom and what they were learning empirically in the community. In the process, they came to ask themselves whether they were intrinsically different from the persons they were following, or rather capable themselves of harnessing the altruistic capacities they witnessed firsthand. For the many students who did see in themselves traces of these capacities, a further question arose: did they have a responsibility to become more like those they were following, to try to build, however slowly, altruistic conduct more and more into their own daily habits and routines? Is altruism something that is bound always to be considered exceptional, or is it a capacity that all members of a community potentially could develop?

There are, to be sure, an abundance of cases that justify an attitude of skepticism about the prospect of "moral development." One of the best and most horrifying is that of twenty-eight-year-old Kitty Genovese, who at 3:20 A.M. on March 13, 1964, was stabbed to death in Queens, New York, while thirty-eight witnesses looked on and did nothing to prevent her murder. When we consider this case with our students, they at first tend to express shock that no onlooker rushed to offer even some minor assistance to the victim, for example, by calling out for help. However, when subsequently prompted by our follow-up questions—"How routinely do you go out of your way to help others in need?"; "Are you sure that you are *so* different from the ones who stood idly by on that fateful early morning in Queens, New York?"—their gut response gives way to deliberate, thoughtful reflection. The pause is to their credit. It indicates honest introspection: the safety of a classroom setting characterized by the consideration of hypothetical scenarios differs from a real-world situation, where one actually acts on behalf of the one in need.

No analysis of altruism should neglect to reflect upon the many examples in which people have the chance to help others but decide not to do so, some of which are far less conspicuous than the case of Kitty Genovese. Most of us forego opportunities to aid someone in need every day. A society such as ours in which the standard assumptions about legality and morality are built around the avoidance of wrongdoing yields citizens who become quite good at providing justifications for their tendency not to be proactively altruistic. Our culture permits, in fact encourages, such rationalizing. Seen in this light the case of Kitty Genovese, or that of the deserters mentioned at the outset of this introduction, is not so surprising. And yet, as we know from watching the news since September 11, the worst crises tend to bring out the best in the otherwise morally ordinary soul. A student in our altruism class— without our prompting and at significant cost to herself—left school at the beginning of the semester in order to travel to New Orleans to help victims of Hurricane Katrina. The altruists in our community in Chico, California, whom our students shadow each semester they take our course, are among the most down-to-earth, accessible, and regular sorts of individuals we know. Proactive altruism is an option exercised by enough of us that it behooves us not to accept uncritically the assumptions of commonsense morality.

The sheer variety of attitudes toward the other in need exhibited by a sample of those who inhabit nearly any society leads us to hypothesize at the outset of this book that it would be hasty to adopt a deterministic attitude about either the frequency or the depth of altruistic conduct in human experience. There is evidence to suggest that altruism, in consideration of the diversity of its applications, is at once rare and ubiquitous, extraordinary and business-as-usual. Altruism is, it appears, at the very least a latent trait within human beings whose potential for manifestation is more limited for some than for others. In this book, we scrutinize the nature of the human limitation to act for the other as well as our possibilities for stretching it. That is, we examine human nature as well as the propensity with which human nature endows us, through nurture, to build upon our initially limited other-regarding capacities. In so doing, we hope to provide the reader with an array of options, presented across the disciplines, for refuting the aforementioned "skeptical view" that baldly asserts that in any society the impulse to act out of self-interest either always trumps or is necessarily incompatible with an altruistic one. Does this mean that we are an "altruistic" species? At the very least, we hope to show that we have the resources to be.

Part One

What Is Altruism?

1

Altruism Defined

WHEN WE REFLECT upon the number of ways in which one can respond benevolently to another in need, the sheer variety of possible acts that would qualify is humbling to consider. We ask you the reader to think about whether you would characterize as altruism such diverse undertakings as: a soldier diving onto a hand grenade to save comrades; a bee stinging and dying in order to protect the hive; a suicide bomber who believes he is saving his people; a suicide bomber who has been enticed by the promise of a tremendous reward in the afterlife; rushing into a burning building to rescue a stranger; rushing into a burning building to rescue a dog; rushing into a burning building to rescue a cockroach; rushing into a burning building to rescue a person, but the motive is that glory and adulation will follow; a physician abandoning her family during a plague to attend to her patients; a man lying to his wife in order to donate his kidney to a stranger who will die without it; a fireman performing his job by rushing into a building to rescue a victim; giving money to charity; giving a small portion of one's enormous wealth to charity for the tax benefits; a mediocre swimmer diving into the icy Potomac to rescue passengers from a plane that has crashed into the river; pulling a drowning child out of a shallow pond at the expense of getting muddy; warning someone who is about to step in front of an oncoming bus. These scenarios are importantly different from one another. Some of them press us to decide whether the act being considered can be deemed morally good, let alone altruistic. Most important, they call our attention to the disparate, sometimes opposing, criteria upon which we can rely for determining what is indicative of altruistic conduct.

The greatest moral philosophers hardly see eye to eye on these issues. For Immanuel Kant, the purity of one's motive in acting constitutes the decisive indicator of moral worthiness, whereas a utilitarian like John Stuart Mill is concerned more with the outcome of any pursued course of action. Biologists object to philosophers' common insistence that for an agent to act altruistically, the agent needs to be aware of the goodness of his or her deeds. Many philosophers and most biologists do not accept the traditional designation of the stranger as the recipient of other-regard, par excellence. Economists, psychologists, and sociologists alike tend to take issue with the widespread assumption that altruism cannot coincide with a self-regarding payoff, much less any calculation that motivates a would-be altruistic act. Theologians from a variety of religious traditions regard self-sacrifice as an essential feature of altruism, thereby denying the self-lessness of beneficial acts that are not costly. Still other religious thinkers, contra Kant, do not comprehend the possibility for selflessness or even moral action apart from some otherworldly or transcendent motivation. Finally, thinkers from a variety of disciplines question seriously whether acts of sheer foolishness judged from the perspective of common sense (such as engaging in high-cost and low-probability rescue efforts) can ever be said to have an altruistic component. How are we to make sense of these competing analyses? What, if anything, lies at the heart of altruistic conduct?

In this chapter, our goal is to boil down the examples just presented, which cover the gamut, to the major issues that arise when one attempts to identify what altruism is. Specifically, we will focus on six concepts whose relevance to other-regard needs clarification before we can arrive at any definition of the term "altruism." They are, in the order we will consider them: (1) the nature of the *object* of altruism (who represents the ultimate sake for which other-regarding acts are performed?); (2) the question of the *cost* of altruistic conduct (must altruism always be self-sacrificial in some sense, and if so, to what extent?); (3) the issue of *intentions versus consequences* with respect to a potentially altruistic deed (are motives more important than results, or vice versa?); (4) the designation of the *recipient* of altruism (who is to be prioritized over whom, the stranger or kin?); (5) the *moral status* of the performed altruistic deed (is it to be classified as required or above-and-beyond?); and (6) the *normative frequency* of altruistic deeds (is altruism a talent with which few are born or a skill that the majority of us, in principle, have the capacity to harness?).

The standard view of altruism has its default answers to the questions raised in debates surrounding these six issues. According to the common-sense understanding presented in the introduction, an act of altruism is construed as a selfless and costly deed undertaken for the noble purpose of aiding one needing help, and, for precisely these reasons, it is both morally optional and infrequently occurring in society. An altruistic action, in the commonsense view, need not result in the successful improvement of another's welfare or well-being as long as it is performed in good faith, but the question of whether the stranger or the near and dear represents the customary recipient of altruistic deeds is a less settled one.

The commonsense understanding, which considers most forms of altruism to be extraordinary and certainly outside the usual sphere of human activity, sometimes leads to the equally intuitive rejection of the possibility of altruism altogether. Subscribers to the theory of "psychological egoism" embrace the commonsense definition of altruism but remain skeptical of its manifestation in real-world human interaction, so characterized. Accepting the dominant understanding of altruism as purely other-regarding and overly costly, psychological egoists reason that the pull of self-interest and self-preservation is too great in everyday life for us to expect even an instance of "genuine" other-regard, although some acts may appear other-regarding to the lesser observer.

Both the commonsense view of altruism as self-sacrificial, rarely occurring, and above-and-beyond and the psychological egoist's denial of the possibility of altruism are restrictive in scope. This is because they make limiting assumptions about what human beings are (or, rather, are not) capable of as well as about the extent to which other-regard is (or, rather, is not) consistent with self-flourishing. In this chapter, by considering several examples, we endeavor to move beyond these restrictive understandings with the aim of arriving at a definition of altruism that accommodates a broader array of positions about human capacity and human flourishing. In service of this goal, by this chapter's close, we tentatively introduce our own working definition of altruism, which we hope will appeal to thinkers from a variety of fields and disciplines. By the same token, we realize that a definition is useful to the extent that it brings into focus the phenomenon under investigation, and we will, where appropriate, make sure to mention what criteria need to be included in any proposed definition of altruism or altruistic conduct.

ALTRUISM AND THE OBJECT OF OTHER-REGARD

In a famous passage from Camus' *The Plague*, the protagonist, Dr. Rieux, has this exchange with a journalist of recent acquaintance who is now poised to follow the majority of residents out of the stricken town of Oran:

"You're right, Rambert, quite right, and for nothing in the world
would I try to dissuade you from what you're going to do; it seems
to me absolutely right and proper. However, there's one thing I
must tell you: there's no question of heroism in all this. It's a matter of common decency. That's an idea which may make some
people smile, but the only means of fighting the plague is—common decency."

"What do you mean by 'common decency'?" Rambert's tone
was grave.

"I don't know what it means for other people. But in my case I
know it consists in doing my job."[1]

At the moment this conversation takes place, we can infer, Rambert is
weighing his love for his family as well as the desire to flee the spread of a
dangerous disease *against* the presumed obligation to do the "decent," or
altruistic, thing. Self-regard is here cast as a good to be pursued at the other's
expense. Rieux, by contrast, acknowledges no such disjunction. Regardless
of whether we interpret Rieux in this passage to be doing only his job (as a
doctor) or to be doing more than his job (as a mere human being assuming
a superhuman task), it is at least clear that he sees his battle against the plague
as *both* the means to helping others and the key to his own fulfillment.
Rieux's self-understanding of his identity requires him to do the "decent"
thing. He does not see his actions as somehow sacrificial or counter to his
own flourishing, although they may be difficult to carry out under the circumstances. Rambert and Rieux in this passage embrace two possible ways
of seeing the relationship between self-regard and other-regard with respect
to altruistic conduct. For Rambert, acting for the other involves self-denial—
the selfish ambition occurs at the expense of the noble one—while for Rieux
the two go hand in hand.

Rambert's assumption is similar to the one most of us accept. Both the
commonsense understanding of other-regard and the skeptical attitude of
psychological egoism proceed from the premise that "altruism," whatever
else it involves, implies a noteworthy divestment of self. For commonsense
theorists, this in turn implies that altruism involves a laudable and valiant
but by no means required departure from the sway of self-regard, while for
psychological egoists it makes altruism mythical, a fiction that would be nice
and most useful in society if true but unfortunately is not accessible in its
pure form. In both instances, altruism is conceived as inimical to human

nature and therefore either rare or impossible. Even Kant, otherwise known to embrace a moral framework far more demanding than the commonsense view, endorses this traditional dichotomy. For Kant, we can only know for sure that an action has moral value if inclination—which extends to all interests of the self, including self-flourishing in a broad sense (beyond mere self-interest)— plays no part in its motivation. In *Groundwork of the Metaphysics of Morals*, he goes so far as to suggest that it behooves us not even to *delight* in providing needed aid and assistance to others, lest the satisfaction corrupt the sake for which duty is undertaken:

> To help others where one can is a duty, and besides this there are many spirits of so sympathetic a temper that, without any further motive of vanity or self-interest, they find an inner pleasure in spreading happiness around them and can take delight in the contentment of others as their own work. Yet I maintain that in such a case an action of this kind, however right and however amiable it might be, has still no genuinely moral worth. It stands on the same footing as other inclinations—for example, the inclination for honor, which if fortunate enough to hit on something beneficial and right and consequently honorable, deserves praise and encouragement, but not esteem; for its maxim lacks moral content, namely the performance of such actions, not from inclination, but from *duty*.[2]

Here, altruism and any interest of the self, including one that could be noble in nature, are cast as diametric opposites. *No* element of self-interested motivation can move the altruistic action. To be altruistic, the action must be *pure*, i.e., completely uncontaminated by inclination of any sort. Commonsense theorists, psychological egoists, Kantians, and others, then, all share the claim advanced in the first view: that altruism refers *exclusively* to other-regard, which in turn implies a suppression of self-regard.

To accept this view, by far the most popular one, is to set up a dichotomy that can never be bridged; other-regard and self-regard are understood to be Venn diagrams that do not overlap. The problem with it is that, as stated, it contradicts the testimony of some altruists themselves, for example, saints, who are known to announce as the crux of their vocation always to be seeking the betterment of others' welfare as well as the alleviation of their suffering and sorrow. The standard view is too strong, for it understands morality in all cases to be opposed to more than naked self-interest. Altruism is, in the common view, not compatible with any and all interests of the self. This conclusion bucks the wisdom of Aristotle, for one, who claims that "the good person must be a self-lover."[3] Is there a way of clarifying the standard view such that it allows for the possibility that other-regard can sometimes also involve self-flourishing in a broader, larger sense? How do we preserve the sensible notion that "altruism" refers directly to the "alter" or "other" without making additional claims about the self that are too sweeping?

Here it becomes helpful to raise a distinction between *ultimate* and *instrumental* objects. An "ultimate" object is an end in itself. If the welfare of the other is the end—the objective—that is being sought, then the welfare of the other is the ultimate object. An "instrumental" object is a means to an end. By extension, if the welfare of the other is sought only as a means to achieving some other ultimate objective, such as a reward, or in order to avoid ostracism, then the welfare of the other is an instrumental object. With this distinction in place, one could conceivably amend the standard view previously presented, which insists that the object of altruism always be the other, to accommodate a more moderate position: for an act to be deemed altruistic, the welfare of the other must be the ultimate, not the instrumental object of the act in question. Subscribers to the theory of psychological egoism claim that altruism is *never* the ultimate object, although they readily grant that other-regarding action leads to self-interest payoffs in a variety of cases. According to our modified view, it is acceptable to identify a "self-regarding" act also as altruistic as long as the altruistic component stands in a hierarchically superior relationship to the self-regarding one. The advantage of tax write-offs or the internal psychological rewards that accrue from just being generous do not, in and of themselves, obviate the altruistic nature of giving charity as long as it is the donation itself that constitutes the primary activity from which these other benefits follow.

To be sure, there is going to be disagreement over the corrupting influence of the "self" in other-regard. Some thinkers who subscribe to a view we might label "radical alterity altruism" maintain that under all circumstances other-regard must issue exclusively from the needs of the "other" and that even mere consideration of how the self might benefit from or even be affected by the supposed altruistic act amounts to a corruption of the act's status. Edith Wyschogrod, for example, contends that the minute our well-being factors into our response to the one in need, we are no longer truly listening to the other, which precludes us from furnishing an effective response.[4] By contrast, Neera Kapur Badhwar contends that it is by virtue of appeal to our own experience with suffering and sorrow that we are able to provide for the other in need, which, in turn, makes us better off.[5] For Wyschogrod, once the self enters into the moral equation, it becomes too hard to act genuinely for the other, while for Badhwar it is because of the self's experience in the world that altruism becomes a possibility to begin with. Both Wyschogrod and Badhwar, however, seem to affirm that regardless of *how* altruistic acts become a possibility for the self, it is the other whose interests represent the primary focus. In this respect, the language of ultimate and instrumental objects becomes a useful device for testing the authenticity of a potentially altruistic act. For the other to benefit from altruism, the self does not necessarily have to suffer; however, the other in need does have to be the one with whom the self is *ultimately* concerned, consciously or unconsciously, in order for an act to be deemed altruistic.

If this is so, then the opposition commonly established between self-regard and other-regard may turn out to be a false dichotomy (although the one between selfishness and selflessness would not necessarily be). That we may also flourish through the performance of other-regarding acts—and perhaps through the cultivation of an other-regarding disposition over the long run—should not definitively preclude the characterization of our actions or intentions as "altruistic," assuming that they are not *primarily* selfish. At the same time, Kant is right to suggest that when we retrospectively notice that we have benefited in some way from performing other-regarding deeds, or from developing an other-regarding character, it behooves us to become a little suspicious of the seductive influence of the joy or gain we do derive in the process over the formation of our motives, for such joy or gain has the potential to cloud our judgment and prevent us from keeping the beneficiary of our altruistic actions in the front of our minds. As almost everyone knows, human beings can be quite creative and skilled with respect to imagining themselves doing good for others when they, perhaps unwittingly, really have the welfare and well-being of the "dear old self" at heart. If our good deeds never, or rarely, cost us anything, then it seems unlikely that the true object of our actions is another.

ALTRUISM AND THE QUESTION OF COST

How decisive *is* the cost to the actor in determining whether an act is altruistic? What if there is a potential cost to an actor considering an other-regarding act, a *risk* to performing a contemplated other-regarding deed, but that cost is never actually incurred? What must we actually or potentially give away of ourselves in order for someone genuinely to receive?

Perhaps the most conventional assumption about altruism is that in a particular act a recipient's gain corresponds to a giver's loss. Indeed, one of the central ideas behind the notion of "reciprocal altruism," which we will discuss at length in the chapter on evolutionary biology, is that over time these sacrifices even out, making it to both parties' symbiotic advantage to divest themselves of their resources when positioned to be the giver. Correspondingly, the most common reason cited for the rarity of altruism is that people are just too selfish. If altruism were not so often costly, this observation would not be so widely invoked.

The idea that cost is central to selflessness has its defenders, not the least of whom is, again, Immanuel Kant. Kant insisted that while it is *possible* for duty to overlap with self-regard, we can never know for sure that we have in fact acted from the motive of duty unless our actions have actually contravened self-inclination. That is, Kant believed that to accrue a benefit from having acted altruistically makes it at least extremely likely that one has acted on inclination unwittingly. The magnetic pull of self-interest is simply too great for one not to become vulnerable to altering one's objective in favor of self-interest unless one has ensured in advance that one's act strains rather than alleviates one's well-being. Therefore, if one is morally honest with oneself, one must at all times be worried that unless one's selfless act is costly, it will not *really* be a replenishing response, although aspects of it may incidentally be so. For Kant, the central concept of "freedom" is the human capacity to reach beyond animal inclination, to forego appetite in all its subtle and explicit forms when other creatures would naturally succumb to it. To act freely in the Kantian sense is thus to act not to make of one's own case an exception, to let only one's duty to help another govern one's actions. This process, as a matter of natural course, involves incurring costs.

Kant's insight is consistent with the fundamental empirical fact that we live in a world of scarce resources to which those who are suffering have the least access. Lack of material goods is the most obvious kind of lack, and when a material good that one stands to enjoy is given to someone who needs it more, the giver naturally suffers the absence of what has been given away. According to this view, it stands to reason that the greater the gift, the greater the cost (acknowledging, of course, that not everyone qualitatively or quantitatively benefits from the same good in the same respect). If cost to self is not a *necessary* criterion for determining whether an act is altruistic, it would at least seem to be something that accompanies such an act with high frequency.

Actual instances of generous monetary and organ donation support the idea that a costly or sacrificial component is central to the concept of altruism. There is the famous case of Zell Kravinsky, a self-made millionaire whose midlife epiphany caused him not only to give away nearly his entire fortune to various needy others but also, against the wishes of his wife, secretly to plan and carry out a plot to donate one of his kidneys to a complete stranger.[6] In successive lifesaving, heroic acts, not only did Kravinsky exhaust his family's resources (setting aside funds only for the future education of his children), but he did so at the expense of maintaining trust and warmth in his own marriage. Interviewed at length in advance of the operation about whether he was psychologically stable enough to be making this decision, Kravinsky claimed that the sanest thing he could do was to "just give all of me to those who need me, whether it is my body, my money, or myself." Putting aside for the moment the question of whether altruists themselves are in the best position to make such explanatory judgments about their acts, it is clear that there is at least a perceived endlessness to the activity of giving whereby the most conspicuous sorts of givers remain uncomfortable ever saying to themselves that they have "given enough." The very notion of "excess" with respect to giving, in this sense, loses its meaning, for as long as there is an imbalance, the giver's resources must flow in the direction of the recipient.

Critics of Zell Kravinsky—and there are scores—maintain that self-interest is, in fact, very much at play in this case of his kidney donation, and dangerously so. Some point to a psychological disorder characterized by self-abnegation and addictive giving, while others attribute to Zell Kravinsky's motives the more rational desire to see himself as a man of high esteem. Still others, including his wife, Emily, accused the controversial benefactor of making an error in judgment by prioritizing a less important virtue (generosity) at the expense of greater ones (honesty or loyalty), or of committing to helping the stranger at the expense of minimally appreciating the obligation of love owed to one's family. These very real consequences of significant and spontaneous giving have been associated with what is sometimes referred to as "the dark side of altruism." Particularly when third parties are involved, the moral issues can become murky. If we assume that helping the impoverished stranger in need is a good thing, the question arises: Just how much of what I own can I give away before my gift becomes inappropriately self-detrimental? How much can I give away when others close to me depend on me for their well-being? To get to the heart of Zell Kravinsky's true motivations (is he a saint or is he crazy?), or even to arrive at an accurate calculus for determining where someone in his position should limit magnanimous charity and donation, would require a considerable experimental undertaking. To be sure, these are in large part empirical questions quantifying the needs of various parties. Nevertheless, it seems that cost at least looms large as a factor worthy of consideration in determining whether or not an act is altruistic. Even if Zell Kravinsky does not see his gift as (relatively speaking) costly for him, or, alternatively, even if we cynically attribute to him selfish motives, the fact remains that he has donated his kidney, a lifesaving act that for him carries with it consequences he will have to bear for the rest of his life.

Does this mean, then, that for an act to be deemed altruistic it must *necessarily* be considered costly? Must genuine gifts substantively tax the giver? Another example will bring the question into clearer focus. Contrast the case of Bill Gates, a self-made billionaire and philanthropist ranked for the last twelve years by *Forbes* magazine as the wealthiest person in the world, with that of an ordinary, impoverished person working for minimum wage who routinely gives food or available dollar bills to the homeless. Bill Gates has donated a staggering 52 percent of his fortune to various charitable organizations and has arguably done more than any other individual alive to ameliorate healthcare in the third world; as a result, he and his wife, Melinda (along with U2 singer Bono), were named *Time* magazine's persons of the year in 2005. The anonymous, struggling, minimum-wage worker gives much less to far fewer recipients, but gives away a much higher percentage of the resources he or she has to spare beyond those strictly required for personal sustenance. Who is the more altruistic? Perhaps we need not answer and be happy simply to grant that both are. If so, however, we need to reexamine the assumption that cost is a necessary aspect of altruistic giving. For, while 52 percent of Bill Gates' assets comes to between twenty-five and thirty billion dollars, the remaining 48 percent is more than enough to guarantee that neither he nor his family will suffer any reduction in comfort or in the lifestyle to which they have become accustomed. Indeed, Bill Gates could donate 99 percent of his fortune before feeling the cost involved; unlike Zell Kravinsky, he has not given away his riches to their very brink, let alone a kidney. To date, though, he has arguably saved more lives than anyone else has. Countless interviews with Bill Gates confirm that his intentions are good, and it is generally not disputed that he has his recipients' interests, and not his own reputation, in his mind.

Life is neither fair nor black and white. Our lives do not begin on a level playing field. For this reason, both Bill Gates and the ordinary, impoverished person have distinctive moral opportunities available to them that the other lacks. It thus seems sensible not to try to rank these two instances of giving in terms of one's superiority over the other. Yet, they remain useful for us to contrast, for they do call attention to the difficulty of arriving at a set of necessary and sufficient conditions for any observable phenomenon, such as altruism. Cost to the giver, we might conclude, is usually a telling component of altruistic activity, but there are exceptions to the rule, as the case of Bill Gates demonstrates. Benefit to the recipient, the far-reaching consequences of one's gift, must also be given weight and consideration.

Our discussion of the question of cost in altruistic conduct should indicate that we endorse what is sometimes called a "family resemblance" approach to defining phenomena such as altruism. According to the family resemblance view, as opposed to the "common core" approach, the presence of certain traits is acknowledged as indicative but not necessarily determining of the phenomenon being defined. In the case of altruism, cost is a perfect example of one such trait. Altruistic acts will frequently involve substantive, if not unusual, sacrifice. Nevertheless, the counterexample of Bill Gates is a compelling one, indeed, one that precipitates a vigorous discussion among our students when we introduce it to them, if for no other reason than that it challenges the conventional view that gifts always correspond to comparable sacrifices.

ALTRUISM AND THE QUESTION OF INTENT VERSUS CONSEQUENCES

A third trait to consider in defining altruism is that of intent. Must we self-consciously be motivated to procure the benefit of another before we perform an action if it is genuinely to be considered a *moral* action?[7] Is action even required for altruism to take place, or is good intention enough? Which is more important, our deliberative, reflective desire to help out someone in need or the actual benefit that the recipient experiences as a result of our conduct? What if we mean well but the outcome of our intervention in the plight of another is disastrous? Conversely, what if we happen to do good for others, but inside we are callous and insensitive? As usual, a concrete example will help to bring these questions into clearer focus.

In the film *Hero* the character Bernie LaPlante, played by Dustin Hoffman, is a troubled scoundrel and an opportunist who rushes onto a crashed plane to steal what he can before the authorities arrive but, through a series of odd events, ends up saving several of the injured passengers from the burning plane. From the context of the scene it is apparent, certainly initially, that Bernie does not regard with any kind of deep moral concern the beneficiaries of the unexpected rescue he undertakes. Are Bernie's actions altruistic? Can good deeds come from poor intentions? Bernie is selfish, but his selfishness turns out "heroically" to save lives. Would it be accurate to characterize him as a reluctant altruist?

We may consider a less obvious example. What shall we make of the college professor who guest lectures for other professors simply because he enjoys it, and through whose competence, enthusiasm, and hard work, students receive benefits well beyond those of their normal classroom experience? In this example the professor is driven by the self-regarding motive of enjoyment. Does the fact that it is his sheer love of teaching that inspires him preclude the characterization of his activity as altruistic? In the case of our professor, unlike that of Bernie LaPlante, the motive is not sheer opportunism. It is arguably a healthy and affirming one, if not immediately other-regarding.

This last example is not unlike many others, in which one's motives are only indirectly in service of the other-regarding result of the performed action. As Kant liked to point out, our motives are often "heterogeneous"; usually more than one reason accounts for why we do what we do. Even we ourselves sometimes have difficulty pinpointing precisely what spurs us to good action. Does this heterogeneity impugn the worthiness of an act that has good consequences, as Kant insisted? The question becomes more complicated when we turn to examples found in the realm of biology. Animals provide critical support for others of the same and sometimes different species without at all realizing that that is what they are doing (as far as we know). As we will see in more detail in chapter three, there are instances in which other-regarding acts are hardwired into, and therefore largely predetermined by, the genetic makeup of the species performing them. Other-regard is in this case instinctive or reflexive. Does the absence of a formed intention on the part of the selfless (animal) actor necessarily preclude the characterization of that act as "altruistic"?

We need not restrict the inquiry into the centrality of motive to counterexamples from the animal kingdom. Saintly persons of exceptionally high moral character arguably do not form intentions when performing their loving deeds, for they have so habituated themselves to sensing and responding to others in need that when they perceive someone suffering, they perform those acts as a matter of course. For these especially virtuous persons, it is as if the question of motive is bypassed. Indeed, some would say that it is actually *more* altruistic for someone to be other-regarding automatically, in a way that requires no thought at all. Kant would of course demur. For him, the deliberate, self-aware process of thought that governs what actions the good will performs stands in a hierarchically superior relationship to actions or the consequences that flow from them. A good will trumps all other subsequent considerations, including bad results that might happen to follow from good intentions. Correspondingly, good results do not make actions retrospectively moral. Only by willing our actions to conform to our duty to care for and assist others in need as we naturally would care for ourselves do we perform a legitimate moral activity. But if this is so—if Kant is right—then neither animals nor some saints, namely, those for whom other-regard and self-regard coincide, can be fully altruistic.

It seems apparent that as with the trait of cost, we can have disputes with one another about the degree to which intent, or motive, is to be regarded as a critical component of altruistic conduct. There are intelligent people on both sides of the debate. It may be helpful to examine four well-known definitions of altruism to see how prominently intent figures in. The political scientist James Ozinga defines altruism as "behavior benefiting someone else at some cost to oneself,"[8] clearly preferring consequence (to the recipient) and cost (to the giver) to intent, which he does not mention. By contrast, the bioethicist Stephen Post maintains that altruism entails acting "for the other's sake as an end in itself rather than a means to public recognition or internal well-being, although such benefits to the self need not be resisted."[9] This definition requires that the ultimate motive be the other's welfare, but it does not require the actor to endure a cost. Psychologist C. Daniel Batson defines altruism at the outset as a "motivational state" whose ultimate goal is "increasing another's welfare."[10] Like Post, Batson defines altruism with respect to the ultimate motive. But since he defines it *as* the motivational state, it is not clear that action is required. And there is no mention of cost. Finally, Richard Dawkins, a biologist, has this to say:

> An entity . . . is said to be altruistic if it behaves in such a way as
> to increase another such entity's welfare at the expense of its own.
> Selfish behaviour has exactly the opposite effect. "Welfare" is
> defined as "chances of survival", even if the effect on actual life and
> death prospects is so small as to *seem* negligible. . . . . It is impor-
> tant to realize that the above definitions of altruism and selfish-
> ness are *behavioural*, not subjective. I am not concerned here with
> the psychology of motives. I am not going to argue about whether
> people who behave altruistically are "really" doing it for secret or
> subconscious selfish motives. Maybe they are and maybe they
> aren't, and maybe we can never know, but in any case that is not
> what this book is about. My definition is concerned only with
> whether the *effect* of an act is to lower or raise the survival pros-
> pects of the presumed altruist and the survival prospects of the
> presumed beneficiary.[11]

This example, which tacitly refers to the process of evolution, relies on the
notion of fitness in the Darwinian sense (i.e., reproductive success). Notice
that here consequences are paramount; intent is irrelevant. And the actor
must incur a cost. This definition evokes a key problem of which Darwin was
aware: how could the ruthless process of natural selection ever produce
organisms capable of sacrificing their own fitness for the sake of another's?
Darwin, whose own proclivities toward the biological perspective led him to
favor consequences over motive, nonetheless pondered how self-sacrifice, a
seemingly intentional overriding of our natural impulse to self-interest,
could ever be possible. In wondering this, Darwin was essentially asking
whether the deliberate formation of other-regarding tendencies was something available to beings that lacked the mental faculty to obey any impulse
other than natural instinct. In other words, was altruism something in which
animals, and not just human beings, could engage? Many of Darwin's successors would go on resoundingly to answer yes by challenging the assumption that reflective, deliberate intent was a precondition of altruistic behavior.
Genetic predisposition could be as well, and perhaps more effectively so.

We conclude that intention, like cost, constitutes a major indicator of
altruistic activity but is not in all cases a necessary feature of altruism. This
conclusion further demonstrates the usefulness of constructing a "family
resemblance" definition of the phenomenon. Certainly, there are cases of
minor giving in which the discovery of a poor, or selfish, intent would seem

to rule out the possibility of an instance of altruism. If, for example, we learn that someone provides comfort to an ailing relative in the twilight of her life in order to obtain a sizable inheritance, then we can reasonably conclude that something besides altruism is going on, even if some good also comes from the act. But this conclusion does not mean that in this case any motive *besides* the direct, deliberative amelioration of her suffering and sorrow will not lead to an altruistic outcome. As the case of the professor who volunteers to guest lecture shows, self-regarding and altruistic motives can coincide. The judgment is in the end a tricky one that needs to take into consideration, alongside intent, a number of other factors (such as cost, benefit to the recipient, etc.). Sometimes even obviously selfish motives, like the opportunism that motivated Bernie LaPlante, can lead to such beneficial results that we should not immediately reject the possibility of altruism.[12]

RECIPIENTS OF ALTRUISTIC CONDUCT: THE NEAR AND DEAR VERSUS THE STRANGER

Who constitutes the "one in need"? Is there an algorithm for determining whether stranger or kin is to be considered a more worthy recipient of altruistic conduct? If we withhold a full disclosure of the truth to protect someone we love from harm's way, at the expense of some social good, or our own good standing with the law, do we act altruistically or criminally? If someone neglects to engage fully in the upbringing of his children because he chooses to go to a foreign land to aid the sick and impoverished, are his actions noble or neglectful, or, if both, both in what measure?

Not only is it unclear whether the ones close to us have the same moral standing as does the stranger about whom we know nothing, but oftentimes helping the former comes at the expense of hurting the latter, if only indirectly. If we buy someone we love flowers to show appreciation for what that person means to us, we do so at the expense of funds that could otherwise be devoted to grand, charitable causes. Conversely, if we devote time to pursuing those causes, how much energy will we have available to invest in those closest to us, arguably the ones most deserving of our special attention? An example by the philosopher Bernard Williams clarifies the tension that can sometimes arise between these two objects of neighbor-love. Suppose a man is in a position to save just one of two drowning people, a stranger or his wife. What should his process of reasoning be prior to his action? Are both of the people in danger equally worthy of his concern? Both are arguably moral agents among other moral agents to whom he owes a positive duty of aid and assistance, just as according to any utilitarian calculation, all other things being equal, both remain legitimate and worthy beneficiaries of any rendered aid and assistance.

Ought he to be impartial in his decision making? Does he at least need an excuse to deflect criticism that may be directed against him for his impulse (and ensuing action) to favor his wife? Bernard Williams answers *no* to both questions. To ask how the prospective rescuer can morally rationalize to himself his preference to help his wife is to ask "one question too many, [for] it might have been hoped by some (for instance, his wife) that his motivating thought, fully spelled out, would be the thought that it was his wife, not that it was his wife and that in situations of this kind it is permissible to save one's wife."[13] According to Williams, the latter qualification is not only excessive but also inappropriate precisely because of the personal relationship in question. The best motivation he can furnish for saving his wife must surely be that it is his wife, and not just anyone, that he stands to lose! Williams' example is intuitively appealing because of the effectiveness with which it describes how we actually form special relations, i.e., by making particular commitments that extend no farther than the one(s) to whom we commit. One of the reasons one presumably chooses one's wife to be one's wife in the first place is because one wants to protect and come to her defense in a way one is not willing to do so for just anyone. Yet, as many would be quick to point out, utilitarians and Kantians for example, intuition does not amount to justification. Our psychologically intuitive, natural impulse to act for the sake of loved ones close to us can often be selfish. That we *do* favor special relations does not mean that we *should*, morally speaking. It seems sensible, then, to try somehow to delineate before the fact the status of the stranger versus the personal relation.

The matter of who constitutes the recipient of other-regard is a classic concern in the literature on altruism and neighbor-love. It may be helpful to turn briefly to an analysis from within the religious perspective in order to provide further clarification, if for no other reason than that it serves as a common model on which many people base their assumptions regarding this issue. Theologians in the Christian tradition are far from settling this dispute; there are staunch defenders of each position who draw from the same body of evidence—the Gospels—to make their case. One of the most famous expressions of neighbor-love in the Gospels comes from the book of Matthew and sets out what is commonly known as the Golden Rule:

> Thou shalt love the Lord thy God with all thy heart, and with all thy soul, and with all thy mind. This is the first and great commandment. And the second is like unto it, Thou shalt love they neighbor as thyself. On these two commandments hang all the law and the prophets. (Matt. 22:37–40)

According to most interpretations of this passage, at least a few things are unambiguous about the second love commandment: the faithful adherent is directed to love the neighbor as a requirement of his or her discipleship (no *options* are afforded by the command); there are no limits to what may become required in this love (and so the love required could turn out to be very *costly*); and no distinctions are set in place with respect to the person to whom the command applies (the ordinary person is just as bound as the extraordinary or saintly one to issue a response). The question of just who constitutes the neighbor, on the other hand, remains unsettled. The Gospels come a little closer to answering this question in Luke 10, wherein, at the outset of the Good Samaritan parable, when explicitly asked "Who is my neighbor?," Jesus answers that the man is the one going down "the Jericho road," i.e., the one in danger, who could be anyone.

In a seminal book, *Agape and Eros,* the twentieth-century Protestant theologian Anders Nygren interprets the generic nature of Jesus' reply to mean that the neighbor has no constraining qualifications—it could be anybody—and that the neighbor's designation as one with whom we have no prior relationship ensures that our loving response is, in fact, agapic rather than erotic and consequently egoistic.[14] According to Nygren, the life of agape, Christian love as specified by the second love commandment, is one of spontaneous, "unmotivated," and total self-giving in which, through God's grace, we acquire the capacity to love the stranger and even the neighbor. This does not mean that agapic love is arbitrary or foolish in some sense, but rather that it is bestowed in a manner indifferent to value: it makes absolutely no distinction among the worthiness of potential recipients.[15] Erotic love, by contrast, is an extension of self-love governed by the normal, prudential, if sometimes subtle calculations that are inevitably accompanied by self-regarding payoffs. We are motivated to love a significant other erotically, for example, because of the psychological benefits we accrue from being and staying in love with that particular person. A corollary to Nygren's thesis about agapic love is that true altruism preferences "suchness" to "thatness," i.e., it designates the "other" as the human being as-such over and against this or that particular friend, family member, or romantic partner. Only our humanity itself, and no other observable characteristic, warrants the loving attention of those in the position to preserve it.

Not all Christian theologians agree with the traditional view espoused by Nygren that prioritizes impartiality over personal relations. Drawing on insights from the field of behavioral biology, the Catholic thinker Stephen Pope argues that kin and friendship preference ought to supplant love of the stranger in terms of what is typically implied in the love commandment. In the tradition of the great Catholic medieval theologian Thomas Aquinas, Pope maintains that sociobiology offers knowledge about both the limiting and the enabling conditions of love of the other, the awareness of which will help us to order love properly as we interpret its meaning from the love commandment.[16] Beginning from the premise that we are embodied creatures whose insights are formed by basic physical and emotional bonds we naturally form with those we concretely encounter in life, Pope goes on to suggest that our love of the special relation can equip us to love everyone, even those with whom we have no familiar bond. In other words, we can build on the loves in our lives that organically form to expand our sphere of concern to include the stranger. If Pope is right, then it is virtuous of us to love the stranger, but our responsibility to cultivate that love does not necessarily trump our duty to our relatives and friends. On the contrary, it is cultivated in virtue of it. In this sense "grace," by which human beings are able to love to begin with (as Pope interprets his Catholic tradition), improves rather than overturns nature.[17] For Pope, unconditional impartiality is neither realistic nor desirable.

We do not need to resolve the dispute between theologians like Nygren and Pope, or thinkers analogously opposed in other disciplines, in order to appreciate the difficulty in pinning down a designation of the recipient of altruism, par excellence. While it is relatively beyond dispute that it is good to try to be loving toward both the stranger and the special relation, and while many times in life the difficulty in doing so is that we would rather serve our own needs instead, genuine moral dilemmas do arise between which kind of recipient takes moral precedence when the two come into conflict. We have already discussed the case of Zell Kravinsky, a heroic and noble Samaritan to some, a defective husband or parent to others. The characterization we are inclined to accept depends on how we weigh the moral claims of the stranger against those of the special relation. This case, we recall, is complicated by the question of cost: Zell Kravinsky genuinely believed that he had a strict duty to give away everything of his to those who needed it more, of whom there are an endless supply. This observation, in turn, led to a consideration of the "dark side of altruism," according to which the altruist potentially becomes seduced by his or her altruistic activity, at grave detriment to him- or herself. Zell Kravinsky's lavish donations were arguably not morally permissible, let alone morally good. Does this mean that universal altruism should never completely trump the needs of the special relation? It is hard to say by referring to the case of Zell Kravinsky because there is more than one issue at stake. It might be helpful to imagine a real-life scenario in which cost and other considerations do not obfuscate the dilemma between the stranger and the special relation.

Let us examine the case of Holocaust rescuers, where the conflict between the stranger and kin takes center stage. Holocaust rescuers, otherwise known as "righteous gentiles," are widely praised for having sheltered hunted innocents facing sure death during Hitler's genocidal rampage through Europe. According to Mordecai Paldiel, who served as director of Yad Vashem's Commission for the Designation of the Righteous for fifteen years:

> The rescuers saved Jews not necessarily because of their love of Jews, but because they felt that every human being, whatever his or her worth and merit, has a right to life and a minimum decent existence; that this most precious gift ought not to be arbitrarily trampled upon. They believed . . . that when confronted with the challenge to save, they had no choice but to help. There is a bottom line that no one dare trespass, or else life loses its ultimate meaning and becomes indeed what the Nazis professed it to be— a brutal struggle for the survival of the fittest.[18]

For such rescuers, the decision to rescue was an easy one, even though rescuers did not know the beneficiaries of their kindness personally. They had "no choice but to help"; to stand idly by, regardless of what they risked by offering their services, would be to acknowledge that life had lost "its ultimate meaning." Paldiel's characterization is consistent with the testimony of scores of interviewed rescuers, all of whom concur that nothing they stood to sacrifice could compare with the shelter they could provide so many that would have otherwise been murdered.[19] Although the question of whether the rescuers' actions should be characterized as required (as they themselves seem to think) or "above and beyond" is an open one, few dispute that they did a morally wonderful thing. Some, however, would take issue with this assumption, for they would point out that rescuers placed not only themselves but also their families at great risk by sheltering Hitler's victims. The Gestapo was known to hunt down and kill anybody offering Jews aid or assistance. In most cases, this threat extended to the families of rescuers as well. This empirical reality, critics claim, should at least have given righteous gentiles pause before engaging in their efforts to rescue Jews. One significant consideration we should take into account in adjudicating the dilemma in this case is the view of rescuers themselves, who vociferously insist that rescuing was not only morally good but morally required. By virtue of the morally commendable consistency with which they involved themselves in the activity of saving others, and resultant designation as "righteous gentile"—an extremely exclusive label among ethicists, sociologists, and other thinkers working on altruism[20]—it would seem that their testimony should count a little more. Yet, one who wishes to call attention to claims of particular attachments would contend that to stipulate as much would be to beg the question, for rescuers partly already see and understand themselves, in advance, as actors specially committed to the welfare and well-being of the stranger in need! The priority of universal altruism, in the rescuer's analysis, seems assumed at the outset, no less than a vow of marriage seems to commit a man to be willing to put himself in harm's way for his wife in a way he would not do for someone else.

In the final analysis, we are hard-pressed definitively to designate a paradigmatic recipient in constructing any definition of altruism. Unlike the qualification that altruism entails identifying the other as the ultimate object of an other-regarding act, and unlike the subsequent qualifications that cost and good intent are *likely* to be indicative of altruistic conduct, the question of just who constitutes the "other" is considerably more open. In philosophical circles, "impartialists" debate "particularists" over which "other" makes the more compelling moral claim, and more generally over whether impersonal morality ought to trump personal relationships. We have seen in this section the split manifest in theological discussions as well, with the difference hinging on the degree to which one incorporates into one's analysis insights from sociobiology about how attachments of love actually form in nature. Finally, we have seen through real and conceived scenarios that where we end up on this issue depends on the self-perception we adopt when addressing it. When someone asks us for help, do we see ourselves as husbands and wives, friends and lovers, or do we see ourselves as "rescuers" of victims as such? How we answer will govern what we decide or decline to do.

Clearly, acts of altruism involve a recipient of some sort; however, saying any more about this recipient will require some context. It appears that the more criteria we consider as candidates to be built into a definition of altruism, the harder it becomes to affirm with confidence their inclusion in that definition.

ALTRUISM AND THE QUESTION OF MORAL STATUS: A MATTER OF DUTY OR SUPEREROGATION?

Another—perhaps the most widely debated in the recent literature—question to ask about altruism is whether it should be considered morally required or morally optional. When somebody needs our help, are we morally bound to provide it, given that we have the resources to do so? Are we bound even if we will incur a great cost in performing the good deed? If not, is there some tacit notion of "undue burden" at work, beyond which, no matter what good lies at stake, we cannot be required to act on behalf of the one in need?

As suggested at the outset of the chapter, the commonsense view of morality endorses the view that acts of altruism should be considered "above and beyond," or "supererogatory," a word derived from the Latin root *erog*, which means "duty." Commonsense morality assumes that we have a *negative* duty not to violate others' rights, that is, to avoid wrongdoing, but not a *positive* duty to go out of our way to help others to whom we otherwise have no obligations. Legal codes in the United States essentially follow this intuition. While we can be prosecuted for stealing something that is not ours, or for attacking someone when we are not acting in self-defense, there are really no Good Samaritan laws alongside such legal prohibitions that criminalize failures to act. The commonsense view certainly considers proactive other-regard good and praiseworthy, but not, strictly speaking, morally compulsory. As such, it is perfectly appropriate to *admire* altruists for performing their altruistic deeds, but we should not necessarily *emulate* them. The view is based on the still prevalent approach to morality and law in our society that prizes civil and individual liberties. Our right to preference our own welfare and well-being above the overall good precludes our having to perform praiseworthy but potentially costly other-regarding actions.[21] Additionally, the commonsense view maintains that spontaneous, or uncoerced, altruism is to be preferred to that induced under moral pressure. The reasoning here is that the very impulse to act altruistically, or the spirit of altruism,

would decline if costly other-regarding acts came to be regarded as mandatory, for it is the optional nature of altruistic conduct that gives altruism its
special quality in the first place.[22]

The commonsense understanding of the moral status of altruistic acts
conforms to how most of us think about our responsibilities toward others.
We tend to resent it when someone else or society determines for us how
much of what we have should be given away; we are adults and should have
the right to make such decisions for ourselves. Yet, when interviewed, altruists known for making the largest sacrifices—and bringing about the greatest benefits to their recipients—aver just the opposite. They insist that they
had absolutely no choice but to act as they did. Organ donors, everyday citizens who risk their own lives to save others in mortal danger, and rescuers
of victims of genocide are remarkably consistent in their explicit denials that
they have done anything deserving of distinctive commendation as well as
in their affirmation that anyone in their shoes should have done exactly the
same thing.[23] To be sure, it seems that the *more* altruistic someone is, the
more they are likely to insist that they have done no more than all of us would
be expected to do, lest we shirk our basic moral obligation to humanity. In
responding in this way, in denying what we so frequently attribute to them,
namely, that they are morally special, altruists place all of us morally "on the
hook," so to speak. To take seriously the implications of their claim, we must
come to acknowledge that at any moment nearly any sort of act of other-
regard could become required of us. To accept the altruist's own account as
true is also to accept that there is no private space into which we can retreat
and say to ourselves, "I have broken no rules today and now I wish to be left
alone to enjoy myself." Add to this implication the reality that the world contains an excess of people who need our help and we may reasonably conclude that there is no end to our moral duty. If what altruists typically utter
were correct, that they act no differently than anyone similarly circumstanced ought to act, then the world would be a very different place. To take
them literally would, for starters, amount to an all-consuming task, beginning with an abrupt modification of our most basic commitments and priorities. This is simply too much for morality to demand of most people.
Thus, from the commonsensical perspective, we interpret the testimony of
altruists who apply their own moral standards to others as laudatory and virtuous but also as out of touch with reality.

Leaving aside for the moment the puzzling observation that altruists
would make such remarks about their commonality given that they are such

a conspicuous minority in our society (and are surely aware of this fact)—
we will come back to this momentarily—the conviction and confidence with
which they utter them does pose a problem for the commonsense view. The
problem is this: It seems disingenuous to praise and admire altruists for their
altruism and moral fortitude on the one hand and then go on to claim, on
the other, that they are not to be trusted as credible moral authorities when
they, in effect, ask us to emulate them by holding ourselves accountable to
the same demanding standard of moral requirement. Indeed, why wouldn't
it be the case that the one with the most courage and virtue is also the one
who possesses the most moral clarity and insight about what is (all of) *our*
duty to aid and assist the one in need? In a famous article, "Saints and
Heroes," the philosopher J. O. Urmson answers this question by asserting
that altruists who claim as much are really being morally modest.[24] Their
contention is noble and well-intended, but it is also misguided, designed not
to bind us to an unreasonably demanding moral framework so much as it is
to take the spotlight off themselves. They are being rhetorical when they
resist attributions of praise. They must be; otherwise, they would become
psychologically unrealistic in their outlook. Human beings have limits to
what they can give of themselves to others. If we were a society that held ourselves accountable to the thoroughgoing altruist's standard, we would over
time come to perceive all of morality as a burden the more we became familiar with the experience of falling short of its demands. In time, we would lose
respect for even the minimal moral constraints that are necessary to keep
society civil and free from chaos, and all of morality would fall into wide
neglect.[25]

On whom do we count to answer the question of moral status for us: a
defender of the commonsense view, like J. O. Urmson, who interprets the
saints and heroes he discusses as "morally modest" in order to leave intact a
moral framework that is psychologically realistic, or saints and heroes themselves, who, when interviewed, seem serious about their claims of ordinari-
ness as well as about us following their lead? If the latter, does the notion of
supererogation even make sense, or does invoking it just become an excuse
for moral complacency?

The truth is that the insights of both parties need to be respected. Supererogation is a vital concept for purposes of acknowledging the difference
between those who possess extraordinary moral virtue and those who do
not. We are not all capable of performing the same other-regarding acts, and
it at least seems plausible that what might be deemed supererogatory for

some is morally obligatory for others. Urmson is correct that it is imperative to embrace a moral framework that can also work. Morality cannot be
too lofty, for it is intended to be applicable for human beings, not angels.
Urmson arguably overshoots the mark by insisting on one objective minimal standard of moral requirement meant to apply to all moral agents, but
it does make sense to employ the concept of supererogation as a way of distinguishing saints and heroes from the rest of us.

At the same time, those who consistently and significantly go out of their
way to help others are so unified in their testimony that they are ordinary
people, no different from anyone else, and in their assertions that they had
no choice but to intervene on behalf of those who needed them, that we
should not be too hasty to interpret these claims as merely rhetorical. It is
probably true that the majority of us, not as inclined to help the one in need
as they are, are quick to cling to commonsense notions like "undue burden,"
which make room for moral options, as a way of deflecting the cumbersome
process of thinking about the disproportionate amount of time and energy
we invest in ourselves. When we reflect upon Gandhi's statement that "whatever is possible for me is also possible for a child," or the founder of the
Catholic Worker movement Dorothy Day's declaration that "I have done
nothing well, but I have done what I could," the effect is to feel moral pressure to ask ourselves in earnest just what *is* possible or realistic for us to do
for others. The answer is likely to be: more than we are bound to do by commonsense standards. How much more? The answer will naturally vary from
individual to individual, and for one individual throughout the course of a
lifetime. As the poet T. S. Eliot once remarked, "[O]nly those who will risk
going too far can possibly find out how far one can go." Assuming that altruism is morally good, and that we *should* do what is morally good if we can,
we may conclude that altruism ought to be considered morally required to
a greater degree in our society than it currently is. Does this mean that moral
requirement ought to be built into the definition of altruism? That would be
a much stronger claim, one that may be too strong to endorse. For it does
seem true that there are times when individuals without much experience
in acting selflessly reach beyond what they believe their other-regarding abilities to be to do something morally special. Perhaps this occurs when one
gives a large sum to charity for the first time in one's life or decides to put
one's entire career on hold and travel to a distant, disaster-stricken part of
the world to contribute to the recovery effort. At such times, these people
genuinely seem to travel the proverbial "extra mile," and so can be said to be

acting supererogatorily. As they do such activities more and more throughout the course of their lives, and begin to acquire an other-regarding character as a result, what was once considered supererogatory will become, for them, a duty. But this does not mean that their optional displays of other-regard when they were moral novices should not also be characterized as altruistic.

Nor should seasoned practitioners of other-regard, compelled by the strictest sense of duty, not be considered altruists simply because they do not consider their actions to be morally optional. To be sure, such figures are replete with virtue and are known for placing others' welfare and well-being above their own. The other is clearly their ultimate object of concern. We should not assume with commonsense theorists that altruism retains its special quality by virtue of being "freely" chosen if "freely" means totally bereft of moral compulsion. Persons who routinely engage in other-regarding activities may, in a larger sense, give of themselves so repeatedly and in so many different ways that over time they choose to become the sorts of people for whom giving is no longer a choice. Indeed, the best kinds of altruists habituate themselves to the practice of giving and as a result cultivate a virtuous character. By so doing, they come to see vividly, where they once saw palely, the other in need who commands our attention.[26] As such, their "canonical expectations" about the world, their assumptions about what is right and proper in the normal course of human behavior, come to entail selfless, generous giving.[27]

We are now in a position to address a question that we temporarily put on hold earlier: namely, how can altruists account for the statistical infrequency of altruism in the world but nonetheless maintain that what they do is nothing special and deserves no special commendation? The answer is that altruists, by disposing themselves to adopt an altruistic orientation, come to possess an insight about the human condition that at present most of us lack or perceive only faintly: we are more morally capable than we think, and expanding our capabilities to attend to those who are suffering constitutes a life we can (and therefore should) lead. Were the rest of us more informed, we too would come to see as mandatory what our society says is legally and morally optional. When altruists assert that it is "impossible" for them not to do the altruistic thing they have done, while knowing that in actuality so many people do not do the altruistic thing, they are implicitly averring that those who ignore the one who needs their help would not do so if they were more informed about humanity, their inherent connection to the suffering other, and the meaning of their own lives.[28] In this view, complacency and (albeit sometimes unavoidable) ignorance cause us to fail to gather evidence that would otherwise convince us of the exigency of various forms of other-regard we currently consider to be morally optional. Now, whether or not seasoned practitioners of other-regard are right in this judgment, it is clear that for them nearly all forms of altruism are a matter of moral requirement. For them, the notion of supererogation is defunct. As such, it would not be prudent to claim we know better than they do by building into the definition of the activity for which they are most known a trait—optionality—they insist is not present (at least for them).

Self-perception, it thus appears, has something to do with whether altruism is to be considered optional and supererogatory, or required duty. This is not to say that the least virtuous among us are excused from becoming more loving and giving people than we currently are. By acknowledging that altruism is *sometimes* optional, or supererogatory, we are not saying that someone who identifies him- or herself as happily selfish has no obligation to change for the (morally) better over time. We all do. The claim we are advancing, rather, is that at any particular snapshot in time different people will have different moral capabilities, which implies that for some people potential acts of altruism will be optional while for others they will be required. With respect to altruism, what should we merely admire, and to what should we as ordinary people aspire? This is a tricky question that must be answered case by case. The question leads naturally to the sixth and final quality of altruism to consider when pondering a definition of the phenomenon: its normative frequency. Is altruism by its very nature something accessible to a few, or is it something that can be built into all our lives on a more regular basis than it currently is?

ALTRUISM AND THE QUESTION OF NORMATIVE FREQUENCY: A TALENT OR A SKILL?

One sunny, spring day, a traveler visiting Venice, Italy, found himself taken in by the beauty of San Marco Square with its pristine plaza, elegant eateries, and scores of aspiring artists, each with palette and brush in hand, painting one scene or another. Caught in the romance of the moment and with the memory of a Nike commercial fresh in his mind ("Just do it"), he decided he would acquire the tools he needed to join the fray, not fully considering that he'd never successfully drawn or painted anything in his life. Soon enough, the traveler had turned himself into an artist, at least in image. Looking the part, he caught the eye of a six-year-old girl who gave him some credibility by approaching and then standing a few feet in front of him, posing with a graceful smile indicating that, unlike him, she was no novice at this. Over the next few minutes, a small crowd assembled around the determined man, as it usually did when someone began to work in this vicinity. The girl played her role well. She stood still, confident that what initially seemed like random smudges and lines would very soon transform into the usual likeness of her. Alas, it was not to be. After twenty minutes, the girl peered over at the easel to see what he had so far produced and, to her horror, witnessed the two dimensional face of what might weakly pass for an alien from outer space. No sooner was she struck by this revelation than huge tears began to well up in her eyes. She ran to her mother at a nearby café, within seconds the crowd dispersed, and at that moment it occurred to our well-intentioned traveler what a fraud he had been. Here, apparently more than a good attitude or concerted effort was required to be counted among the artists. Dejected for a time, the man got over his humiliation and took a few painting lessons. Sadly, however, his ambition was never to be realized, for he lacked a certain something, the intuition or knack perhaps, that could have made him a painter worthy of San Marco Square.

The protagonist in this story happens to be one of the authors of this volume (who will remain nameless). We tell this story to our students as a way of introducing a contrast between *talents*, which are innate and can never really be taught, and *skills*, which can be acquired through practice over time. There are certain activities, such as singing an aria or hitting a baseball traveling at close to a hundred miles an hour, in which success is clearly more a matter of traits with which we are born than anything else. Is the same true of altruism? Are heroes and saints, for example, born heroic and saintly, or did they become so through repetition and effort? This is all a roundabout way of asking: Are altruists ordinary people that we encounter in everyday society, and if so, what does this imply about our own capacity to dispose ourselves to become altruistic throughout the course of our lives? Just how phenomenal is the phenomenon of altruism?

At stake in answering this question is the issue of the centrality of morality to ordinary human life. Arguably there are certain activities in which it is beneficial for everyone to take part, such as maintaining good physical and mental fitness and cultivating friendships and other relationships. There are things we both can and should try to do regardless of who we are or where our strengths lie. Is altruism to be mentioned alongside these things, as altruists of a variety of stripes passionately insist? Aristotle, the great philosopher credited with spelling out what is involved in the pursuit of the human good, our "eudaimonia," may be a helpful resource to consult in addressing this issue. In a famous passage from the *Nicomachean Ethics*, Aristotle writes that we should "strain" ourselves to the utmost degree to perform "the finest actions" and goes on to assert that those who succeed in doing so are "welcome and praised by everyone" because they have pursued the virtuous life with seriousness and focus.[29] We should, in other words, always aspire to become better people than we currently are, acknowledging the potential to develop our virtuous faculties instead of remaining static. A little later in the text Aristotle adds that we ought to be "pro-immortal, and go to all lengths to live a life that expresses our supreme element."[30] Clearly, Aristotle advocates harnessing virtue with whatever wherewithal we can muster. What is up for debate—and debated vigorously—is whether in these passages Aristotle is referring to those moral and nonmoral traits for which we already have a propensity (so long as they are conducive to our happiness) or to the other-regarding traits that are specifically indicative of moral virtue. Although neo-Aristotelians tend to espouse one view or the other, Aristotle himself is ambiguous on this issue. Our interpretation of him depends on the extent to which virtue, the pursuit of which Aristotle unconditionally advocates, is understood to refer to other-regard. Some interpreters of Aristotle hold that the balanced life involves the pursuit of moral ambitions and nonmoral projects. According to this view the realization of eudaimonia does not prioritize one aim at the expense of the other, barring some special circumstance that involves the consent of a particular individual to do so because he or she feels a special proclivity to engage in altruistic activities. Others interpret "virtue" more narrowly, as a primarily moral trait whose payoff always resides in the improvement of others.

In our course on altruism, we treat the possibility that altruism is a ubiquitously worthy ambition as an open hypothesis, which we test throughout the course of the semester. In an average community, in this case Chico, California, is altruism generally pursued as a vocation or calling by a select few who have already identified in themselves a talent to be altruistic, or is it something that constitutes a more regular sort of activity in which a broader swath of society can participate? On the first day of class, we assign each student in the class a particular "altruist" whom we have identified in advance for the student to shadow for four months. By the end of the semester, our students almost invariably report back to us that even though they are impressed, and sometimes awed, by the goodness of the ones they are following, they can also identify with them. The altruists are, in the students' words, "ordinary," "sometimes flawed," and certainly not do-gooders singularly governed by their altruistic motivations. Our students impart to us that altruism is conveyed by their altruists as something that enriches their lives, just as working out at the gym or deriving satisfaction from their profession does. In other words, altruism is presented as an activity that is generally conducive to human fulfillment.

The more weight we place on this anecdotal evidence, the more, it would seem, we ought to see altruism as a skill that is both learnable and worth learning rather than as a talent in which only a limited few should participate. To lean in this direction is not necessarily to restrict altruism to only a few kinds of activities. The view that altruism is a skill more than it is a talent is consistent with recognizing that different people may have different sorts of preferences with respect to which altruistic activities they choose to explore. One person may find working with mentally handicapped children to be more enjoyable or feasible than assisting the elderly, and so this activity becomes better suited for him or her; another may prefer to donate large sums of money rather than big chunks of time. Altruism pertains to a set of activities with several subsets. Our hypothesis is that these cover enough of a range to be applicable to the vast majority of us, and that our involvement in any one of them is something that is intrinsically worthy. Nor is the view that altruism is learnable meant to preclude the possibility that, for reasons that cannot perhaps be fully understood, some people *are* distinctively talented, either with respect to their capacity to resist the pull of self-interest or with respect to their capacity to love the other in a more immediate way. Not everyone is capable of the same sorts of other-regarding acts. Some people, moral saints for example, are morally extraordinary in a way that the rest of us are not. Again, however, all that is being claimed here is that regardless of our initial capacity for other-regarding activities, not only can it be developed, but it behooves us to make the effort to develop it to the extent that we can.

In the final analysis, we see altruism more as a skill than a talent, though we acknowledge that some individuals are especially talented at participating in altruistic activities. This conclusion is in line with one of the main arguments running throughout this book, namely, that the motivation to be altruistic is intrinsically valuable to the human experience and can spring from several sources, explained in various ways by the different disciplines. If we are right, then the tendency some people have to make comments such as "Since it is not in my nature to be heroic, it is futile for me to aspire toward moral heroism in the first place" downplays the opportunity people do have to *move in the direction* of heroism by taking seriously an ideal that in itself may (admittedly) be unrealizable. As the psychologist and philosopher Owen Flanagan once remarked, the greyhound runs after the rabbit it can never catch, although it would not run so fast if it were not for the rabbit.[31] The faster the greyhound runs, the better; catching the rabbit is not what is of most importance. If other-regard lies closer to the center rather than the periphery of human flourishing, then it behooves us to try to become more like especially altruistic individuals even if it is unlikely that we will ever be just as they are.

In contending that altruism is primarily a learnable skill that has ordinary *and* extraordinary aspects to it, we do not wish to diminish the distinctiveness or noteworthiness of altruistic activity within the larger spectrum of human behavior. Indeed, in the ensuing chapters, we hope to uncover various motivations for human altruism, partly in the hope of bringing some understanding to why altruism, regardless of its frequency, is a special sort of activity. We believe that both scientific and nonscientific evidence converge to demonstrate that we are an altruistic, or benevolent, species, potentially to a greater degree than any other.

Toward a Tentative Definition of Altruism

We have just examined six critical issues, the clarification of which moves us in the direction of a definition of altruism, which we will now tentatively offer. While the traits we have considered above are commonly associated with altruistic behavior, they are for the most part neither necessarily indicative nor precluding of it. Perhaps the only exception to this is with respect to the first of these issues considered, the *object* of altruistic behavior. We did contend that in order for altruism to be taking place, the other has to be the ultimate, and not merely the instrumental, object of other-regard. This qualification aside, our definition is fashioned more from a "family resemblance" than a "common-core" model. That is, we do not purport to announce the definitive list of necessary and sufficient conditions that need to be present to identify a behavior as "altruism." We will present a considerably broader understanding of the concept, one intended to accommodate the use of the term in the context of the different disciplines in which it will be examined in the rest of this book.

Without further ado, then, we will now offer our own characterization of altruism, which reads more like a description than a traditional definition. Altruism occurs when *one acts for the sake of another or others and their well-being and welfare become the ultimate object of one's concern. Altruism will usually, but not always, entail a cost borne by the actor and a benefit to the recipient(s). It will also often be an activity in which the actor deliberately intends to bring about the good of his beneficiary, although it can sometimes occur at an instinctive or prereflective level. The object of other-regard in altruistic activity can be the stranger or it can be the personal relation. Altruism is one's moral duty or it is supererogatory, depending on the context and on who is performing the altruistic deed. Finally, altruism is an activity that is fundamental to the human experience, an activity in which the vast majority of us can and should participate, and, as such, more resembles a learnable skill than a God-given talent, even though there are a few extraordinary persons for whom the aptitude for altruism comes much easier than for the rest of us.*

One thing to note in this understanding of altruism is that we do not oppose other-regard to self-regard. While selfishness, which does stand in contrast to altruism, takes place when one makes oneself the ultimate object of concern, there can be and frequently are self-regarding payoffs to behaving altruistically, not the least of which is the larger fulfillment one experiences by living an other-regarding life.[32] This assumption is not shared by everyone. In fact, it is controversial. We will now turn our attention to the principal opponent to the view that other-regard and self-regard constitute overlapping sets, the psychological egoist.

Part II

What Motivates Altruism?

2

The Perspective of Psychological Egoism
A Sheep in Wolf's Clothing

IN JACK LONDON'S NOVEL *The Sea Wolf*,[1] erudite literary critic Humphrey Van Weyden is forced to examine his idealistic beliefs about the basic goodness of humanity when he finds himself conscripted into service aboard a seal-hunting schooner, the *Ghost*, captained by a ruthless brute called Wolf Larsen. Although Van Weyden is grateful to have been plucked from the sea by Larsen and his crew following a ferry accident, he is dismayed at Larsen's unwillingness to return him to shore. But Wolf Larsen, who is himself fairly well read, is pleased to find himself in the company of someone with whom he can discuss matters of philosophy, and he has no compunction about subjecting Van Weyden, or anyone else for that matter, to his whims. In his new role as cabin boy, Van Weyden witnesses a sort of existence he has never before imagined. Aboard the *Ghost* brutality is commonplace, routine even, and order is maintained not by any sense of civility, but rather by the sheer force of the captain's will, enforced by his awesome physical might.

During occasional interludes in the violence that characterizes life on the ship, Wolf Larsen articulates to Van Weyden his philosophy—a worldview that Van Weyden finds profoundly repugnant but at the same time compelling in its parsimony and resistance to refutation. Life, even human life, Wolf explains, is nothing more than the brief crawling and squirming of creatures that, like yeast, exist for no purpose other than to satisfy their own selfish biological urges. "The big eat the little that they may continue to move, the strong eat the weak that they may retain their strength. The lucky eat the most and move the longest, that is all,"[2] says Wolf. From this Darwinian foundation, Wolf extrapolates the ethical conclusions that justify his own conduct. Natural selection favors those individuals who are strong; therefore, it is good to be strong. "Might is right, and that is all there is to it. Weakness is wrong. Which is a very poor way of saying that it is good for oneself to be strong, and evil for oneself to be weak—or better yet, it is pleasurable to be strong, because of the profits; painful to be weak, because of the penalties."[3]

But, one might object, surely there is more to human life than just that? Don't we have responsibilities to one another? Doesn't morality necessarily entail consideration of the interests of others? "Not at all," Wolf answers. "One man cannot wrong another man. He can only wrong himself. As I see it, I do wrong always when I consider the interests of others. Don't you see? How can two particles of the yeast wrong each other by striving to devour each other? It is their inborn heritage to strive to devour, and to strive not to be devoured. When they depart from this, they sin."[4] So what of altruism? "Any sacrifice that makes me lose one crawl or squirm is foolish,—and not only foolish, for it is a wrong against myself and a wicked thing."[5] Despite Van Weyden's contention that the power of Wolf Larsen's argument lies in its stark simplicity, Wolf seems to have muddled two distinct points, each of which deserves further examination. The first is a descriptive claim about the nature of life and by extension about the nature of humanity, namely, that human beings, like all beings, are inevitably committed to furthering their own aims, interests, and ambitions. This is roughly the view that we will identify as *psychological egoism*. The second claim is not descriptive but normative, although one Wolf believes follows from the first. It is the claim of *ethical egoism*, namely, that because it is ultimately in our nature to be selfish, we *should*, in fact, aspire to be this way. We distinguish Wolf Larsen's two claims in turn.

The first of Wolf Larsen's claims is so accessible in its clarity when stated in its most basic form that it is frequently taken for granted by laypersons and scholars alike. According to psychological egoism, each individual harbors one ultimate objective: the betterment of his or her own welfare. Wolf explains this as a truism based in our own biology: because all creatures are competitors in a Darwinian struggle for existence, it is inescapably our nature to seek our own well-being. Self-preservation has been programmed into each of us by eons of natural selection. In the past, those who lacked the strength or fortitude to preserve their own lives in the face of intense competition from their more resolute conspecifics quickly perished and became the ancestors of no one. So their constitutional weaknesses were not passed on. Those who were endowed with more favorable personal characteristics, including the good sense to put their own interests ahead of the interests of others, had better odds of surviving and reproducing, thereby passing on those characteristics. Because the individual organism is the unit upon which natural selection acts—meaning that it is the individual organism that either survives and reproduces or fails to do so—any inclination to subordinate self-interest to the interests of others will be dealt with harshly. It follows that there is no place in nature for true altruism or altruistic motivation. Intentionally acting to further the interests of another is like kicking the ball into the wrong goal; you are only scoring points for the other team. Even if nature occasionally produces mutants with other-regarding motives, their altruism is a weakness, like a mutant tiger born without claws, which is doomed to pay the ultimate price for its unfortunate defect. For Wolf Larsen, to make any sacrifice for the benefit of another is nothing other than a foolish failure to act in accordance with the exigencies of nature.

Many have accepted such a view of "nature, red in tooth and claw," to use Tennyson's colorful phrase, as an accurate descriptor of the world inhabited by other animals while simultaneously exempting human beings as standing outside or above the natural order. But, notwithstanding the impact of culture, socialization, and technology, surely a Darwinian understanding of our relationship to the natural world demands that we not consider ourselves removed from the laws of nature. We are one species among many, and, as in all other species, our characteristics, physical and psychological, were shaped by millions of years of natural selection. We may be unique, and even quite extraordinary as a species in many respects, but we are not immune to the laws of nature, which must be manifest as much in our psychology and behavior as in the form of our bodies. Darwin knew this, and Wolf Larsen, knowing Darwin, knows this too. A Darwinian world is a world of strife and competition, not a world of peace and self-sacrifice. So even if it seems that people occasionally act for the welfare of others, they are really motivated by some self-interested end. That's just the way of nature. Or so Wolf Larsen believes.

But is this really an accurate portrayal of human nature? Or of nature itself? Is it true that the ruthless process of natural selection necessarily produces only ruthlessly selfish organisms? These are difficult questions to answer, and major portions of the following two chapters will be concerned with developing answers to these questions and analyzing the extent to which Wolf's view of nature, and of human nature, is correct.

Wolf Larsen goes farther than merely insisting that human beings, as products of natural selection, are not in fact altruistic. The second point that merits examination is his claim that even if it were possible to behave altruistically, it would be wrong to do so. Notice the sleight of hand that he has used here. He has advanced a claim that it is only natural to be selfish at all times and in all matters, from which he deduces that only selfish conduct is ethically justifiable. Implicit in this argument is the normative premise that that which is natural is that which is right. And the obverse is then also implicitly held to be true: that which is not natural is wrong. Altruism is a violation of the laws of nature. In defiance of the principle of natural selection, one who behaves altruistically has compromised, even if only in some small measure, his or her fitness. Therefore, altruism is ethically wrong. But is this argument sound? Wolf Larsen's first claim is that all actions *are* motivated by self-interest. It reflects, to repeat, the position called psychological egoism, while the second claim, that all actions *should* be motivated by self-interest, is known as ethical egoism. As we shall see, affirming the latter by demonstrating the former, as Wolf Larsen has attempted, is not a valid line of reasoning. Even if the theory of psychological egoism turned out to be correct, ethical egoism would not necessarily follow as a logical consequence.

Wolf Larsen is a fictional character. We have used his arguments as the backdrop for what follows because he makes a strong case for both psychological egoism and ethical egoism, and he does so in part by appealing to the principle of natural selection. Any theorist who wishes to affirm the existence of true altruism, as we wish to do, must contend with evolutionary theory. Can altruism exist as a product of natural selection, or must it be understood as an anomaly that natural selection automatically acts against? If altruism does occur among human beings, is it a product of our biological nature, or is it dependent upon socializing forces that transcend, overshadow, or negate our biological nature? Can evolution and altruism be reconciled? We intend to advance the argument that the strongest case *against* psychological egoism, and therefore in favor of the existence of altruism, actually comes from the modern gene-centered view of evolution. This argument will be presented at length in the following chapter. First, however, we will consider in more detail some arguments for and against psychological egoism by developing, throughout this chapter, a dialogue of sorts between us and a hypothetical apologist for psychological egoism.

Two Views of Human Nature

Clearly, one's conception of human nature affects how optimistic or cynical one is concerning the prospect of altruism. In order to discern the essence of our nature as individual human beings, Thomas Hobbes and Jean-Jacques

Rousseau have both performed the thought experiment of conceiving of humans existing without government or society. Their famously different conclusions illustrate, perhaps, the limitations of this sort of mental exercise, but they also illustrate how fundamental is the issue of egoism versus altruism in painting a picture of human nature—so much so that each of these thinkers offers his respective take on the issue with little argument, as though the absence of truly unselfish benevolence (Hobbes) or its presence (Rousseau) were practically self-evident.

Although Hobbes' main concern in *Leviathan*[6] is to establish a justification for rule by a sovereign, he builds the case by beginning with the psychology of the individual. In typical reductionistic fashion, Hobbes reasons that society must be explicable in terms of the individual.[7] So to understand the genesis of civilization, Hobbes imagines what it must be like to be a person without society, a person for whom the only cause of action is one's own nature. In such a condition, Hobbes supposes, all are equal.[8] Of course, there are differences among people in strength and intelligence, but Hobbes imagines that these differences are not so great that the weakest or least astute could not find a way to dispatch the strongest or shrewdest. The consequence of such equality, however, is not harmony, but danger.[9] All are equal not only in the capacity to harm one another, but also in their aspirations to attain their own good. Conflict is the inevitable result of each pursuing his own interests by obtaining and using whatever he deems conducive to survival and security, including the property and person of others, while simultaneously defending his property and person from others who would do likewise in pursuit of their own survival and security. There is also, according to Hobbes, another cause of conflict: each naturally, but naïvely, wishes to have his own interests valued by other people to the same degree that they are valued by himself, which other people obviously will not do since they too care only for themselves. So, in the absence of government, people live in a "condition which is called War; and such a war, as is of every man, against every man."[10] Such an existence would be miserable for all and would be characterized by "continual fear, and danger of violent death; and the life of man, solitary, poor, nasty, brutish, and short."[11]

In this condition of nature, this war of all against all, each person's security is greatly threatened, and everyone has both a right and an obligation to preserve one's own life, using any means available. In such a state, Hobbes reasons, because everyone is responsible only for self-preservation, there can be no limit on an individual's right to do whatever is deemed necessary to promote personal security. There are no such things as law, injustice, or morality. Everyone has a right to all things.[12] But exactly because the condition of war is so definitively not conducive to self-preservation, then each person has good reason to seek peace, the attainment of which will necessarily entail giving up the right to all things and agreeing not to harm others in exchange for the assurance that they will do likewise.[13] The result is something akin to the Golden Rule, albeit a negative version: do not do unto others what you would wish them not to do unto you. Civility begins when all extend to others the consideration they would have others extend to themselves. This is, however, a civility that is realized not by way of individuals developing any real concern about the welfare of others, but rather by individuals doing that which best promotes their own security, which includes seeking peace. Compared to the condition of war, peace is so advantageous that it is simply reasonable to give up the right to all things that characterizes a state of nature. So sociality emerges from each person's pursuit of self-preservation. Of course, since some might be tempted to cheat on this arrangement and receive the benefits of their neighbors' restraint while showing none themselves, a powerful government—the Leviathan—is required to enforce the rules.

Notice that, for Hobbes, psychological egoism is practically axiomatic. It is directly derivative from the principle that *is* axiomatic in his psychological theorizing: self-preservation is our most basic impulse. So he is able to claim broadly that "of the voluntary acts of every man, the object is some Good to himself"[14] without offering much evidence for such a claim except an appeal to common sense. He asks us to consider that we all recognize that others will harm us if they are able, as shown by the care we take in locking our doors and otherwise observing precautions to protect ourselves.[15] And that's how we behave when there are laws and authorities to provide protection. Imagine the extent of our distrust—and how justified it would be!—in the absence of laws and civil authorities to enforce them.

But hold on just a second. Doesn't the exercise of common sense, or even just a moment's reflection, reveal that we do care about each other? Benevolent action (or refraining from malevolent action) may often be motivated by the anticipation of reciprocation (or the fear of retribution), but surely that's not always the case, is it? Yes, self-preservation is a powerful motivational force, but do we not also have impulses that have as their objective the good of others? If our motives are always self-interested, then how can we account for those who give to charity, particularly when it is patent, as it often is, that the recipients of the charitable act will never be in a position to reciprocate? Hobbes recognizes that such behavior occurs, of course, and he accounts for charity by invoking a return that he believes is quite salient: power. "There can be no greater argument to a man of his own power than to find himself able not only to accomplish his own desires but also to assist other men in theirs."[16] And what about those pangs that we feel when we see someone suffer? Do they also somehow spring from self-interest? "Grief, for the calamity of another, is pity," Hobbes allows, but it "arises from the imagination that the like calamity may befall himself."[17] These rather uncharitable interpretations, ad hoc though they may be, neatly reconcile Hobbes' foundational belief in psychological egoism with the empirical observation that human beings often help one another and experience vicarious distress at the misfortune of others.

Rousseau agrees with Hobbes that human beings in a "state of nature" would be characterized by a rough equality, but, in stark contrast to Hobbes, Rousseau paints a fairly rosy picture of the life of the "savage," while regarding the emergence of sociality as the source of iniquity, inequity, and misery. Living as a solitary creature, without language, property, or commerce, the natural human would be a more impressive physical specimen than the civilized human, though perhaps not as strong or agile as many animals, and would also be quite clever, with the capacity to adopt a variety of subsistence strategies (which could be arrived at by imitating various animals) and thereby obtain a relatively easy living.[18] With plenty for all, there would be no need for strife. Rousseau proffers the pleasant image of a man "satisfying his hunger under an oak tree, quenching his thirst at the first stream, finding his bed at the foot of the same tree that supplied his meal; and thus all his needs are satisfied."[19] What need is there for hostility in this tranquil utopia?

Moreover, not only is conflict unwarranted by the conditions of natural existence, human nature itself dictates against it. Whereas Hobbes assumes that human beings naturally possess a single primary impulse, that of self-preservation, Rousseau proposes two: self-preservation and compassion, or "a natural repugnance to seeing any sentient being, especially our fellow man, perish or suffer."[20] Rousseau agrees with Hobbes that pity involves identification with someone who is suffering, but pity is a truly compassionate feeling for the other, not an abstraction produced by the faculty of reason that warns of the potential for a similar fate befalling oneself. "Pity is what, in the state of nature, takes the place of laws, mores, and virtue, with the advantage that no one is tempted to disobey its sweet voice."[21] So in a state of nature, people live happily and harmoniously, without ill will, indeed without much contemplation at all, living as they do in the immediate present, in direct contact with their world, experiencing it through their senses and enjoying their leisure and the easy fulfillment of their appetites.

For Rousseau, it is reason that is dangerous. Where Hobbes argued that reason is instrumental in guiding one to enter into the covenants with others that will obviate the condition of war of all against all, Rousseau sees reason as a corrupting influence that generates incorrigible self-interest. For self-interest is a condition that depends on the capacity to consider oneself as compared to others, a capacity that he believes would not have existed in the presocial human. It comes about gradually as tool use, language, cooperation, competition, and reason—all of which are social constructions— take hold, and it becomes endemic once people begin staking claims to private property, which inevitably leads to disparities in wealth, and also to oppression and even enslavement of the poor, to distrust, and, given the circumstances, to a not unreasonable preoccupation with advancing the interests of the self. Morality becomes connected with duty and legal responsibility, rather than springing spontaneously from our capacity for compassion. The end result is a sort of egoism. Egoism does not necessarily inhere in our nature, but it is nevertheless established in us by the corrupting influence of the institutions of society, masking our capacity for true compassion and interfering with our potential for happiness. Happiness would be possible for us, Rousseau suggests, without any requirement that we divest ourselves of our enlightenment and our civilization, if we were to restore equality and freedom to all, under which conditions our intrinsic goodness could reassert itself.[22]

So which vision of human nature is correct? Are we swept along only by the implacable current of self-interest, or can we also be moved by an irreducible other-regard that runs equally as deep in us? One way to answer is to say that neither Hobbes nor Rousseau has really done much to forward an accurate depiction of human nature, in part because both assumed that the essence of humanity could be ascertained only when the complicating encumbrances of society were removed from consideration. This is naïve and ill-conceived because human beings are inherently social creatures. Whether Hobbes and Rousseau considered the idea of humans without society to be a hypothetical abstraction conjured for strictly heuristic purposes or considered it to be a real historical stage in the evolution of our species

(Rousseau, in particular, seems to hold the latter view, and Hobbes, referring to Native Americans, suggests that such a condition has existed at some times for some peoples),[23] the thought experiment is moot, for the simple reason that it is expressly *unnatural* for a human being to exist without society. Even on those exceedingly rare occasions when the discovery of a feral adolescent offers a glimpse at the psychology of the completely unsocialized person, little can be inferred about human nature, because these children's experience has been distinctly inhuman. Did our species, or our primate ancestors, ever exist as isolated ships in the night, with no intercourse among adults except of the sexual variety, as orangutans today live? The answer appears to be an unequivocal no. For at least the last several million years, our ancestors have lived in social groups, dependent upon one another for survival. The gregarious chimpanzee, not the solitary orangutan, appears to provide a closer model of human beings in a state of nature, if by a state of nature we mean a condition in which it is actually natural for humans to exist.

Hobbes may also have been naïve to think that human psychology can be reduced to a single ultimate motive. Indeed, Hobbes reduces not only psychology but moral theory itself to a single principle: hedonism. According to Hobbes, those things that we call "good" are simply those things we desire (or "love") because they produce pleasure, while those things we call "evil" are those things we avoid (or "hate") because we find them to be unpleasant.[24] Although Hobbes allows that we have many words to express a wide variety of psychological states, he shows how they all reduce to (or can be defined in terms of) our appetites and aversions. Hedonism is therefore a particular form of psychological egoism that holds that self-interest is indexed, at least roughly, by net pleasure attained and pain avoided. We shall have more to say about the relationship between the pleasure/pain dimension and motivation, but the point for now is that Hobbes' form of egoism hangs on his psychological theory. If his theory of motivation is incorrect, then his version of psychological egoism collapses. Of course, the same argument can be applied to Rousseau: if he is wrong that compassion is a basic human motive, then he might also be wrong to reject psychological egoism. Ultimately, then, the question is an empirical one, and a deeper understanding of psychology will be required to adjudicate the issue. Suffice it to say at this point that both Hobbes and Rousseau most likely have oversimplified the nature of human motivation by reducing it to one or two fundamental impulses.

Another way to answer the question of which of these two characterizations of human nature is closest to the mark is simply to address the central issue: is psychological egoism correct, or does altruism exist? Historically, psychologists, economists, political scientists, and other social scientists have tended to accept psychological egoism as a kind of truism. It has long been upheld as a sort of null hypothesis, a formulation that is accepted as true by default unless and until an alternative formulation—which, in this case, would be that altruism exists—is convincingly demonstrated to be true. For the remainder of this chapter, we would like to adopt the reverse tactic and assume that the burden is on the psychological egoists to prove their case. In the chapters that follow, the burden of proof will shift back to us as we attempt to provide positive evidence for the existence of altruism.

We ask the reader at this point to allow us a degree of liberty with respect to our use of pronouns. As mentioned earlier, we wish to present the arguments for and against psychological egoism through the rhetorical device of a dialogue between us and a hypothetical subscriber to psychological egoism. Since much of the debate will necessarily concern itself with the nature of motivation, and since motivation is clearly a personal phenomenon, it will seem awkward if we confront the egoist with the condition of "our" motivational states. Thus, in the following section we will introduce another hypothetical character to help us argue our position, a character who will speak with our voice but will be identified as "I" or "me." The word *we* will still be used where appropriate to refer to us as the authors of this book, or in the way that it is often used generically to indicate other collectives such as all human beings. The word *you* will often be used by our hypothetical egoist to refer to our singular alter ego, "me." Even though the egoist is directing his comments at "me," not at you, when he says "you," we hope you will find yourself identifying with "me" (us).

The Choice

It's a Sunday morning in Denver and although the sky is now clear and blue, a major snowstorm has just ended and everything is blanketed by nearly a foot of snow. The Broncos have a home game today, and I'm going. I go to every home game. In fact, I pretty much spend the entire week looking forward to the game, and the entire off-season looking forward to football season. My mother is the same; we go to the games together. We've always been very close, and this is perhaps our favorite thing to do together. So today I'm particularly glad to have my four-wheel-drive tucked snuggly inside the garage. No toiling away out in the cold with a snow shovel or an ice scraper for me! Of course, lots of ticket holders won't make it out to the stadium today, because of the weather, but we'll be there, doing our part to cheer the Broncos on to victory. We never allow inclement weather, or anything else for that matter, to dissuade us from going to the game.

My confidence in my vehicle turns out to be justified. Even though these early-season snowfalls are wet and heavy, my truck slices through with just a bit of wheel spinning, and I make it down the driveway and onto the roadway. I'll be out of the side streets and onto a plowed thoroughfare in just a couple of minutes; then it will be smooth sailing. We'll be right on time for the kickoff.

I'm barely out of the driveway when I notice my neighbor, whom I know only as Ed (is he an Edward, an Edgar, or maybe an Edwin, I wonder?), struggling to move the heavy snow with a cheap-looking plastic snow shovel. What in the world is he thinking? I don't know Ed well at all, but I do know that he's well into his eighties and that he has fallen at least once—in better weather than this—which landed him in the hospital for a couple of days. He's lucky he didn't break anything. And he'll be even luckier if he doesn't hurt himself with this foolishness. Or worse. The old guy is going to give himself a heart attack. Really, what's he thinking? Okay, sure, I know there's a law that requires people to clear their walks, and I know the law has the good intention of providing safe passage for pedestrians, but who's going to be out walking around today? Nobody, that's who. It's Sunday, so there's not even mail delivery. And it's not like he's going to get a ticket or anything. No one really pays attention to the shoveling ordinance, and the snow will probably be nearly melted off by tomorrow anyway. Come on, Ed, what are you doing? Put the shovel down, go inside, and have a nice mug of hot chocolate or something.

But Ed's not going to do any such thing. He knows his duty, and he's going to see to it. That much is clear. Maybe I should stop and help him. Maybe I could get him to go inside if I told him that *I* want some hot chocolate, and then I'll take care of the sidewalk while he prepares the chocolate. How long could it take to clear his walk? I mean, obviously, it's going to take *him* practically forever, frail and stooped over as he is, but I bet I can zip it out in a few minutes. Fifteen minutes, max. Maybe. Well, probably more like half an hour. Oh, who am I kidding? He'll probably want the driveway done as well as the sidewalk. If I stop to help, I'm going to be stuck here for a good hour. By the time I pick up Mom and we get to the game, we will have missed the whole first quarter. I'd better keep going. I'll just pretend I didn't see him. I can barely see him in the rearview mirror now anyway. He'll be okay—hey, maybe the exercise will be good for him!

Once again, my vehicle impresses me with its power and traction as I whip a tight 180-degree turn and head back to Ed's house. I hope the Broncos will get through the first quarter all right without the encouragement of our cheers.

THE CHOICE-IMPLIES-DESIRE ARGUMENT

In the preceding hypothetical vignette I decided to go back and help Ed. Why? By definition, psychological egoism requires my reason—my true reason, anyway—to be self-interested, since ultimately, according to the theory, all voluntary actions are motivated by self-interest. But what could this mean? How could anyone possibly argue that my assistance to Ed is an example of the pursuit of self-interest?

The egoist might argue in the following manner: Yes, you stopped to help your neighbor, and yes, doing so caused you to miss part of the game. But that doesn't mean that it wasn't a self-interested act. You behaved voluntarily, which means that you acted on the basis of your own desires. In short, you did what you wanted to do. You were faced with a choice between two options: (1) see the entire game and disregard poor old Ed, or (2) miss part of the game and help Ed. You chose the latter option, which means that, ultimately, you preferred that option. If you had preferred the first option, you would have chosen it. So, given the circumstances, and taking nothing away from the exertion of your deliberations or from the fact that both options entailed sacrifice, you did what you most wanted to do. That's not to say that you wouldn't have preferred it if Ed had been safe and cozy inside his house all along so you could have gone straightaway to the game without any concern for his well-being, but that wasn't one of the options. Of the options actually available to you, you chose the one you preferred. You did what you wanted to do. And not just in this particular instance, for it is always the case that voluntary actions are those which we choose, and that they are therefore reflective of our desires (again taking into account the constraints of reality and the fact that in any situation only certain courses of action are actually available). Whatever we have done voluntarily, it is what we wanted to do. Otherwise, we would have done something else.

As James Rachels has pointed out, this is a strange way to define what it means to "want" to do something.[25] I surely *did* want to go to the football game, and I decidedly did *not* want to spend an hour shoveling snow. To say that I chose as I did because it is what I "wanted" deeply mischaracterizes the nature of my motivation. The force that I felt was not one of desire, but of obligation, along with a strong sense of concern for the well-being of my neighbor. I also felt, quite powerfully, the pull of self-interest, of my desire for my own pleasure—but had I heeded that call I would have kept moving toward the football game. The force that turned me around was of a different sort, which not only was not reflective of my self-interested desires but stood in opposition to them.

A moment's reflection will reveal that we all voluntarily do things that we don't want to do. How many times have you heard someone say, with a heavy sigh, "I don't want to go to work today," an utterance that is promptly followed by the person heading off to work? Are people lying when they say such things? Or would it be more reasonable to allow that people often voluntarily do things that they don't really want to do? It seems perfectly legitimate to accept the notion that motivation consists in more than just desire. Yes, we often do things for self-interested reasons, and sometimes the impetus is rightly described as desire. But even when our ultimate goal is some benefit to self, desire is not always an accurate characterization of the tenor of the motive. I don't want to go to work, but I do have responsibilities to fulfill, and yes, I do want to keep my job and receive a paycheck. Admittedly, going to work is a self-interested act, or at least a means to a self-interested end. But that doesn't mean that I *want* or *desire* to go to work, in the sense that we usually use such words. I can say with no contradiction or duplicity that I don't want to go to work—and then still go to work. Motivation and desire are not necessarily the same thing (although desire might constitute one important class of motives). So even if psychological egoism were true, the egoist's present argument couldn't possibly establish its veracity, because even self-interested acts cannot all be said to be reflective of our wants or desires. It just is not true that we always do what we want to do. And if the argument fails in cases where self-interest is indisputably at work, how can it succeed in proving the presence of self-interest in arguable cases, such as in the case of my decision to turn around and help Ed?

Perhaps, though, the egoist's argument could still generate some traction if we could be convinced to ignore the idiosyncratic use of the words *want* and *desire*. Remember, the egoist says, we're considering the example of your choice between two options, and you freely chose one course of action over the other. You object that you didn't really "want" to shovel snow and miss part of the game, but the argument was not about the absolute strength of your desires: it was about the relative strength of your desires. You may have loathed the course of action for which you opted, but you loathed it less than any alternative course of action, which is to say you preferred it. You weighed the alternatives and you picked the one that was least objectionable—to you! So while it's understandable that you object to the characterization of your motivation in this case as "desire," the foundation of the argument stands unperturbed, and your choice was, after all, self-interested. You did what you wanted to do, or what you preferred to do, or what you least detested doing—pick your descriptor; the point is the same.

Setting aside for the moment the important question of *why* I might prefer helping Ed to indulging my love of football, we can now put to rest once and for all the egoist's argument by admitting that it is true. The egoist has shown that when I voluntarily select a course of action, I do so because of some psychological impetus, which can go by many names—want, desire, preference, relative preference, and so forth. And how does the egoist know what I prefer? How does the egoist establish that I prefer helping Ed to getting to the ball game on time? That's easy. Whatever I choose to do *must* be what I prefer to do. So preference now means nothing more and nothing less than the selection of a course of action. It no longer connotes anything in addition to the choice itself, such as actual desire (in the way that we ordinarily use the word). The egoist's claim is this: I choose to do what I prefer to do. But since preference is the same as choice, this translates to: I choose to do what I choose to do. Brilliant. And while, like all tautologies, the claim is true by definition, it seems to have fallen a good bit short of the mark with respect to what the egoist hopes to prove. At best, the egoist has merely asserted what no one denies, that behavior is motivated. To go further than mere tautology and establish something meaningful about the nature of motivation—namely, that the basis of all motivation is self-interest—the egoist will have to do better than simply point to the existence of choice.[26]

THE IDENTITY ARGUMENT

The egoist at this point might object that we have misunderstood the argument. The point is not the degree to which the qualities of various motivational states can be captured by terms such as "want," "desire," and "prefer." And the point is not to suggest that it is okay to adopt an oversimplified view of the complexities of motivation or render the concept meaningless by obscuring the distinction between motive and action. The point is that, whatever their various qualities and however multifaceted and diverse they may be, surely your motives are *your* motives. Who else's could they be? If you are motivated to go to the game and you do so, you do so to satisfy that motive, which is yours. If you are motivated to help your neighbor, and you do so (despite your grumbling that you don't really want to), you do so to satisfy that motive, which is also yours. So again, the conclusion must be that all voluntary behavior is self-interested, since it is undertaken to satisfy motives (whether we call those motives desire, obligation, compassion, or something else) that belong to the person performing the actions.

Again, as in the previous argument, the refutation lies not in showing that the egoist's premise is false, but rather that, while true, it is merely tautological and does nothing to adjudicate the issue at hand. Of course *my* motives are *mine*! No one would suggest otherwise. But the fact that I am the possessor of my motives does not imply at all that they must be exclusively self-interested. If I say that I am motivated to secure the welfare of someone else, I am certainly not denying that it is *my* motive of which I speak. Yet few would see such a statement as anything other than a declaration of concern for someone *other than me*. Why is that? What is it about such a statement that conveys the implication of other-regard, that makes it manifest that my motivation is *not* self-interested? As we argued previously, not all motives are identical, and furthermore, distinctions made between any of my motives cannot logically be based on who possesses them, since that will always be me. Distinctions must be made on the basis of the goal to which the motive is directed.[27] Surely, there is a legitimate distinction to be made between "I was motivated to go to the football game" and "I was motivated to help my neighbor Ed." The egoist's argument allows no such distinctions, however, because it takes the possessor of the motive as its sole defining quality, a tactic that would allow no distinctions of any sort ever to be made between an individual's motives. As Joel Feinberg writes, "*not where the motive comes from* (in voluntary actions it always comes from the agent) but *what it aims at* determines whether or not it is selfish."[28] The argument applies with equal force to any basis upon which one might want to parse motives, except to whom they belong. My motives can be distinguished from yours on the basis of which are possessed by whom. No further parsing or characterization is possible, however, unless we allow the object of the motive to count. With respect to self-interested versus altruistic motivation, surely the difference lies in whether the objective is benefit to myself or benefit to someone else, a distinction to be found in the predicate's object, not in the subject, of sentences like "I want to go to the game" and "I want to help Ed."

THE MOTIVE-SATISFACTION ARGUMENT

But perhaps we are still missing the point. It's not just the fact that your motive is yours that is being asserted, the egoist might say. And no one is denying that motives can be distinguished on the basis of their objects. One must think carefully about what a motive is and what it means to act on a motive in order to understand why psychological egoism is necessarily true. A motive is a reason for acting. It specifies an end to which an action is a means. Identical acts by different people, or by the same person at different times, can have different motives. Most of the time, the reason for driving an automobile is that it is a convenient way to reach a certain destination. On other occasions (perhaps on a pleasant day with the convertible top down), a person might drive for the sheer enjoyment of driving. The behavior in both instances is similar, but the motives are quite different. Conversely, it is also the case that identical motives can result in different actions. Two people are both motivated to make it to work, but one drives and the other cycles. There are many ways potentially to satisfy a motive. But the result, if the action is successful, is always the same: the motive is satisfied. If your reason for driving was to get to work, and you did so successfully, then your end was achieved, and the motive was satisfied. (Of course, not all action results in successful attainment of its goal, in which case the motive is not satisfied, but that does not detract from the present argument.)

Now, the egoist continues, given that you *act* on a motive, it only makes sense to say that your action was intended to realize the state of affairs indicated as the motive's end. If you drove in order to get to your place of employment, then you intended to arrive at your place of employment, and driving was the means by which you realized that goal. It would be ridiculous to suggest that you had the goal of getting there, and you acted on that goal by driving there, but you had no interest in achieving that goal. You might have possessed other motives, such as a desire to stay home and watch daytime television, upon which you didn't act, but in the case of those motives it makes no sense to assert that you also had the objective of realizing their ends. Only in the case of motives upon which one acts does it make sense to say that one also intended that the objectives of those motives come to fruition. This means that whenever one does act upon a motive, there are always two objectives: the specified end state to which the action is a means and the realization or attainment of that end state. It is only in the realization or attainment of the end state that we say that the motive has been satisfied. If you successfully arrive at work, your goal has been realized, and your motive has thereby been satisfied. Should you fail to arrive at work (perhaps because of a mechanical failure in your automobile), nothing about the relationship between the act of driving and the end it was intended to achieve (arriving at work) has been altered, but your other objective, that of actually realizing the specified end, has been thwarted.

To reiterate, the argument is that whenever people act voluntarily, they have as a goal—a superordinate goal, if you will—the successful attainment of the objective of the action, which is to say that they have as a goal the satisfaction of their motive. Now, to whom does this satisfaction accrue if the objective is attained? Obviously, it accrues to the actor, since it is the actor who is in possession of the motive that is satisfied. So in the case of any motive upon which a person acts, it must be conceded that the person is, in fact, seeking to satisfy his or her own motive, which renders every voluntary act self-interested. This is just as much the case for acts intended to promote the welfare of others as it is for any other act. You say you returned to help your neighbor shovel snow because you were impelled by a motive that had as its goal the promotion of his welfare. That's fine, as far as it goes. If it is assumed that you were successful in the job, that you convinced Ed to let you shovel his walk while he retired to the warm safety of his house, and that your motive was thereby satisfied, then to whom does the satisfaction belong? You, of course, exactly as you intended. (Remember that when one acts on a motive, one *always* has the intention of satisfying that motive.) Ed may well have also been pleased to have the help, but on the other hand, he might have taken umbrage at your patronizing insistence that he shouldn't be engaging in such strenuous tasks. He might have been quite displeased! But that wouldn't necessarily have mattered much to you, since your goal was not to endear yourself to Ed but to keep him safe. The point is that in an ultimate sense you didn't help to satisfy Ed: you helped to satisfy yourself, to attain an end that was specified by your motive. So your act, compassionate though it was, was ultimately self-interested. Since the same thing can be said for any act, psychological egoism must be true.

The reader at this point has probably discerned that the egoist's foregoing argument has the same flavor as the previous two, and as we will now show, it is similarly flawed. To begin with, the egoist has subtly conflated two meanings of the word *satisfaction*. The word is often used in one sense to indicate a particular psychological experience that could also be described as pleasure or contentment. There is no disagreement that in some cases we are motivated to achieve an objective entirely or in part because it will produce this agreeable state of mind, and in such cases it is legitimately said that the ultimate motive is self-interested. I might desire to get a massage, for example, exactly because I expect the massage to result in this sort of satisfaction. But in many cases, what we seek is not expected to bring about an experience of satisfaction of this sort. If I miss part of the football game to help Ed shovel snow, I do so with the expectation that, far from being contented, I will be uncomfortable and irritated. Furthermore, even if my act *does* result in pleasure to me, that does not mean that I was motivated by pleasure attainment as an end. Feinberg makes this point with the apt example of taking a hot bath, an activity that is sometimes undertaken explicitly because it is pleasurable, but that is usually motivated by other concerns, such as a desire to get clean.[29] One may well find the hot bath pleasurable regardless of the motive for bathing, but there really is a difference between bathing for pleasure and bathing to get clean, and in the latter case it is simply not empirically accurate to describe satisfaction (qua pleasure) as the bather's objective.

So why did the egoist's argument initially seem to have an aura of plausibility? Part of the reason is that through most of the argument, "satisfaction" was used in another sense, one in which it means something more like "fulfilling certain conditions." For example, a job announcement may state that applicants are required to type at least fifty words per minute. If an applicant can in fact type at that rate, then the applicant has fulfilled, or satisfied, the stated requirement. When the word is used in this sense, it is certainly true that by acting on a motive, we seek to satisfy it, which is to say that we seek to achieve its end by fulfilling the conditions specified as its object. But that does not imply at all that we seek satisfaction in the former sense (as pleasure or contentment). And it is nonsensical to claim that satisfaction in the latter sense entails an additional end that necessarily accompanies the explicit objective. The egoist says, "Whenever one acts on a motive, one must also seek to satisfy that motive." But the last eight words could be omitted without subtracting any meaning from the sentence because they add nothing to what has already been said. To act on a motive *is* to seek to satisfy it. The egoist claims that whenever I act on a motive, I am seeking satisfaction (of the motive), which means that I am seeking to fulfill the conditions specified by the motive, which is exactly the same as acting on the motive. All that is meant by satisfaction, though, is that my action was successful. No additional end has been generated by virtue of my action. If I help Ed, I have the objective of securing his welfare—that is the end to which my act is directed—and if I am successful in doing so, then it can be said that my motive has been satisfied, but only because its end was achieved, not because satisfaction, however defined, was ever an end in itself. Moreover, satisfaction of a motive, in that sense, *cannot* be an end unto itself, at least not in any meaningful way, because it means precisely the attainment of the explicit end state specified by the motive. To say that we seek satisfaction when we act on our motives is no different than saying that we seek to attain what we seek to attain. Once again, we find that the problem with the egoist's argument is not so much that it is false as that it is merely tautological. The egoist has proved nothing more than the notion that when we act, we intend to attain certain goals, a point that no one denies, but a point that does nothing to advance the claim that all voluntary acts are rooted in a self-interested motive.

PSYCHOLOGICAL HEDONISM

The preceding arguments for psychological egoism all had a certain flavor; that is, they had a common logical structure. Each one attempted to show that psychological egoism is inevitably true, that it is a logical necessity to be demonstrated by argument, without need of marshaling empirical evidence. Each argument failed because it turned out that nothing synthetic was being claimed. Under scrutiny, the arguments were revealed to say nothing more than "I choose to do what I choose to do," "My motives are my motives," or "I seek to attain what I seek to attain."

The most powerful statement of psychological egoism, however, is not based on logical arguments but on a theory of human psychology that says that we are, as a matter of empirical fact, constituted in such a way that our voluntary actions always have as their ultimate objective our own self-interest. This theory has been so influential that it is often not even recognized as a theory but taken as a kind of truism. We have already met it in the philosophizing of Thomas Hobbes and the fictional character Wolf Larsen. Among political philosophers, it probably reached its apogee (or nadir, depending on your point of view) in Jeremy Bentham's utilitarian "pleasure-seeking machine"[30] (which is not to say that all utilitarianisms espouse hedonism).

It has been adopted in psychology, at least implicitly, by theorists as divergent as Sigmund Freud and B. F. Skinner. It is the theory known as psychological hedonism.

Psychological hedonism, like psychological egoism, says nothing about how we ought to behave. It asserts, rather, that we are psychologically constructed such that the only thing we are capable of pursuing as an ultimate end is our own pleasure. (Ethical hedonism, in contrast, is a normative theory that says that we *ought* to do that which maximizes pleasure and minimizes pain, regardless of our actual psychological constitution.) Obviously, psychological hedonism is a particular brand of psychological egoism, since pleasure attainment is a particular example of a self-interested end. So if psychological hedonism is true, psychological egoism must also be true. Or so it would seem. Later we will make a case that there is a way to reconcile psychological hedonism, or at least something similar to it, with the existence of altruistic motivation, which would seem to suggest that psychological hedonism (or something like it) could be true without psychological egoism also being true. But first we will bring back the voice of the egoist to present the arguments in support of psychological hedonism.

Our egoist friend might begin by asking us to recall the arguments we employed to counter the motive-satisfaction argument for psychological egoism. The argument failed, we said, because "satisfaction" did not mean satisfaction in the sense of pleasure, but in the sense of "fulfilling certain conditions," which is not an end to be sought at all. But, the egoist says, satisfaction *should* be taken to mean pleasure. Ultimately, it is the only thing we are capable of pursuing. This claim might seem obviously false, as some of the examples previously considered seem to demonstrate. After all, isn't it true that usually one bathes not to attain pleasure (although the bath might be pleasurable) but to get clean? No argument there. So hasn't psychological hedonism, with this one example, been disproved?

Well, no. At this point, it is important to raise the distinction between that which is an ultimate motive and that which is instrumental. The behavior of taking a bath can be deconstructed into a virtually limitless set of subsidiary behaviors. First you twist the faucet handles, an act that is motivated by the desire to start the water flowing. Then you adjust the water temperature, an act motivated by the desire to make the bath comfortable. Once in the bath, you reach for the soap, an act motivated by the desire to, say, begin washing your face. The list goes on and on, but the point is that all of these individual actions are subordinate to the larger goal of getting clean. Each minute action can be said to have its own goal, its own specified state of affairs that it is intended to achieve, and therefore its own unique motive; but at the same time each of these motives serves the superordinate goal of getting clean. So among all of the various particular motives that drive your behavior during a bath, none of them is an end in itself, which is to say that none of them is an ultimate motive. Getting clean is the ultimate motive; everything else is instrumental to that end. Right?

But wait! Now we should consider why anyone wants to be clean in the first place. Is getting clean really an end in itself? Or is it instrumental to some other ultimate goal? In fact, you may have various reasons for wanting to be clean. One might be that it feels good. Another might be that you fear (with justification) that you will be shunned by others if you don't maintain a certain level of personal hygiene. So the goal of getting clean is itself a means rather than an end; it is a subordinate goal to other, grander concerns, such as the desire not to be shunned. And why do you wish not to be shunned? Perhaps you want to have friends, a romantic partner, and a job, things that you would risk losing if you quit bathing. And why do you want friends, a romantic partner, and a job? Because all those things bring you great pleasure, and their absence would bring great misery. So when you bathe, even when you do so not for the immediate pleasurable sensations that it provides but in order to get clean, you are still doing that which, in your estimation, best promotes the maximization of your own pleasure.

Moreover, it turns out that this is true for any motive upon which a person acts. Consider a student struggling to master organic chemistry. Does she find the arduous task of studying for the exam immediately pleasurable? Admittedly, some do enjoy such tasks, but let's say that, as with many students, she does not. So what is her motive? If the task is intrinsically unpleasant, then how can we say that she is engaged in the pursuit of pleasure? It is interesting that the answer is not only obvious but is, if anything, even more compelling in instances such as this where the activity itself is inherently aversive. In such cases, we all intuitively recognize that there must be some extrinsic motive, some way in which the activity is expected to turn a profit in the student's hedonic bookkeeping; otherwise, the student would not willingly suffer such torment. Of course, performing well on the exam is a powerful motive, and a good mark is likely to be accompanied by considerable pleasure. Failing the exam would produce great distress, so studying is done to gain the pleasure accompanying a good grade while avoiding the distress attendant on a poor grade. Furthermore, the attainment of a good grade is instrumental to passing the course, which is instrumental to getting a degree, which is instrumental to getting a job, which is instrumental to earning money, which is instrumental to having a comfortable and fulfilling life, which is instrumental to the only end that is superordinate to all others: pleasure. No matter where we begin, we can trace our motives to one ultimate motive, to the one thing that we are capable of pursing as an ultimate goal: our own pleasure.

Let's return to the example of stopping to help Ed shovel the snow from his sidewalk. You claimed (the egoist says) that in so doing you weren't seeking your own pleasure, and that in fact, quite to the contrary, you expected to be uncomfortable and irritated. So you discounted the possibility that your ultimate aim was self-interested, much less the particular condition known as pleasure. But no one is saying that you would enjoy shoveling snow or that you would relish missing part of the football game. The point is that you willingly paid that steep price to avoid a consequence that you deemed even more unpleasant, which was (perhaps) the worry that would have nagged at you the rest of the day, possibly preventing you from enjoying the game. Or maybe you acted to avoid the guilt you would have felt at leaving Ed to his own feeble devices, not to mention the remorse you would have felt had Ed actually experienced a heart attack. There's no need to be so cynical as to suggest that you helped Ed to receive adulation from those who know you, but perhaps you pride yourself on being the sort of person who helps neighbors in need. Maintaining such a self-conception results in substantial feelings of pleasure, and failing to help would obliterate those feelings. Whatever the pathway through the hierarchy of motives, we can be sure of one thing: you acted compassionately because you expected that doing so would result in the best overall outcome—*for you.*

Some clarifications are now in order. The foregoing argument might have been taken to imply that people always consciously weigh alternative courses of action and select the course of action that maximizes pleasure in the long run. This is not quite correct in two respects. First, the deliberation need not be entirely conscious. In fact, it would be surprising if it were entirely conscious, and it would be even more surprising if we were always aware of how our actions actually serve the cause of promoting our own well-being. This is true for the simple reason that we will be more likely to attain our particular goals (which are subordinate to the one ultimate goal of maximizing pleasure) if we *believe* those goals to be ultimate ends, even though they really are not! If we recognized the subordinate goals as merely instrumental, our zeal in pursuing them might be diminished, with the result that we would be less likely to realize the full measure of potential well-being. So a certain amount of self-obfuscation concerning the true nature of our ultimate motivation is adaptive because it improves the likelihood of fulfilling the ultimate objective. If you will be better off, ultimately, having helped Ed than not having helped, and if the probability of helping Ed is increased when you believe that doing so is an end in itself, then this belief, although a self-deception, serves a useful function. Like much of our cognitive functioning, our true motives are often hidden from us.

The second clarification is an answer to an objection that is often leveled against psychological hedonism, which is to point out that people often do things that fail to maximize their pleasure over the long haul. One way to answer this objection is to point out that actions often have unintended consequences, and people are often unable to judge accurately which course of action will *actually* best serve their interests. But psychological hedonism does not require that people actually maximize their pleasure: it only requires that all action is *intended* to do so. But then it might be objected that people sometimes do things that they have good reason to believe will produce unpleasant results. Some people smoke cigarettes, knowing full well the potential health consequences. Many people eat poor diets, elevating their risk for heart disease, diabetes, and other unpleasant, debilitating conditions. These examples, it turns out, actually provide strong support for the theory of psychological hedonism, because the only way to account for such behavior is to acknowledge the immediate gratification that it garners. People do things that are bad for them in the long run, not because they are not self-interested, but because self-interest tends to slant toward immediate pleasures. Human beings (and other animals as well[31]) overweigh immediate consequences compared to delayed consequences when selecting courses of action, for the good reason—or at least for the adaptive reason—that immediate consequences are more certain than delayed consequences. In nature, and in our evolutionary history, a bird in the hand usually really is better than two in the bush, and this fact of nature has shaped our psychology such that we give more weight to immediate pleasures and pains than we give to delayed pleasures and pains in our (not necessarily conscious or omniscient) hedonic calculations.

This raises one more objection. What about those cases in which a person acts to save others at the cost of his own life, such as when a soldier throws himself on a live grenade? Surely, you might say, such an act could not be intended to garner any personal pleasure, either now or later. The ultimate motive, you will say, must be truly other-regarding, or at least it must be rooted in a sense of duty, but it surely can't be self-regarding. Admittedly, there is no pleasure to be attained in such a scenario. But there is pain to be avoided. Those who have survived horrific ordeals during which they demonstrated a willingness to sacrifice their lives to save others report that they felt they "couldn't have lived with themselves" if they had done otherwise.[32] In (not necessarily consciously or accurately) calculating the best course of action, the looming possibility of a lifetime of guilt and remorse evidently weighs quite heavily—so heavily that the person would rather die than endure it.

Finally, the egoist says, although it has become obvious by now, let's explicitly lay out the implications of psychological hedonism for altruism. The one essential definitional attribute required for an act to qualify as altruistic is that the welfare of the other must be the ultimate goal and not a means to some other end. But it has now been demonstrated that this is never the case, because all action is undertaken with the ultimate goal of obtaining pleasure for the self. Therefore, altruism does not exist.

REFUTATIONS OF PSYCHOLOGICAL HEDONISM

We have attempted to do justice to the arguments in support of psychological hedonism by presenting them in a convincing fashion through the voice of a hypothetical apologist for egoism. But we are not convinced. Indeed, it is somewhat astonishing that psychological hedonism (or any form of psychological egoism, for that matter) is still considered credible among psychologists and other social scientists, considering that straightforward and persuasive refutations are widely known to philosophers and theologians. One of the best known and perhaps still the best of these refutations was published in 1726 by Bishop Joseph Butler in his *Fifteen Sermons on Human Nature Preached at the Rolls Chapel.*[33]

Butler acknowledged, as we all do, that people desire their own happiness, a desire which he calls self-love. And among desires, self-love has the unusual characteristic that, being self-referential, it requires no external object as a referent. In addition to self-love, we also have a host of particular appetites and passions, but unlike self-love, these are directed toward external things. That we have an appetite for food, for example, is evidenced by the fact that we take pleasure in eating food, but not in eating a stone.[34] Now, while it is

true that each passion of mine *is* mine, and although the pleasure in grati-
fying it is *my* pleasure, we should not therefore dismiss the distinction between self-love and the passions themselves. "How much soever therefore is
to be allowed to self-love, yet it cannot be allowed to be the whole of our
inward constitution; because, you see, there are other parts or principles
which come into it."[35] The point is that the existence of self-love (or desire
for happiness or pleasure) does not negate the existence of our particular
non-self-referential desires.

Quite to the contrary, although we desire happiness, we never attain it by
seeking it directly; rather we attain it by satisfying our particular appetites
and passions. If you have a passion for playing soccer, then you will pursue
opportunities to play soccer and thereby derive pleasure. If you have an
appetite for knowledge, then you might read everything you can get your
hands on and thereby secure your pleasure. At first glance, these examples
might seem to bolster the egoist's claim that all our motives are merely
instrumental to the ultimate motive of self-satisfaction, but Butler's argument is different in an important respect that turns the egoist's theory on its
head. Because happiness is never attained by seeking it directly, then its very
existence presupposes the existence of other desires, the fulfillment of which
is required in order to derive pleasure. And all of these particular desires
must have as their ends the particular conditions that they specify, and *not*
pleasure, since pleasure cannot be attained by seeking it directly. So with
respect to our particular desires, their ultimate ends *must* be their explicit
objects, not pleasure. Pleasure (or satisfaction or happiness) is not, in this
view, really an end at all, if an end is something that can be sought. It is a
rather more like a psychological barometer that measures the extent to
which our actions have been successful in achieving *their* ends. When a
mouse seeks cheese, it is really seeking cheese, not pleasure, even though
obtaining the cheese may well result in pleasure. The same is true of us.

To see why it is true that happiness cannot be achieved by seeking it
directly, consider what it would be like to have no desires other than the
desire for happiness (which is in essence what psychological hedonism
claims). How would you fulfill your desire for happiness? Not desiring food,
you would take no pleasure in eating. Not desiring companionship, you
would take no pleasure in the company of others. Without a passion for
reading, or watching television, or skiing, or listening to music, or gazing at
the stars, or chatting with friends, or anything at all, you would have no way
to attain any pleasure.[36] As Butler put it, "So that if self-love wholly engrosses

us and leaves no room for any other principle, there can be absolutely no such thing as happiness, or enjoyment of any kind whatever; since happiness consists in the gratification of particular passions, which supposes the having of them."[37] This reveals the paradox of hedonism, as it has been called. If psychological hedonism were true—if the only thing we were capable of seeking was pleasure—then we would find ourselves in the perfectly futile position of having no possibility whatsoever of attaining it. The fact that we do ever experience pleasure demonstrates that we must have desires for things other than pleasure, which means that pleasure is not the only end we are capable of seeking.

Far from negating the existence of motives other than the desire for pleasure, the realization of pleasure can expose our true motives! Your belief that you have a passion for playing soccer is substantiated, not disproved, by the fact that you really enjoy yourself when you play soccer. The pleasure that you experience when you learn new things likewise validates rather than contradicts the contention that you have an appetite for knowledge.

These arguments apply with no less force to altruistic motivation. In the first place, once we understand the relationship between motivation and pleasure, we should have no reason to discount the existence of a motive on the basis that attaining its end is attended by pleasure. This is true just as much for altruistic motivation as it is for any other sort of motive. In Butler's words, "... there is no peculiar contrariety between self-love and benevolence; no greater competition between these, than between any other particular affections and self-love."[38] To say that altruism is an illusion because helping others is pleasurable is like saying that hunger is an illusion because eating food is pleasurable. Furthermore, if pleasure is derived from an act of helping, then this fact actually provides good reason to believe that altruistic motivation *does* exist. If someone obtains pleasure from eating food, we are not being unreasonable if we suggest that hunger was a motivating force, and in fact we are more likely to believe so than if eating had produced no pleasure! This is not to say that all instances of charity or helping are altruistically motivated (or that all instances of eating are motivated by hunger). In many cases, the motive for giving to charity is to obtain a tax break. In some instances, a person may help another with the goal of getting something in return, such as adulation or a monetary reward. But if no other beneficial consequence to self is sought or received, *other than pleasure*, then we should take this as strong evidence in support of an altruistic motive.

The Compatibility of Self-Interest and Other-Regard

In the preceding chapter, we offered a "family resemblance" definition of altruism in which we proposed that the sole requisite constitutive feature of altruism is that the ultimate object of concern must be the interests of the other rather than the interests of the self. The foregoing discussion suggests the possibility that altruistic motivation is compatible with certain forms of self-interested motivation, as long as it can be established that the welfare of the other is truly an end in itself rather than merely a means to a self-interested end. Taking pleasure in helping others seems to fit this criterion. As the paradox of hedonism illustrates, it would not be possible to obtain pleasure from helping others if their welfare was not already valued as an end in itself. This interpretation of the relationship between pleasure and altruistic motivation seems to accord well with the phenomenological experience of altruism, as indicated by exemplars of altruistic behavior themselves (such as those who rescued Jews from the Nazis) when they say things like, "Oh, yes, sure it feels good to know that you helped someone. But that's not *why* you do it." We will discuss the phenomenology of altruism in more detail in chapter four, but for now we wish to consider the possibility that various benefits to self might be compatible with true altruism.

Neera Kapur Badhwar has argued persuasively for precisely such compatibility where the self-interested motive is something she calls self-affirmation.[39] The essence of the argument is that if someone holds a particular value, then that person has an interest in acting in accordance with it. To do otherwise is to commit an act of self-betrayal and thereby do damage to the self. Moreover, the more deeply held the value or the more central it is to one's sense of identity, the more one has a real self-interested stake in upholding it. So a person who cares deeply for the welfare of others has a lot at stake in the encounter with a stranger in need. To help might cost a lot (this was certainly the case with the rescuers of Jews), but not to help would entail a devastating loss of a central part of one's self-concept. Lest the egoist be tempted to exclaim, "See, it really is self-interest motivating these actions after all," let us emphasize again that the mere fact of experiencing this sort of motivation presupposes a real, and not merely instrumental, concern for the welfare of others. The existence of an altruistic motive logically cannot be contradicted by the presence of a self-interested motive if the altruistic motive is a necessary precondition to having the self-interested motive in the first place.

Badhwar's larger concern is to show that in certain special cases an act can be considered morally praiseworthy despite being motivated by self-interest (in contrast to the traditional thesis that only altruistic acts have moral worth). In making her case, she asks the reader to consider the same act of helping performed by two different hypothetical actors. In one case, no self-interest enters into the equation, and the actor helps the other solely for the other's sake, with no concern whatsoever about the role that her actions play in affirming her own values. This would seem to contradict the very notion that other-regard is a deeply held value, since if it were, she would have an interest in affirming it. In the other case, the actor is motivated to affirm his concern for others as a central disposition of his character and to avoid the psychological damage that failure to do so would entail. In which case does the act have greater moral worth? Badhwar concludes that the presence of the self-interested motive of self-affirmation adds to the moral worth of the act. Under such circumstances, altruism can be characterized as "whole-hearted."[40] But in the case of altruism unaccompanied by an interest in self-affirmation, the act loses some of its moral worth because the values exemplified by the act are not very much valued by the actor! In much the manner in which Butler reconciles altruism with pleasure, Badhwar has successfully demonstrated that altruism and at least one form of self-interest (self-affirmation) are compatible.

Of course, not all forms of self-interest are compatible with altruism. As Badhwar points out, some rescuers of Jews seemed to be motivated primarily by financial gains.[41] Since the desire to earn money by arranging to hide or transport desperate refugees does not presuppose real concern for the welfare of those refugees, these rescues do not qualify as instances of altruism. Their helping acts saved lives, and they may have even cared about the Jews whom they rescued, but if a monetary incentive was necessary to impel action, then the desire for money and *not* the good of the refugees was the ultimate motive; and, therefore, in these cases the welfare of the other was merely a means to a self-interested end. Badhwar identifies two other kinds of self-interested motives that she deems incompatible with altruistic motivation: psychological rewards (which include pleasure attainment and guilt avoidance) and the desire to become a better person.[42] If one's primary motive is to obtain these goods for oneself, then the welfare of the other is merely an instrument to the self-interested end, and the act is not altruistic.

We have already presented the argument (from Butler) that pleasure attainment is not necessarily incompatible with altruistic motivation and that in the absence of any other rewards to self, the realization of pleasure via an act of helping actually validates the altruism of the act. We would now like to scrutinize more thoroughly guilt avoidance as a motive to determine whether it really is the case that it negates the possibility of considering an act altruistic in the same way that seeking external rewards does. In conducting this analysis, we return to the case of our old neighbor Ed and his snow-covered sidewalk. What was my primary motivation for returning to help him? Was it concern for his well-being, as an end in itself? Or was it concern for myself: a desire to obviate the guilt I would have felt had I continued on without stopping? There is no denying that I anticipated guilt, perhaps even remorse, as a consequence of not helping. Would I have helped Ed in the absence of guilt avoidance as a motive? Perhaps not. Let's say I wouldn't have helped him. That would mean that guilt avoidance was the ultimate motive, and securing Ed's welfare was merely a means to that end, wouldn't it? So my act wasn't altruistic after all, right?

That all depends on what it means to feel guilty. If we mean that I feared ostracism once it was discovered by others that I could have prevented Ed's heart attack (supposing he actually did have one and that my helping would have prevented it), then labeling my act self-interested seems justified. Clearly, we use the word *guilt* in this sense, which could also be labeled "fear of getting caught." But the sensation of guilt doesn't always entail fear of getting caught and being subjected to scorn or some other external punishment. On the contrary, the guilt of which we speak when we aren't afraid of getting caught seems to be a sort of self-punishment, a painful psychological consequence of failing to act in accordance with our own values. Guilt, in that sense, would seem to presuppose genuine caring for the other. After all, if, as the egoist says, I don't *really* care a whit about Ed for his own sake, then why should I feel any guilt if something bad happens to him? There aren't going to be any real consequences to me, first of all because no one will know that I could have helped him but didn't, and second of all because even if others did know they surely wouldn't blame me for going to the football game. It's more likely that, seeing my distress upon hearing of poor Ed's demise, people in the community would offer comfort and explain to me why it wasn't my fault. But I would still feel guilty. Why? The only possible answer seems to be that I must have cared about Ed as an end in himself. The very concept of guilt in this latter sense is rendered incoherent in the absence of altruistic motivation.

So it seems that there may be a variety of psychological states that co-occur with altruistic motivation without negating it. Indeed, it is difficult to imagine an altruistic act that does not involve some element of self-interested motivation. One can *imagine* someone acting in a purely altruistic fashion, without even a shred of self-interested motivation, but the image seems strangely robotic and, well, inhuman. Considered carefully, the image even seems a bit absurd: a person who chooses to endure costs or risks in order to help others, without conditions or limitations, but who finds no satisfaction in doing so, who has no apprehension about adverse psychological consequences to self that might result from not helping, who cares for others but doesn't care *about* caring for others. Do such people exist? Selflessness such as this sounds more like a description of a honeybee than of a human being.

Perhaps the point of view that we are defending could be dubbed a weak form of egoism, because it admits that altruistic motivation activates other psychological mechanisms that entail self-interest. But we should like to resist the label of egoism, however weak, because our position is that the defining tenet of egoism, which is the claim that the only things we are capable of pursuing are self-interested ends, is false. Without the ability to pursue the welfare of the other as an end, the psychological consequences to the self that we have been considering are moot. But all of this leads to an important question: If altruistic and self-interested motives are so inextricably entangled, how can it be determined which *is truly* the ultimate motivation, the interests of the other or the interests of the self? And if our "true" motives are often hidden, even from ourselves, how are we to know what they are? Is it, even in principle, possible to determine whether an act is altruistic? It turns out that it might be possible, despite the difficulties, and we'll see in chapter four that some experimental work has been done on just this question. The test is whether one would choose to receive the same benefits to self (and perhaps simultaneously avert some of the costs or risks associated with helping) via a different route that does not ensure the good of the other. Imagine that as I drove past Ed and began considering my options, I had in my pocket a magic pill that would completely alleviate any subsequent guilt that I might experience if I neglected him, no matter what happened to him. Perhaps the pill works by making me forget the entire episode, so that later, when I learn of his death, I will have no idea that I was ever in a position to prevent it. Will I take the pill and drive on? That depends—on whether I *actually* care about Ed! If I don't care about him—if my ultimate motive in helping him is merely to avoid the aversive experience of guilt—then I will take the pill. But if I really do care about Ed, then I will *still* turn around and help him, despite the easy availability of a painless way out. Does it really strain credulity to think that someone in a situation like this would choose to help rather than take the magic pill? Would Roger Olian and Lenny Skutnik, both of whom jumped into the icy waters of the Potomac River in an attempt to save survivors of the Air Florida Flight 90 crash, have taken the magic pill had they had it in their pockets? Would André and Magda Trocmé, who organized efforts by the poor villagers of Le Chambon that resulted in saving about five thousand Jewish lives, have taken the magic pill when the first frightened Jewish refugee arrived on their doorstep?[43] One thinks not.

A Final Objection to Psychological Egoism

Discussions of psychological egoism seem inevitably to include the following passage, which first appeared in an Illinois newspaper and describes an argument for psychological egoism purportedly advanced by none other than Abraham Lincoln:

> Mr. Lincoln once remarked to a fellow-passenger on an old-time mud coach that all men were prompted by selfishness in doing good. His fellow-passenger was antagonizing this position when they were passing over a corduroy bridge that spanned a slough. As they crossed this bridge they espied an old razor-backed sow on the bank making a terrible noise because her pigs had got into the slough and were in danger of drowning. As the old coach began to climb the hill, Mr. Lincoln called out, "Driver, can't you stop just a moment?" Then Mr. Lincoln jumped out, ran back, and lifted the little pigs out of the mud and water and placed them on the bank. When he returned, his companion remarked: "Now, Abe, where does selfishness come in on this little episode?" "Why bless your soul, Ed, that was the very essence of selfishness. I should have had no peace of mind all day had I gone on and left that suffering old sow worrying over those pigs. I did it to get peace of mind, don't you see?"[44]

Proponents of egoism are fond of making such arguments, but as we have already seen, the argument does not work because for Mr. Lincoln to help the pigs in order to secure his own peace of mind, he had to care about the welfare of the pigs in the first place. His self-interested desire for peace of mind presupposes an altruistic motive. As Rachels puts it, "If Lincoln 'got peace of mind' from rescuing the piglets, does this show him to be selfish or, on the contrary, doesn't it show him to be compassionate and good-hearted? (If a person were truly selfish, why should it bother his conscience that others suffer—much less pigs?)."[45]

The story of Mr. Lincoln and the pigs reveals what is perhaps the deepest problem with psychological egoism: it begs the question. If someone gains pleasure from helping others, far from taking that as evidence that we should dismiss the possibility of an altruistic motive, we should ask *why* anyone would take pleasure in promoting another's interests. Cynical answers, such as Hobbes' suggestion that charity is an attempt to demonstrate one's power, do not seem to accord with the psychological facts, as we shall see when we examine the phenomenology of altruism in chapter four. It seems more concordant with subjective experience and no less parsimonious to assume, with Rousseau and Butler, that true other-directed compassion is a part of our psychological makeup, and that as is true with other parts of our psychological makeup, we take pleasure in successfully satisfying its impulses. The same goes for guilt. To point to guilt avoidance as the "true" motive for an act of kindness begs the question and leaves us wondering: If we aren't really concerned about the interests of others except insofar as they affect us, *why* do we experience guilt? Hobbes shows that it is *possible* to account for all charitable and compassionate impulses from an egoistic stance, but that does not mean that his interpretations are correct. The very existence of concepts such as compassion, empathy, generosity, pity, and guilt, not to mention their universality in human experience, suggests, on the contrary, that other-regard is an integral facet of human psychology. In any case, these are matters to be resolved empirically. Psychological egoism will stand or fall not on the basis of logical arguments or ad hoc revelations of the supposed "true" motives underlying every instance of compassionate behavior; rather, it must contend with the facts of human psychology. We shall see how well it holds up.

Before we delve into the psychology of altruism, however, we must still contend with Wolf Larsen. In his arguments, we have one more argument for psychological egoism to consider. If we are products of natural selection, then must not it be the case that we, like all creatures, are necessarily designed to promote our own reproductive fitness? Isn't it going to turn out to be an unavoidable fact of nature that all creatures are programmed to do at all times whatever is prudent in advancing their own selfish interests? Wouldn't behaving otherwise constitute an unnatural departure from the very exigencies of nature? Although the egoist has failed to prove the case for psychological egoism, our job is far from done. Now the burden shifts back to us, and we must begin our attempt to make a positive case for the reality of altruism. The first challenge is to show how altruism can be reconciled with natural selection, indeed how we should *expect* altruism to come about as a *result* of natural selection. That is the task that we shall take up in the next chapter.

☙ 3

The Perspective of Evolutionary Biology
The Genetic Dynamics of Caring and Cooperation

GROWING PAINS

THE FOUNDER and most famous practitioner of psychoanalysis, Sigmund Freud, took the vitriol with which his theories were received in some quarters as evidence that he was onto something big. After all, Freud noted, the great discoveries of science have a way of ticking people off, because they tend to displace us from our presumed position of privilege in the cosmos. In Freud's judgment, there already had been two such great blows to human self-esteem. The first resulted from the Copernican revelation "that our earth was not the centre of the universe but only a tiny fragment of a cosmic system of scarcely imaginable vastness."[1] The second blow to human self-esteem came at the hands of Darwin and the revelation of biological evolution, which "destroyed man's supposedly privileged place in creation and proved his descent from the animal kingdom and his ineradicable animal nature."[2] Both of those scientific revolutions were greeted with scorn, ridicule, or outright contempt, despite the strength of the evidence in their favor and their promise for advancing human knowledge by leaps and bounds (a promise that continues to be dramatically fulfilled). Then, in one of the great moments of back-patting self-adulation of all time, Freud identified a third scientific revolution at least as momentous as the previous two: his own insight that the human ego "is not even master in its own house, but must content itself with scanty information of what is going on unconsciously in its mind."[3]

Of these great blows to human self-esteem, Freud considered the psychological blow to be the most painful to our narcissistic sensibilities, but history seems to have proved him wrong. Although many of the particulars of Freud's theorizing have become little more than historical curiosities, the basic notions of unconscious mental processes and human irrationality are as well accepted today, among both professionals and laypeople, as Copernicus' heliocentric solar system. Only the biological revolution continues to inspire indignant disbelief and invective wrath from large numbers of otherwise well-educated people (although it must be noted that the "controversy" exists only among laypeople; professional biologists have no doubt about the reality of evolution). Freud's misjudgment may have been a conceit regarding the importance of his own theory, but it also may have reflected a failure to appreciate the depth of the insult issuing from the Darwinian revolution. For the insult cuts far deeper than the mere fact of our descent from animals and our relatedness to them. Indeed, most people who are already mortified by the idea of biological evolution scarcely imagine the degree to which a proper understanding of it—which entails an appreciation for advances made in population genetics and molecular genetics since the time of Darwin—smashes any pedestal upon which we would like to place ourselves. Even people who cheerfully accept the basic idea of evolution are often little aware of its deeper, and profoundly humbling, implications.

Stephen Jay Gould, perhaps the greatest modern popularizer of evolutionary ideas, began an essay entitled "Can We Complete Darwin's Revolution?" in much the same manner as we opened this chapter, by citing Freud's criterion of damage to our sense of self-importance as an index of the significance of a scientific revolution.[4] Gould observes that the way in which it is commonly understood (or rather misunderstood), the idea of evolution has been distorted in various ways to allow us to preserve a sense of our own special status among the creatures of the earth. Of the misconceptions that Gould identifies, perhaps the most pervasive and most face-saving is the view of evolution as a progression along an inevitable trajectory toward "more evolved" creatures, a pathway that finally arrived, as it was destined to do, at what are so far the most evolved creatures of all—us. This trajectory, it is also often assumed, will continue, and human beings of the distant future will have massive craniums to house their enormous brains, which will be even "more evolved" than ours.

Interestingly, the popular spin-doctored (to borrow another apt term from Gould's essay) view of evolution has found a way to incorporate into its framework two historically cherished notions that are in fact decidedly refuted by a proper understanding of evolution. One of these is the *scala naturae*, or great chain of being, which is the idea that organisms, and everything else for that matter, can be rank-ordered from low to high. Of course, among those who hold such a view, human beings are seen as being at the pinnacle of the ordering (but perhaps below more ethereal beings such as angels). The other is the notion that evolutionary change inevitably entails progressive improvement and that there are predetermined objective standards of perfection that impart to beings a purposive drive toward their evolutionary destiny. Both of these notions are roughly captured in countless cartoons showing a sequence of animals beginning with a fish crawling out of the water and ending with a human being, as though that were the only possible sequence of evolutionary transitions. The implication that fish, amphibians, reptiles, and various mammals are "less evolved" precursors to humanity is nonsense. Of course, these cartoons may well depict with some accuracy a few exemplars of creatures representing the long lineage of ancestral species from which we are descended. And we shouldn't be blamed for being parochial in emphasizing our own lineage. But we go too far when, because our recent ancestors resembled modern nonhuman primates and our much more distant ancestors were some sort of fishy creatures, we ascribe to ourselves a "more evolved" status than primates, fish, or any other extant life form. Everything currently alive on earth has an ancestral lineage that ultimately traces back exactly as long as ours.

Perhaps one reason for the ease with which the notion of inevitable progressive advancement is erroneously incorporated into the idea of evolution is that we are, after all, most interested in our own species. And members of our species are particularly large and complex. If we are allowed selectively to examine only the lineages of organisms that, like ourselves, are large and complex, then we will inevitably find that those species have evolved from smaller, less complex forms. The earliest life forms were tiny, relatively simple creatures, so these select lineages will describe trajectories from those tiny, simple forms to the larger, more complex forms that exist today, seemingly confirming the presupposition of directional evolution. Given such exemplars, how could the evolutionary path appear otherwise? But if we select an organism *at random* and examine its evolutionary ancestry, we will find little evidence for increases in either size or complexity. How can that be? The reason is that, if we select at random, we will almost certainly select a bacterium, simply because there are so many of them. Our randomly selected organism, our representative portrait of life on earth, will be a single-celled creature without even a nucleus in which to carry its DNA. Despite evolving and accumulating mutations in its DNA for 3.5 billion years, it will be markedly similar to its ancestor of 3.5 billion years ago. And yet, this is, in fact, an accurate representation of the typical life form. By nearly any objective measure—total number of individuals, number of species, length of existence on the planet, range of habitats, even the ability to affect climate—the dominant form of life on earth is, and always has been, and probably always will be, bacteria. In contrast, human beings constitute no more than a brief footnote in the book of life. Put differently, and invoking a better metaphor, if the history and diversity of life on earth were depicted as a massive branching bush, the twig representing our species would be so tiny as to be practically invisible, even if one knew where to look for it. The upshot of all this is that the insult to our dignity is much deeper than is widely recognized. Contrary to the popular misconception, our species is no more *the* culmination of eons of evolution than one minuscule twig is *the* culmination of an enormously arborescent bush.

There is, though, an even more punishing blow to be endured at the hands of the biological revolution, one that Gould himself seemed reluctant to embrace. You may recall learning about the role of DNA in reproduction. That's what DNA is for; it is what we use to reproduce ourselves, right? Well, not exactly. It is more accurate to say that DNA uses *us* to reproduce *itself.* From a strictly objective point of view, it turns out that we exist as a tool for our DNA, not the other way around. This gene-centered view of life was the subject of Richard Dawkins' famous book *The Selfish Gene,* in which he explains that the fundamental unit upon which natural selection acts is not the individual organism, but the gene.[5]

Life began when molecules with the strange property of being able to make copies of themselves came into existence. Among such molecules, those that were most resistant to destruction and best able to replicate themselves proliferated, for no reason other than the adventitious possession of those very characteristics. Accidental changes—mutations—occurred frequently and were undoubtedly, as they are now, usually deleterious. But some mutations produced molecules that were even better able to survive and replicate, and these molecules, with their adaptations, proliferated. Eventually, the accumulated mutations produced more and more sophisticated adaptations, including the capacity to make rudimentary protective cells in which to live. Further mutations resulted in the ability to manufacture ever more elaborate structures. Today, the descendants of those molecules have formed coalitions that live in our bodies as DNA. They still build their protective structures, which range from the relatively simple single-celled body of a bacterium to the spectacularly complex multicellular body of a human being. These bodies all have the same function: to serve as vessels for the replicating molecules that created them—the genes.

We can forgive Freud for not fully appreciating the gravity of the biological revolution and just how much it demotes our importance in the overall scheme of nature. After all, nothing was known about molecular genetics in Freud's day. But now that we better understand our place in nature, what are we to make of it? Darwin wrote, "There is grandeur in this view of life, with its several powers, having been originally breathed by the Creator into a few forms or into one; and that, whilst this planet has gone cycling on according to the fixed law of gravity, from so simple a beginning endless forms most beautiful and most wonderful have been, and are being evolved."[6] An understanding of the genetic basis of our existence, deeply humbling though it is, does not seem to repudiate the essence of Darwin's sentiment. On the contrary, the gene-centered view of life opens up new possibilities for how we might conceive of ourselves. In the preceding chapter, we encountered the argument that because natural selection rewards only ruthless selfishness, true altruism cannot exist (except perhaps as a short-lived and maladaptive anomaly). We will see in this chapter that the argument is sound—when applied to the entities upon which natural selection directly acts, the genes. Among genes, there is no place for altruism. But what about us, humble vessels and servants of our genes? It turns out that the gene-centered view unexpectedly restores to us some of the dignity that we feared we had lost as products of evolution.

So the point of this chapter is not the depth of the insult levied on us by evolutionary theory. The point is that an examination of evolution from the gene-centered viewpoint actually rescues from the red teeth and claws of nature the possibility of altruism. It will take awhile to lay the groundwork, but we will eventually argue that when one understands how natural selection works, then it becomes apparent that it not only can but is quite likely to generate altruism. Our first task in making such an argument will be to explain in a bit more detail the genetic basis of natural selection. Then we will consider the general conditions that would have to be satisfied in order for altruism to evolve. Three mechanisms have been proposed that satisfy those conditions—kin selection, reciprocity, and group selection. We will examine each of those mechanisms in turn and then analyze the extent to which they shed light on the central question of this chapter: can natural selection and altruism be reconciled?

MECHANISMS OF BIOLOGICAL CHANGE

The immediate results of the human genome project have done little to salvage any impression of exceptionality for our species. It appears that about

25,000 genes are sufficient to create a human being, which is about the same as the number required to make a mouse (with which we are about 88 percent genetically identical), fewer than the number used by corn (about 40,000 genes), and not many more than the number needed to make the thousand-cell roundworm *Caenorhabditis elegans* (about 19,500 genes).[7] The rather low number of genes in the human genome came as a considerable shock to all concerned, as it had long been assumed that the number of genes must at least equal the number of proteins manufactured in the body. Since the human body can make at least 90,000 different proteins, that figure had been taken as the lower limit on the requisite number of genes. Clearly, the "one-gene, one-protein" dogma has been decisively overturned, and biologists have recently gained greater insight into how a single gene can produce a variety of protein products. Of course, much work remains to be done. Sequencing the human genome and counting the genes are a bit like counting the recipes in a cookbook—where the cookbook is written in code and in any case only lists the ingredients of each recipe, omitting the instructions for combining them. One is still a very long way from understanding how to make a soufflé.

We do not wish to get too bogged down in the details of molecular genetics, but a brief overview of some of the main concepts will be helpful in developing the primary arguments of this chapter. Of course, our genetic material is made of deoxyribonucleic acid (DNA), which in its overall structure is somewhat like a very long, tightly twisted spiral staircase. As staircases go, however, this one is unusual in that it can be split right down the center of the stairs. Each side of the staircase is made up of a chain of molecular subunits called nucleotides, each of which comprises a sugar, a phosphate group, and a nitrogenous base. The sugar and the phosphate groups form what is commonly called the backbone of the DNA (of which there are two, like the two side rails of the spiral staircase), while the bases pair up between the dual backbones to form the connecting stairs. The nucleotides that make up DNA come in four varieties, which differ only in the structure of the base: adenine (A), thymine (T), cytosine (C), and guanine (G). Each type of base has a monogamous relationship with only one of the other types of base. A and T always join together, and C and G always join together. The recipe for life is coded in the sequence of these complementary base pairs. In human DNA, there are slightly more than three billion base pairs distributed among twenty-three separate stretches of DNA called chromosomes (and there are two slightly different versions of this twenty-three-volume tome in each cell, one set inherited from each parent). To read the code, cellular machinery unzips a portion of the two strands of the DNA, breaking the weak hydrogen bonds between the complementary bases. The sequence of bases on one of the strands can then be transcribed into a similar single-stranded polymer (RNA), which is then translated by other cellular machinery into a sequence of amino acids (a protein). Sequences of three bases, called triplet codons, specify particular amino acids. For example, the four-codon DNA sequence CCTGAGGAGAAG translates into the four-amino-acid sequence praline/glutamic acid/ glutamic acid/lysine. Substituting thymine for adenine in the middle base of the second triplet (CCTGTGGAGAAG) changes the amino acid sequence to praline/valine/glutamic acid/lysine. Sickle-cell anemia is caused by a mutation of just this sort.

So what, exactly, is a gene? A simplified and inexact answer is that a gene is a segment of DNA that codes for a particular protein product. Such a segment of DNA is also called a cistron. This definition is not quite accurate, though, in part because it turns out that in some cases the final product is not a protein at all, but an RNA molecule that serves some function other than arranging amino acids into proteins. The definition also obscures the fact that, particularly in human DNA, the sequence of bases that codes for a protein is typically fragmented into sections called exons, which are interspersed amid long stretches of noncoding DNA, called introns. (In fact, it appears that the roughly 25,000 genes of the human genome comprise only about 2 percent of the total base pairs present in the DNA.) Before a protein can be sequenced, the RNA transcribed from the DNA must be sliced up and spliced back together to eliminate the noncoding regions. The RNA that is finally produced, and that guides the sequencing of the protein, is called messenger RNA. The discovery that a single gene can be spliced in various ways to form a variety of messenger RNA transcripts explains how 25,000 genes can produce more than 90,000 proteins. It also suggests that the fractionation of the genome into exons and introns serves the useful purpose of contributing to alternative splicing, thereby allowing more complexity to be milked out of a relatively small number of cistrons.

The definition of a gene as a cistron is not the preferred definition of some. Dawkins, for one, conceives of a gene in more abstract terms, as "any portion of chromosomal material that potentially lasts for enough generations to serve as a unit of natural selection."[8] Thus, a set of genetic material that is closely associated on a particular chromosome, such that it would be very likely to remain intact through many generations of reproductive transmission, constitutes a gene, even though that section of DNA might contain several cistrons. Of course, this definition does not at all neglect the effects that the gene has on the bodies it inhabits; on the contrary, it is precisely those effects upon which natural selection acts, thereby either increasing or decreasing the number of copies of the gene that are conveyed into the future. Indeed, Dawkins' definition has the decided advantage of emphasizing the broader phenotypic effects of a gene rather than the particular protein and RNA products. (The term "phenotype" refers to the combined bodily effects of an individual's genes. Clearly, there is a correspondence between the whole set of genes—the "genotype"—and the traits possessed by an individual, but the relationship between genotype and phenotype is complicated by the fact that most genes have multiple effects, and most characteristics are influenced by multiple genes as well as by nongenetic environmental factors.) Despite the productive use that Dawkins makes of his rather fluid definition, it appears that the gene-as-cistron definition has become the more conventional usage. For the purposes of this book, there seems to be no particular need to choose between definitions. We are satisfied to note that both consider a gene to be a portion of genetic material much smaller than a chromosome; it can be replicated and passed on intact to offspring, and it has an effect or effects, at least potentially, upon the morphology or behavior of the body in which it finds itself.

A question frequently asked about the human genome project is, "Whose genome was sequenced?" In a sense, it hardly matters, since base pair for base pair we are all about 99.9 percent genetically identical. But obviously, the 0.1 percent difference between individual genomes makes a real difference. Since cistrons range in length from several hundred bases to hundreds of thousands of bases, the variability among bases provides ample opportunity for a large number of genes to vary from one individual to another. Thus, many of our approximately 25,000 genes exist as various versions, like different hand-typed copies of the same manuscript, identical except for a few typos in each. A particular typo might not affect the meaning of the text at all, but on the other hand it might. Likewise, a difference in a base between two versions of a gene may or may not produce a difference in the phenotype. A bigger typo, like deleting or repeating a section of text, will likely have a more pronounced impact, and, likewise, deleted or repeated sections of a gene will tend to produce significant consequences for the organism. The various versions of a gene are called its alleles. In fact, often when we use the word *gene* we really mean a particular instance of the various alleles of that gene. Despite our overwhelming genetic similarity, we each have a unique set of particular genes (i.e., alleles), which gives each of us a unique phenotype. It is this variability that provides the raw material upon which natural selection acts.

A Gene for Altruism?

Of central concern in this chapter is the question of whether natural selection could favor a gene for altruism. Such a statement immediately irritates many readers, and rightly so, because to say that a gene is "for" something is grossly to mischaracterize the relationship between genes and their phenotypic effects. There are at least three qualifications that must be made to the notion of a gene being "for" something, particularly when that something is a complex behavioral effect such as altruism. First, nearly all traits, whether they are morphological or behavioral, are influenced by many genes, and the contribution to a trait made by one gene is not independent of other genes. This means that a particular allele, finding itself in a particular genetic milieu, might have a very different net effect than it would have had in a different constellation of genes. So a gene "for" altruism might be so only when certain other genes are present, or it might fail to be so in the presence of certain other genes. Second, a single gene can have effects on a very large number of phenotypic characteristics, so, even if natural selection does favor propagation of the gene, it might be quite difficult to establish the exact effect or set of effects that earns it such favor. It is possible, for example, that selection pressures could generally work against the evolution of altruism, but it could appear nonetheless as an ancillary effect of genes responsible for other traits that provide adaptive benefits sufficient to outweigh the liability of a bit of altruism. Finally, even apart from the interaction of a gene with the rest of the genotype, the effect of a gene is far from invariant. Gene expression is modulated by a variety of factors, and the phenotypic manifestations of a gene depend not only on its genomic environment but also on the developmental and experiential circumstances in which the organism finds itself. As Matt Ridley puts it in his excellent book *Nature via Nurture*, "Genes are designed to take their cues from nurture. . . . Genes are not puppet masters pulling the strings of your behavior but puppets at the mercy of your behavior."[9] In saying this, Ridley is not minimizing the role of genes; he is simply refusing to dichotomize "nature and nurture" or to elevate the role of genes at the expense of experience, or vice versa. The actual interactive relationship between genes, bodies, environment, and behavior is too complex, and much too interesting, to be captured by any simplistic "nature versus nurture" dichotomies.

Where does this leave us? Keeping in mind these qualifications, we can still consider the possibility that natural selection might favor a gene that, all other things being equal, would tend to increase the likelihood of altruistic behavior. In other words, what we really mean when we speak of a gene for altruism is an allele that, when it occurs as part of a more or less typical genome residing in the cells of a more or less ordinary human being who has had more or less normal human experiences, has the net effect, on average, of increasing the likelihood of altruistic behavior, given that certain circumstances and opportunities arise, relative to other alleles of that gene. The rhetorical advantages of employing an imprecise but economical phrase such as "a gene for altruism" should now be obvious. However precisely we phrase it, the question that remains is: Could such an allele survive for long in the gene pool, where other alleles of that gene produce (on average) a lower probability of such recklessly self-disregarding behavior? How could such an allele persist in the face of ruthless natural selection? Before we can begin to answer those questions, we need to examine more closely the idea of natural selection and how it produces evolutionary change.

For natural selection to operate, three conditions must exist. First, there must be variability in the traits possessed by individuals. Second, the source of those variable traits must be replicable and heritable such that it (the source) can be copied and passed on to offspring. Third, individuals must experience different rates of success in passing on the source of those heritable traits, and at least part of that differential success must owe to the differences in the traits themselves. Under these conditions, natural selection will produce evolutionary change.

All of these criteria are met in biological populations. Individuals vary with respect to practically any trait that can be described, and some of that variability is related to differences in their genotypes. In fact, variability is constantly infused into the genetic material through errors that occur during copying of the DNA. Many of these mutations have no effect on the phenotype of the organism and will be invisible to natural selection. Other mutations are harmful (where harm is defined with respect to the likelihood of reproduction); natural selection will tend to remove them. A few are beneficial to their lucky possessors; natural selection will favor them. The point is that mutation provides a constant source of allelic variation upon which

natural selection can act.[10] Of course, to be passed on to offspring, the mutation must be present in the gametes (sperm or ova). But that happens often
enough, and when it does, offspring will inherit the mutated gene. If the offspring are viable, they might well pass the mutated gene on to their offspring,
and so on. Thus, new alleles constantly enter the gene pool. The linchpin is
this: organisms live in a competitive world where not every individual manages to survive and reproduce. The traits possessed by an individual, however, can affect the likelihood of surviving and reproducing. An allele that
has the effect of helping its possessors in this competition for existence will
tend to be propagated through generations at higher rates than other alleles
of that gene.

This raises an interesting point about the unit of selection. Natural selection comes about as a result of differential success of individual organisms. It
is the organism itself that either survives and reproduces or fails to do so. It is
the organism itself that has the strong muscles, sharp teeth, keen senses, warm
coat of fur, clever camouflage, or whatever trait, that gives it a slight competitive advantage over its conspecifics. But the *effect* of natural selection—evolution—takes place among the genes, and not even among the genes of any
individual, but among the constituent genes of the population, which is called
the gene pool. So evolution can be thought of as a gradual change in the allele
frequencies of a population's gene pool. Of course, the change in allele frequencies will have an effect on the phenotypes of the population as well, such
that those traits that were beneficial to the ancestors of the current generation will tend to be more common in subsequent generations.

A more concrete example is in order. Consider the simplified case of a
gene that exists in two versions in a population. For convenience let's call the
two alleles A and B, where A is our hypothetical "gene for altruism" (keeping
in mind what we really mean when we say that). For the sake of simplicity,
let's say there are one thousand individuals in the population. Now, since
each individual has two copies of each chromosome, everyone will have two
copies of this gene as well, and there will be two thousand total copies of the
gene in the gene pool. The two copies present in an individual could be the
same (AA or BB), in which case the individual is said to be homozygous for
that gene, or the two copies could be different (AB or BA), in which case the
individual is said to be heterozygous for that gene. Let's add some more
assumptions: 10 percent of the existing instances of this gene are version A
(which means there are 200 As and 1800 Bs); there will be no further mutations in either version of the gene; individuals select mates at random, but

only within the population; only half of the members of the population reproduce successfully, but each successful mating couple produces four offspring (so the next generation will also comprise one thousand individuals); generations are discrete and nonoverlapping; and finally, reproductive success is not affected by this gene. The very low likelihood of all of these assumptions holding true in a real population is immaterial at this point.

These assumptions create a situation in which each reproductive event is no different than what would happen if one were able to obtain a random sperm from the population and combine it with a random egg from the population. Now, it is important to know that sperm and eggs, unlike the other cells of the body, have just one copy of each chromosome, so they each will have just one copy of the gene with which we are concerned. So, what is the probability that a sperm or an egg has the A allele? Given our assumptions, it is the same as the frequency in the population, 10 percent. So 10 percent of the sperm and 10 percent of the eggs will have allele A. The other 90 percent will have allele B. And since the sperm and the eggs are combining randomly, only 10 percent of the A sperm will combine with A eggs, so only 1 percent of the next generation will be AA homozygotes. The other 90 percent of the A sperm will combine with B eggs, so 9 percent of the next generation will be AB heterozygotes (with the sperm contribution indicated first, for no particular reason). Likewise, only 10 percent of the B sperm will find themselves joined with A eggs, so 9 percent of the next generation will be BA heterozygotes. There is no compelling reason to distinguish AB heterozygotes from BA heterozygotes, so let's combine them and call them all AB heterozygotes. Together they will make up 18 percent of the next generation. The remaining 90 percent of the B sperm will fuse with B eggs, so that 81 percent of the next generation will be BB homozygotes.

Now let's do some counting. We have 10 AA homozygotes, 180 AB heterozygotes, and 810 BB homozygotes. If we count up all the alleles in this generation, we find that we still have 200 As and 1800 Bs. As long as the specified conditions continue to hold, the population will remain in equilibrium and the frequencies of the alleles will remain the same. This is known as a Hardy-Weinberg equilibrium. Of course, many things can disrupt the equilibrium, and we should not expect a Hardy-Weinberg equilibrium to be the normal state of affairs for very long with real genes and real populations. That's why evolution occurs. Among the disruptive influences are genetic drift, mutation, migration, nonrandom mating, and our main concern, natural selection, the primary engine of evolutionary change.

So let's take the population that we ended up with after the previous exercise and throw some selection pressure into the model. This just means that reproductive success *is* affected by the gene under consideration. If possession of the A allele conferred a benefit such that 90 percent of our 10 AA homozygotes and 70 percent of our 180 AB heterozygotes reproduced successfully, but only about 45 percent of our 810 BB homozygotes managed to reproduce, then 14.4 percent of the fruitful eggs and sperm would contain allele A and the other 85.6 percent would contain allele B. No longer is there equilibrium; rather, the next generation will be different from the parent generation. The next generation will include 21 AA homozygotes, 246 AB heterozygotes, and 733 BB homozygotes, accounting for 288 A alleles and 1712 B alleles. Iterating another generation with roughly the same selection pressures (and adjusting family size slightly to keep the population size of each generation constant at 1000), we end up with 40 AA heterozygotes, 322 AB heterozygotes, and 638 BB homozygotes. Again, the composition of the gene pool has shifted, so that there are 402 A alleles and 1598 B alleles. We could continue to iterate the model generation after generation, but the message of this exercise is by now clear enough. The A allele, by providing its possessors with a selective advantage, has managed to increase the number of copies of itself from one generation to the next. The population is evolving.

There is an important implication that follows from this, and it goes directly to the core of the gene-centered view of evolution. Genes, in a sense, control their own destiny. If allele A has a phenotypic effect that results in a systematic increase in its own frequency across generations, relative to its rival alleles, then it will tend to displace those rival alleles in the gene pool. So the genes that become prevalent are the genes that are best at doing just that. This makes it seems as though genes are "trying" to get more copies of themselves made or that all a gene really "wants" is to propagate copies of itself. But let's be clear that these psychological metaphors are just that—metaphors—as genes do not literally have motives or desires but simply do what they do without thought or intention. Furthermore, such metaphors mischaracterize the nature of evolutionary change by implying that it is forward-looking. A gene is what it is because the phenotypic effects of the ancestral genes from which it is copied worked well enough to get those genes copied through the generations. But having said as much, it can nevertheless be heuristically useful to think of genes *as though* they want to propagate themselves and try to produce the effects that will best serve that end.

We have described these effects as "benefits" to the individual, but what is and what is not a benefit are defined only with respect to propagation of the genes that produce those effects. A mutation in the gene that directs the manufacture of hemoglobin might allow that allele to get lots of copies of itself into the gene pool by providing heterozygotes with a greater resistance to malaria, but that is of little comfort to homozygotes for whom the effect of the mutation is sickle-cell anemia. Propagation of an allele does not even necessarily require that the allele produce more *personal* reproduction, as long as it somehow gets more copies of itself into the next generation. If allele A had the power to make its possessors throw themselves off cliffs, and if that somehow resulted in more copies of A being transmitted to the next generation, then soon a large proportion of the population would be jumping off cliffs. Never mind the liberties that this example takes concerning the ability of any gene to directly cause a particular complicated behavior. The point is that genes do not care about what is "good" for their possessors. And of course, we wouldn't expect that a gene would be able to propagate itself very effectively by disposing its possessor to such self-destructive behavior; but there are lots of examples in nature of behavior that does not *seem* adaptive, but turns out to be when examined from a gene-centric point of view. The sacrifice that a honeybee makes (its life) when it stings an intruder is but one example. So, after all this, we return to a restatement of the central question of this chapter: could human altruism, despite entailing self-sacrifice, be a manifestation of genes doing what they do, that is, producing effects that result in the production of more copies of themselves?

KIN SELECTION

Imagine that you have a gene that disposes you to take risks or endure costs in the interest of promoting the welfare of others, but only certain others. You don't help everyone, just certain individuals. What determines who merits your beneficence? Let's say that you have only one criterion: there has to be a good chance that the recipient also has a copy of that particular gene. Indeed, you mete out the amount of assistance and gauge the risks and costs you will accept in direct proportion to the likelihood that the recipient shares that gene with you. You might even step in front of a bus if doing so would prevent the bus from mowing down two or three other individuals, as long as you had good reason to believe they probably possess that special gene. Of course, the gene would produce similar dispositions toward self-sacrifice in its other possessors. How effective could such a gene be in getting copies of itself into subsequent generations?

The answer is that it might do quite well. The key is that the costs to you would have to be outweighed by the benefits gained by the recipients (where costs and benefits are ultimately measured by net fecundity). So there are a number of circumstances in which offering your help would work to the advantage of the gene. If you were absolutely certain that the potential recipient of your help had the gene, then the benefit to the recipient would only have to be slightly greater than the cost to you. The net effect to the gene itself, since it has a copy in each of you, would be a slight increase in its chances of being passed on. If, however, there was a 50-50 chance of the gene being in the potential recipient, then over many such interactions, there would be an average fitness gain for the gene only if the benefit to the recipient was just more than twice the cost to you. But if you could help more than two people (each of whom has a 50 percent chance of possessing the gene) without increasing your cost, then you could do so where the benefit to each recipient is equal to the cost to you and the gene would still gain ground overall.

Many more such situations could be described, but let's consider a more general way to discuss such scenarios. Each of these scenarios has three quantifiable elements: (1) the cost, c, endured by the helper; (2) the benefit, B, to the recipient; and (3) the probability, p, that the recipient carries the gene. The gene will propagate itself if the cost to the helper is less than the benefit to the recipient multiplied by the probability that the recipient carries the gene; i.e., if $c < Bp$.

Where multiple recipients could be helped without increasing the cost to the helper, the cost would have to be less than the sum of the products of the benefit to each recipient times the probability of carrying the gene; $c < \Sigma Bp$. When these conditions are met, the gene will, on average, get more copies of itself into offspring than a rival allele that does not dispose its possessor to help others under these circumstances. A fascinating and seemingly paradoxical implication of this is that an individual can be quite fit without reproducing at all, even though fitness is defined in terms of fecundity! All that is required is that the individual somehow contributes to the reproduction of others who have the same gene complement. After all, the effect on the gene pool is the same whether you or someone else contributes the sperm or egg that contains a copy of this particular allele.

But what are the chances of running into such people? And how could you possibly recognize them or gauge the probability that they share any of your genes? Well, it turns out that some of them might be at the table with you for Thanksgiving dinner. The people with whom you share the most alleles are your blood relatives. The probability that any rare allele is shared by two people could be virtually zero for unrelated individuals (the exact probability would depend on its rarity). But if you carry a copy of the allele, and assuming that it did not crop up for the first time in you as the result of a mutation, then one of your parents must have transmitted it to you, so the probability that each parent has it is 50 percent. Likewise, since half of your genes are sorted into each of your gametes (sperm or eggs), there is a 50 percent chance that a child of yours will get the allele. For siblings, the calculation is a bit more complicated, but the result is the same. Your full sibling gets a random half of your mother's genes and you get a different random half of your mother's genes. Statistically, the overlap between the two sets is expected to be 50 percent, so about half of the maternal half of your DNA should be shared with your sibling. Of course, the same calculation applies to the DNA received from your father, so on average full siblings will share 50 percent of their genes. Half siblings will share 25 percent of their genes, on average. (These proportions are even higher if there is inbreeding. If two siblings parent a child together, the genetic similarity between the parent-siblings greatly increases the probability that a particularly rare allele will be inherited not only once, but twice—once from each parent. That's why certain genetic diseases and abnormalities are likely when inbreeding occurs. They arise when a rare allele is present in both the sperm and the egg that combine to form the offspring, a circumstance that is much more likely when the parents are closely related.) Cousins are, of course, not as closely related as siblings, but for every allele you have, there is a one in eight chance that your first cousin has also inherited a copy of that same allele.

These probabilities are known as coefficients of relatedness (r), and they can be plugged into the cost-benefit equations expressed above to yield a formulation known as Hamilton's rule.[11] Inclusive fitness is the term given to Hamilton's demonstration that two components must be factored into measurements of fitness. One is direct fitness, which is realized through personal reproduction. The cost associated with an altruistic action is measured in terms of its detrimental effect on direct fitness. The other component of inclusive fitness is indirect fitness, which refers to reproduction on the part of relatives. Hamilton's rule says that an allele for altruistic behavior will spread if the cost to the altruist is less than the benefit to the recipient multiplied by the coefficient of relatedness; i.e., $c < br$. Likewise, where a single act benefits multiple recipients, the allele for that behavior will propagate when $c < \Sigma br$.

An appreciation of this relationship reportedly led geneticist J. B. S. Haldane to quip that he would not lay down his life for his brother, but he would for two brothers or eight cousins. Notice that Haldane's tradeoffs represent an equilibrium. With respect to the number of "my" alleles that remain in living bodies, there is no statistical difference between my death and the death of two of my siblings. This means that from a fitness point of view, I might as well sacrifice my life to save two siblings. Of course, if I could additionally manage to save one cousin as part of the deal, "my" alleles would come out ahead in the exchange.

In practice, there are often various asymmetries that should be factored into the decision. Perhaps I have greater reproductive potential than my siblings, simply because I am younger. Each of my grandparents will share with me, on average, 25 percent of my alleles. Does that mean that in terms of the replicative interests of my genes, it's a toss-up whether I save myself or save all four of them? Of course not. They're done reproducing; I'm not. Conversely, if my grandfather had to choose between saving himself and saving four grandchildren, there would be no contest in terms of the best interests of the genes. There is also the issue of uncertainty about the true degree of relatedness between two individuals. Cuckoldry is surprisingly common, which means that lots of people are laboring under misconceptions about who their real biological relatives are. Perhaps my willingness to help a sibling ought to be weighted by a factor that takes into account the possibility that, unbeknownst to me, we do not have the same father.

But let's hold on for just a second. Who thinks like that? Who goes around calculating costs to self and benefits to relatives before deciding whether to help out? Who ever bothers to calculate a coefficient of relatedness under any circumstances, much less factor it into such a decision? And who conceives of costs and benefits in terms of the potential for reproduction? No person of whom we know thinks in those terms. The point is that we don't have to. The calculations, so to speak, have already been performed over long periods of time through the action of differential selection of the alleles that foster such behavior. The manner in which the genes get their vessels to carry out the behavior is quite indirect, as they specify the plans for a nervous system that has various capacities and potentialities and has the day-to-day responsibility of directing behavior. This indirectness in the path between genes and behavior is likely to leave a lot of room for imprecision in the implementation of the behavior that best propagates the genes. Neverthe-less, if the selection pressures are strong, the fidelity of the process may be quite good. In any case, we can expect that at least to an approximation, we will find ourselves willing to sacrifice for the sake of relatives when the ben-efits to them outweigh the personal costs, in proportion to the degree of relatedness (or at least perceived relatedness).

The case for kin selection is not merely theoretical. Examples appear to be fairly commonplace in nature. In one of the most cited studies,[12] Belding's ground squirrels were observed to produce distinctive alarm calls when approaching predators were detected. When the predator was an aerial ani-mal such as a hawk, the squirrel sounding the alarm improved its own chances of survival as well as the chances of all the other squirrels, as every-one scrambled for cover. So there is no need to invoke altruism to account for alarm calling in the case of aerial predators. But when the predator was a terrestrial animal such as a coyote, the caller was actually more likely to be targeted and killed by the predator. So why would anyone risk being the caller? Well, not just anyone did step up to the plate. Females emitted calls much more frequently than males. This appears to be explained by the fact that these squirrel colonies were composed of clusters of related females liv-ing with unrelated male immigrants. Thus, in terms of inclusive fitness, females have more incentive to sound the alarm for the benefit of their mothers, aunts, sisters, and nieces, as well as for their direct offspring. In sup-port of this hypothesis, it was found that the likelihood of a female sound-ing the alarm correlated directly with the presence of relatives and offspring. But even in the absence of offspring, females were still likely to make the call if there were relatives in the vicinity. In the absence of either offspring or other relatives, females acted more like males.

Perhaps the most exemplary altruists of all are the social insects, more properly known as the eusocial insects. We have already mentioned the altru-istic sacrifice made by the bee that dies by employing its stinger in defense of its colony. But in a genetic sense, the worker bee has lost nothing, because it has already sacrificed everything—it is sterile. Direct fitness can make no contribution to the inclusive fitness of the sterile worker. Its only hope of replicating its genes lies in furthering the reproduction of its fertile relatives, namely, its mother, the queen. It has been designed to be the ultimate altru-ist, prepared to work its whole life, and to give its life, entirely in service to others. How could such a condition have evolved? Before Hamilton developed the concept of inclusive fitness, the evolution of whole castes of non-reproductive workers seemed to present a real problem for evolutionary theory, one that perplexed Darwin himself, who, without benefit of the subsequently discovered principles of genetics, nevertheless was able to intuit a reasonable solution. Darwin suggested that the challenge to his theory presented by sterile castes, "though appearing insuperable, is lessened, or, as I believe, disappears, when it is remembered that selection may be applied to the family, as well as to the individual."[13] Hamilton's development of the notion of inclusive fitness vindicated Darwin's intuition. By helping the queen to produce offspring, workers produce sisters, a few of which become the queens of their own colonies. Thus, workers are in fact able to pass on "their" genes, albeit indirectly. Moreover, for some of the eusocial insects, sisters are actually more closely related than mother and daughter. This occurs because the male of these species is born from an unfertilized egg, which provides it with only one set of chromosomes, which means that all of its sperm are identical. Females who have the same father are therefore 75 percent genetically identical, on average. Under these circumstances, sibling altruism pays particularly high dividends, such that investing in the interests of sisters is potentially a better strategy than investing in offspring.

These examples raise an important question, which we will pose but will not attempt to answer at this point. When an organism sacrifices some of its own direct fitness for the sake of a close relative, with an attendant increase in its indirect fitness, can this legitimately be called altruism? Or should such acts be considered fundamentally self-interested because they enhance the net inclusive fitness of the actor? Clearly, the gene-centered point of view raises some interesting issues concerning the boundary between self and others. We shall consider these issues at some length, but first we must examine the prospects for altruism between *unrelated* individuals. In so doing, we will find ourselves entering another realm of scientific exploration of which Darwin could have had no inkling: game theory.

RECIPROCITY AND THE
DYNAMICS OF COOPERATION

For a seemingly simple game, the Prisoner's Dilemma has generated a lot of interest. This does not mean that people are rushing to stores to buy the game or logging onto Web sites that provide interactive access to the game. The interest is all on the part of academic types who want to understand the dynamics of the game and discern what those dynamics reveal about the nature of competition, cooperation, and social interactions in general. In the simplest form of the game, there are two players (let's call them "you" and "I"), each of whom has been arrested and charged for comitting a crime in which they allegedly both took part. The players are separated and each is interrogated. If both players clam up and refuse to implicate the other, the prosecution will have to content itself with lesser charges, so both players will do just a bit of jail time. But if you clam up and I squeal, they'll let me go and they'll throw the book at you. Ha! Oh, but wait; the same deal applies to you. If you squeal on me while I clam up, you'll get off and I'll do the hard time. If each of us squeals on the other, we'll both be convicted, but our sentences will be reduced a bit in consideration of our helpfulness to the prosecution. What should you do? Well, let's break it down. You don't know what I'm going to do, so consider first what your best option is if I clam up. If you clam up, you'll do some jail time, but if you squeal, you'll be a free person. So if you think that I'll stay quiet, you should squeal. But what if I squeal? In that case, if you clam up, you'll get the maximum sentence. If you squeal too, at least your sentence will be reduced. So if you think I am going to squeal, then you should squeal too. So no matter what I do, you're better off if you squeal. What about me? What should I do? The same exact reasoning applies to me, so I will also conclude that no matter what you do, I am better off if I squeal. The net effect, then, is that we'll both conclude that the best course of action is to squeal, and as a consequence we'll both have to serve substantial jail time. Right? But wait. Shouldn't we have both kept quiet? That would have resulted in much shorter sentences for both of us. Yeah, that's true, and I really hope *you'll* think that way because then when I squeal I'll get off entirely! Of course, you'll realize that, and you won't want to risk being the sucker—and we'll find ourselves right back at the same result: we both squeal. The logic is airtight.

There are a variety of stories that can be spun around this basic dynamic, so let's develop some generic terms that will serve our rhetorical purposes. The interpersonal relationship of interest is the one between the two players, so if a player makes the move that would benefit the other player (clamming up), we'll call that cooperation. If a player makes the move that harms the other player (squealing), we'll call that defection. Let's also change the nature of the consequences so that players are awarded different numbers of points depending on the outcome of the game. For example, let's say the payoff for mutual cooperation is 3 points, but the payoff for mutual defection is only 1 point. And if only one of us defects, the reward for doing so is 5 points. The other player, the sucker who cooperated while the other defected, gets no points. The goal of each player, by the way, is to get as many points as possible, which does not necessarily mean getting more than the other player. Games of this type are called non-zero-sum games, which means that one player's profits are not necessarily the other's debits. In any case, the dynamic is unchanged. If you think I will cooperate, you should defect and earn the full 5 points. If you think I will defect, you should defect and take the 1 point rather than the 0 points. I will reason likewise, so we'll both defect and we'll each get only 1 point.

Now, another twist. Let's play repeatedly, an infinite (or at least indeterminate) number of times. Does this change the strategy? Indeed it does. You risk getting the sucker's payoff by cooperating, but you might be able to elicit my cooperation on subsequent moves by extending such an olive branch. And though you might lose a couple of points enticing me to cooperate, you will more than get them back if you are successful in doing so. More generally, the dynamic in a repeated Prisoner's Dilemma game is affected by the fact that each player can formulate a strategy that takes into account the other player's previous moves. If you notice that I always defect, no matter what you do, then you might as well defect every time, and each iteration will be the same as the one-shot game. If you notice that I always cooperate, no matter what you do, you will also want to defect every time, and you'll reap the benefit of the best payout on each iteration. But if you notice that I tend to respond flexibly to your behavior, then a different strategy might suggest itself. Perhaps I mirror your responses, such that I respond to your defections by defecting on the next iteration. Likewise, I respond to cooperation by cooperating with you on the next iteration. In this case, the most sensible thing for you to do is to cooperate because then I will cooperate in return and we'll both get a better return compared to the poor payoff earned by doggedly sticking it to each other in cycles of mutual defection. And once you begin cooperating, you won't be tempted to defect, not because you've suddenly become all warm and fuzzy about our relationship, but because you've discovered that I won't allow you to treat me like a sucker. If you do defect, I will just go back to defecting myself, and we'll both be worse off. These strategies have been dubbed with various names, but let's call the player who always cooperates a dove, the player who always defects a hawk, and the strategy of mirroring the other player's previous move "tit for tat."

Of course, many other strategies are possible. What if someone scheduled a round-robin tournament, in which many different strategies competed over a large number of iterations? What kind of strategy would end up with the most points? Before we answer that question, let's make it even more interesting. Let's say that there are several rounds to the tournament, and the strategies that do well in each round get to enter more copies of themselves in the subsequent round, and the strategies that do poorly get weeded out. This, obviously, is intended to model evolutionary effects, and this is exactly what Robert Axelrod did.[14] He solicited from academics with interest in game-theory programs encoding strategies for playing the repeated Prisoner's Dilemma, and he received sixty-two entries. Some were aggressive and hawkish; some were meek and dovish. The simplest program submitted was the one that implemented the tit-for-tat strategy. It was also the winner.

Why is tit for tat such an effective strategy? The reason is that it is eager to get along and reap the benefits of mutual cooperation, but it won't let itself be played for a sucker. So when it meets a dovish strategy or another tit-for-tat player, mutual cooperation will emerge from the interaction, to the benefit of both. When it meets a hawkish player, it won't do as well, but neither will the hawk. Hawks, however, will do well against dovish strategies, so strategies that are too dovish will be driven to extinction by the exploitation of the hawks. But once the hawks have taken out all the dovish suckers, then they are stuck with strategies that pay them back in kind. So they have no opportunity to do any better than the small payout that accrues for mutual defection. Tit for tat, however, can chalk up points as long as there are other tit for tats or similarly "nice" strategies remaining in the competition, so it will begin outcompeting the hawkish strategies.

The point of this is that it demonstrates that evolutionary dynamics can favor cooperative strategies, as long as there are enough cooperators in the population that they encounter each other fairly frequently. It is plausible that there are many such situations in nature. Consider a species that is prone to get ticks.[15] It would be quite helpful to me if you would remove the ticks from the places on my body that I can't easily reach. Once you have done so, I might like to defect on you and not return the favor. But if you reciprocate my defection, then I will lose out on your future tick-removal services, so my best bet is to reciprocate your kindness and return the favor. And likewise, if I do you the service of removing your ticks and you fail to return the favor, I will retaliate by refusing to help you anymore. If we live in a society of individuals who employ various strategies with respect to the issue of tick removal, and if ticks have detrimental effects on their hosts such that those who do not get cleaned are at a selective disadvantage, then, as in Axelrod's computer tournaments, the tit-for-tat strategy should ascend to dominance. This will particularly be the case where individuals interact often and repeatedly, where the benefits of being helped are great and the costs of helping are low, and where individuals have the cognitive wherewithal to recognize each other and remember previous interactions. There are probably a large number of mammal and bird species for which these conditions are realistic. Humans would seem to be one of them.

Another, rather exotic example comes from vampire bats.[16] Vampire bats venture out at night in search of blood, but like most big game hunters, they frequently fail to find prey. When a bat is successful in getting a meal, it will load up and drink a lot of blood. Even so, if it suffers several successive nights without a meal, it is in real danger of starving to death. Its conspecifics could help it, though. A bat that was lucky enough to have found a good meal could regurgitate some of the surplus for the benefit of a hungry friend. In a careful study of this behavior, G. S. Wilkinson found that vampire bats do just that. In many cases, the hungry bats that were fed were offspring or relatives of the donor, in which case parental care or kin selection could account for the behavior. But in some cases, the donor and the recipient were unrelated. However, familiarity with each other was an important determinant of the helping behavior. Wilkinson was able to demonstrate that these bats recognize one another as individuals and that they have a much greater tendency to help roostmates than strangers. This scenario corresponds very closely to a repeated Prisoner's Dilemma dynamic. Individuals interact repeatedly with others that they recognize, and the benefit to the recipient of the blood donation is greater than the cost to the donor (which is, nevertheless, significant). It is worth emphasizing at this point that reciprocal altruism occurs not because it benefits the group, but because the individuals who participate in the reciprocal interactions benefit from their participation and they therefore pass on their genes at higher rates, including the genes that disposed them to engage in reciprocal altruism in the first place.

Once again, an obvious question arises. Is reciprocal altruism really altruism? It does have the effect of helping others at a short-term cost to the helper, but doesn't the fact that it ultimately evolves because of the benefit to the helper render it self-interested? Again, we will defer our analysis of these issues to a later section of this chapter. First, we must consider one more evolutionary mechanism that potentially could generate altruistic behavior.

GROUP SELECTION

One of the popular misconceptions about evolution that Gould identifies is the idea that evolution works for the good of the species. If this were true, then the existence of altruism would hardly be a puzzle. But, as should be clear from our earlier discussion of the genetic basis of natural selection, evolution does not work that way. Genes do not care about the good of the individuals who possess them, and, if anything, they care even less about the good of the species to which the individual belongs. Nevertheless, and notwithstanding the personal sacrifices involved in kin selection and reciprocity, it is not unreasonable to assume that most often a gene best promotes its own replicative interests by making the body that it inhabits in some way better suited to the survival challenges it is likely to face. Thus, the ubiquity of self-interest bewilders no one. Could the same kind of argument apply to entities larger than the organism? Do genes best serve their selfish interests not only by providing for the survival of the bodies they inhabit, but also by providing for the interests of the groups inhabited by those bodies? The general thesis of group selection is that where there is competition between groups, such that one group can potentially supplant another, natural selection can favor characteristics that benefit the group itself, even if those characteristics are not advantageous to individual members of the group.

Darwin considered such a process to be a plausible explanation for the evolution of morality in humans:

> It must not be forgotten that although a high standard of morality gives but a slight or no advantage to each individual man and his children over the other men of the same tribe, yet that an increase in the number of well-endowed men and an advancement in the standard of morality will certainly give an immense advantage to one tribe over another. A tribe including many members who, from possessing in high degree the spirit of patriotism, fidelity, obedience, courage, and sympathy, were always ready to aid one another, and to sacrifice themselves for the common good, would be victorious over most other tribes; and this would be natural selection. At all times throughout the world tribes have supplanted other tribes; and as morality is one important element in their success, the standard of morality and the number of well-endowed men will thus everywhere tend to rise and increase.[17]

More recently, V. C. Wynne-Edwards proposed that natural populations have evolved mechanisms of population control that subvert the short-term reproductive interests of individuals for the benefit of the species.[18] Noting laboratory research indicating an inverse relationship between population density and individual fecundity, plus the ethological observation that natural populations tend not to proliferate to the point where they deplete the resources necessary for their survival, Wynne-Edwards reasoned that species must possess innate mechanisms for population control. Such mechanisms could have come about through a sort of group selection. Species that failed to control their population size would have outstripped their food sources and doomed themselves to extinction, but species that practiced restraint in their reproduction could prosper and endure. As a result, population self-regulation has become the norm among extant species.

The problem with theories of group selection such as these is that they do not seem to be supportable in light of the genetic mechanisms of heredity and selection.[19] The essence of the problem is that selection at the level of individuals can much more easily undermine the interests of the group than the converse. Consider, for example, a bird belonging to a population that has evolved a mechanism of population control wherein each breeding pair has only one offspring per breeding season. A mutant individual who violated this convention and produced more than one offspring per season would, by virtue of its greater fecundity, be more fit than its relatively restrained conspecifics; and because its mutation would be transmitted to some of its offspring, they would also be more fecund, and so would their offspring, and so on, with the eventual effect that the restrained individuals would be supplanted by the unrestrained. This argument should not be taken to mean that reproductive restraint cannot evolve or that natural selection always favors the most fecund individuals; but it does mean that the mechanisms that regulate such things as clutch size or litter size must be explicable in terms of individual selection.

A similar argument applies to the contention that altruism might have evolved because of the advantage that it confers to the group. As Darwin imagined, intergroup competition might favor those groups with greater numbers of self-sacrificing individuals, but the altruism of such groups would always be vulnerable to subversion from within. Selection within the group would tend to favor those individuals who were less self-sacrificing, who would therefore eventually displace their more altruistic comrades.

In light of these difficulties, most biologists simply dismissed the concept of group selection altogether, and students were taught that it was an idea that had been conclusively refuted. Recently, however, Elliott Sober and David Sloan Wilson have shown how something similar to group selection can operate under certain ecological conditions without violating selfish-gene principles.[20] Consider, for example, a pathogenic organism that reproduces in the body of its host. Among the individual pathogens, those that are best able to multiply rapidly are in a short-term sense the fittest. They are also, by virtue of their rampaging reproduction, more virulent and more harmful to the host. But the harm done to the host, particularly if it is fatal, may make it substantially less likely that the pathogens are transmitted to another host. Heightened virulence may well evolve within certain unlucky individuals, but it is less likely to evolve as a typical characteristic of the pathogen, because the less virulent forms will be more successful in transmitting themselves to new hosts. Pathogens whose contagion depends on the continued social activity of their hosts, which is particularly the case for airborne organisms, do tend to be less virulent, which suggests that group selection can counter the effect of within-host individual selection.[21]

The same general process could result in the evolution of altruism in a population that is regularly segregated into subgroups that subsequently reintegrate into the larger population. To illustrate this process, Sober and Wilson consider a hypothetical population, initially composed of equal numbers of altruists and selfish types, that splits into two subgroups of equal size. One of the subgroups includes a large proportion of the altruists; the other has only a few altruists. By definition, the altruists behave in a way that has the immediate effect of reducing their individual fitness. But everyone in each subgroup gains some measure of fitness from the altruists in the group. In terms of reproductive output, within each group selfish types naturally do better than altruists, because they profit from their altruistic compatriots' beneficence without enduring the cost. Altruists also reap the benefits of their fellow altruists' charity, but they must also pay the cost for their altruism. If each group is examined individually, it would appear that the altruistic type is headed toward extinction. But there is also a between-group difference in reproductive output, and the altruist-rich group produces more *total* progeny than the altruist-poor group, for the simple reason that everyone's reproduction is enhanced in the altruist-rich subgroup because of the large number of altruists. In fact, reproduction of altruists in the altruist-rich group may well exceed reproduction by the selfish individuals in the altruist-poor group. The somewhat surprising net effect when the population is reconstituted is that the proportion of altruists in the global population has actually increased, despite having decreased within each group.[22] This happens because progeny of the group with the large proportion of altruists are more heavily represented in the next generation, so the proportion of altruists in the global population shifts in that direction.

If some are not satisfied that the ecological conditions specified in this model are sufficiently realistic, or in particular that they represent conditions that likely prevailed for ancestral humans, it should nevertheless be conceded that Sober and Wilson have demonstrated that intergroup dynamics at least have the potential to counter the selective effect exerted against altruism within groups. Certainly, human beings have long existed in groups that at times competed, at times joined forces, at times exchanged mates, and so on. It does not seem too far-fetched to suppose that complicated intergroup dynamics such as these could have produced a situation favorable to the replication of alleles that disposed their possessors to behave altruistically. Furthermore, although we have examined kin selection, reciprocity, and group selection separately, it may well be that these mechanisms are not entirely independent of one another, but that the net selection pressure exerted on any allele affecting social behavior reflects a synergistic interaction among all three of these processes. However complicated the selection dynamics truly are, it should now be clear that when self-sacrificing altruistic behavior is analyzed as a function of the replicative interests of genes, it no longer seems impossibly enigmatic.

TOWARD AN EXPLICATION OF ALTRUISM: IS ANY OF THIS REALLY ALTRUISM?

In this chapter we have described three mechanisms that could result in the propagation of genes that dispose their possessors to behave in ways that appear to be altruistic. But in showing that such behavior is explicable in terms of the replicative advantages to the genes of the actor, haven't we implicitly shown that these acts are *not* altruistic? Isn't this just another form of egoism, albeit a form of egoism in which self-interest means genetic self-interest? When you offer assistance to a relative, do you do so for the sake of the relative, or for the sake of your own genes, which may also be present in that relative? When you offer a favor to a friend, do you really do so because of the payback that you are likely to receive when you are in need of a helping hand? When you work for the good of your community, do you do so because your genes will tend to prosper to the extent that your community prospers? It is easy to see why people have regarded the gene-centered view with skepticism, suspecting that it can generate nothing but a cynical outlook on human nature and our ultimate motives. We wish to argue that such suspicions are unwarranted, and that the genetic blurring of the boundaries between individuals is part of what makes altruism possible. In other words, it is our contention that the intrinsic selfishness of genes not only does not preclude altruism or imply that individuals must be inherently selfish; it actually creates the conditions of interconnectedness that make altruism possible, even likely.

The suspicion that a gene-centered view inevitably leads to cynicism is probably rooted in a couple of fundamental misunderstandings about precisely what is being claimed. The first misunderstanding stems from an overly literal interpretation of the rhetorical device of describing a gene as being "for" a particular behavior. We have already noted that this usage is merely a semantic shortcut. Nevertheless, it is easy to see how such a usage could be taken to imply actual goal-directedness on the part of genes, inadvertently resurrecting something akin to the teleological fallacy discussed by Stephen Jay Gould, which we mentioned earlier. When behavior is explained by reference to its effects on gene frequencies, it is all too easy to infer that it is additionally being claimed that the purpose of the behavior is to have just such an effect on the gene pool. For example, in describing kin selection, it might seem as though the claim being advanced is that an organism helps its kin not for the sake of the kin, but for the sake of its own genes. The inference is unwarranted, however; indeed, it reflects an inversion of the relationship between genes and behavior as that relationship is properly understood. To understand evolutionary arguments correctly, we must appreciate their specifically nonteleological character. Evolutionary analyses of behavior claim that certain behavior has evolved because *in the past* it had the effect of promoting replication of the genes responsible for the behavior. These analyses do not claim that the behavior exists in order to exert further effects on gene frequencies. Thus it makes no sense to say that a behavior occurs for the *sake* of gene replication. That would imply a sort of forward-lookingness contrary to the principles embodied in the idea of natural selection. If we want to talk about the purpose of a behavior, we will have to switch to a different level of analysis, because evolutionary analyses do not literally invoke purpose.

The second misunderstanding comes from the reductionistic structure of evolutionary arguments, which may create the impression that the individual is nothing more than a constellation of genes. If the organism is equated with its genes, and if the mechanisms of kin selection, reciprocity, and group selection can be shown to advance the replicative interests of those genes, as they do, then it is only natural to assume that part of what is being asserted is that those mechanisms serve the interests of the organism. But the concern that exposing the genetic mechanisms responsible for altruism will inevitably reduce altruism to self-interest reflects a confusion among types of entities. Genes, as we have said, cannot be altruistic. Genes are professional replicators; they have no choice but to do the best they can at generating copies of themselves. For a gene to sacrifice its good for the benefit of another gene is for the gene to be unfit. But a gene that disposes its vessel to sacrifice for the sake of others could very well be fit. This does not necessarily mean, however, that the interests of the vessel are being advanced. The individual organism may well suffer injury or death as a result of its beneficence; how does that advance *its* interests? So the question is not whether genes are ever altruistic. We already know the answer to that question, which is a given by virtue of the very nature of genes. The real question is whether individuals are ever altruistic.

To a large degree, the question of whether an instance of behavior qualifies as truly altruistic depends on how one defines altruism. Dawkins, you will recall, defined altruism as follows: "An entity, such as a baboon, is said to be altruistic if it behaves in such a way as to increase another such entity's welfare at the expense of its own."[23] Now, it is possible to define "welfare" so broadly as to include all possible forms of fitness gains to the entity in question. In this case, no act inculcated into a species' behavioral repertoire by the mechanisms of kin selection, reciprocity, group selection, or any other form of selection, could qualify as altruistic. The mere demonstration that the behavior was a product of natural selection would indicate that it has tended to confer a fitness advantage, in the sense of an enhancement of overall gene replication, to those who have possessed the genes underlying the behavior. Thus, no matter the cost to the actor, the cost will be redefined as a benefit if the behavior is positively selected, thereby negating the altruism of the act. In other words, if we equate welfare with inclusive fitness, then altruism, defined this way, cannot evolve. Helping behavior can evolve, but it cannot qualify as true altruism. Evolutionary theorist Lee Dugatkin appears to subscribe to just such a definition. In explaining how kin selection could favor the evolution of alarm calling among ground squirrels, he writes, "What this means is that when a squirrel risks its own life to save the lives of its relatives, it is not being completely altruistic, because its relatives most likely carry the same genes that it does."[24] Once again, this seems to reflect a conflation of the interests of the organism with the interests of its genes, interests that, while certainly not independent of each other, nevertheless do not necessarily coincide perfectly. Just ask the squirrel whose chirping earned it the attention of the hungry coyote. Such behavior may be good for its genes, via kin selection, but what good is that to *the squirrel itself* when it becomes the coyote's next meal?

Few people, however, would define welfare so broadly. More plausibly, one might point to the distinction between direct fitness and indirect fitness, and define the welfare of our ostensibly altruistic entity exclusively in terms of impacts upon its direct fitness; that is, upon its prospects for survival and personal reproduction. With welfare defined in this way, the possibility of altruism is not precluded a priori by the definition itself. Behavior contributing to the reproductive potential of unrelated group members at a cost to the direct fitness of the actor, that is, behavior generated by group selection, clearly qualifies as altruistic. What about kin selection? Some sacrifices made for the sake of relatives count as altruistic, but interestingly, sacrifices made for offspring do not count, because parental care is considered, by definition, to subserve direct fitness. This probably accords with most people's intuition that parental care has a distinctly different quality than other forms of helping behavior; but from a strictly theoretical standpoint, is such a distinction justified? Why characterize sacrifice for the sake of one entity with whom you share about 50 percent of your alleles—a sibling, say—as altruistic, while characterizing sacrifice for the sake of another entity who also happens to share about 50 percent of your alleles—your child—as nonaltruistic? From an objective, genetic point of view, doesn't such a distinction seem a bit arbitrary? What about reciprocity? From the current definitional point of view, "reciprocal altruism" must be considered something of a misnomer, because reciprocity evolves via direct-fitness advantages that accrue to the participants in these reciprocal exchanges. Over time, the cost of helping is repaid, and the repayment exceeds the original cost, so the helper ultimately nets a direct-fitness profit.

Of course, we don't have to guess what Dawkins means by "welfare" because he tells us. "'Welfare' is defined as 'chances of survival,' even if the effect on actual life and death prospects is so small as to *seem* negligible."[25] Defined this way, welfare has nothing to do with gene replication. Rather, it means something far more conventional and intuitively pleasing. There is no trickery in Dawkins' definition. If you endanger yourself while helping some-one else—meaning precisely that you increase, however slightly, the chance that you will die, while simultaneously increasing, however slightly, the chance of another surviving—then the act is altruistic. So, is a personal sacrifice made for the sake of unrelated group members altruistic? Of course.[26] Is the ground squirrel who sounds the alarm to warn its relatives of an approaching preda-tor behaving altruistically? Definitely. What about a killdeer (a type of bird) who performs a broken-wing display to lure an approaching predator away from its nestlings? It seems likely that the adult killdeer exposes itself to a greater risk of predation by doing so, in order to reduce the risk of predation to its offspring. This raises the interesting question of whether parental care is altruistic. For Dawkins, if kin-selected behavior qualifies as altruism, then parental care does as well, because parental care *is* an example of kin selection in action. "The truth is that all examples of child-protection and parental care, and all associated bodily organs, milk-secreting glands, kangaroo pouches, and so on, are examples of the working in nature of the kin-selection princi-ple."[27] Dawkins makes the point even more directly when he writes, "The com-monest and most conspicuous acts of animal altruism are done by parents, especially mothers, towards their children."[28]

As before, reciprocal altruism presents more of a puzzle. Is the vampire bat that donates blood to an unrelated "friend" behaving altruistically, according to Dawkins' definition? How we answer seems to depend on the time scale and number of interactions over which we integrate the costs and benefits. Remember that reciprocity evolves because on average the paybacks that individuals eventually receive more than offset the costs of helping. The net long-term average consequence to the donor is an increase in its survival prospects. For this reason, reciprocity is often characterized not as altruism but as a form of "mutualism" in which both entities involved in the exchange come out ahead in the long run. But if we look only at the immediate effect of the bat's blood donation, then we might get away with calling it altruis-tic. After all, the donation can save the life of a hungry recipient, and the donor is really giving up precious nutrients that might have gone to preserv-ing its own life just a bit longer. Although the donation pays dividends in the long run *on average*, it is entirely possible that in some particular instances a bat starves to death a few days after having donated blood to one of its broodmates, when it might have lived to see one more hunt had it kept the blood in its own stomach. If so, what is the benefit to the donor? Its benefi-cence saved a friend but cost it its own life. Isn't that altruism?

However one classifies particular cases, the general point has been made. Natural selection is entirely capable of producing individual organisms that are disposed to behave in ways benefiting others at a cost to self. This is possible because genes, not individuals, are the fundamental units of selection. If it were true, as Wolf Larsen implicitly believed, that the fundamental unit of selection is the individual, then a cynical view of any apparently other-regarding act would be justified. But the gene-centered view obviates that cynicism and puts Wolf Larsen's arguments to rest. That is not to say that natural selection doesn't strongly favor self-interested behavior; obviously the replicative interests of genes are often best served when individuals put their own interests above those of others. But natural selection need no longer always connote the ruthless selfishness advocated by Wolf Larsen. Genes must be selfish, but organisms don't have to be. Human beings in particular are social animals whose flourishing is predicated on highly developed capacities for cooperation and nurturance. Yes, of course self-preservation is a powerful drive in humans as in other animals, but the Hobbesian thesis that self-preservation is the sole source of our motivation appears quite naïve in light of an informed appreciation of the genetic mechanisms underlying behavior. Demeaning as it might initially seem that, biologically speaking, we exist as vessels for transmitting genes through time, this condition frees us to be something other than the selfish pawns of natural selection. Unlike genes, we can care about the welfare of others.

But this brings up another reason that people are often skeptical about the prospect for true altruism. This reason harkens back to the idea of "hidden" motives. When one considers that evolutionary mechanisms such as kin selection, reciprocity, and possibly group selection provide the basis for altruism, it is tempting to think that the "real" motive for the behavior must somehow address the fitness gains that drive these mechanisms. The biologically informed skeptic might say something like, "You know, the *real* reason that you do so much for your family is that, unbeknownst to your conscious mind, you want to do whatever you can to get copies of your genes into the next generation." Or, "Sure, she seems nice, but of course her kindness is *really* motivated by a desire for reciprocation, even if she doesn't know it consciously." The skeptic might even say, "So you see, what you're calling altruism isn't really altruism at all. The underlying motive—the ultimate motive—is always directed toward the satisfaction of your own biological imperatives." Egoism doesn't give up easily.

Still, we have made substantial progress toward our goal of establishing the reality of altruism. In chapter two, we showed that the possibility of altruism cannot be eliminated on strictly logical grounds. In this chapter, we have shown that the principles of evolutionary biology in no way preclude the possibility of altruism. We really have yet to get to the main point, though. We wish to defend the reality of altruism according to *our* definition, which, in contrast to Dawkins' definition, specifically *does* refer to the psychology of motives. We will have to make a case that the kind of mechanisms detailed in this chapter are likely to produce not only behavior that benefits others, but also motivational states that fulfill our psychological criteria for what constitutes a true instance of altruism. To accomplish that, we shall need another chapter.

4

Psychological Perspectives
Nurturing Our Nature

NATURE AND NURTURE

IN THE PRECEDING CHAPTER, we emphasized that genes are the entities that replicate themselves through generations, and that we, the bodies they build, are their inventions and their servants, designed to promote their replication and transmission to new bodies. Doubtless, many genes have done well for themselves by participating in the production of behavior that serves the interests of the self. Self-preservation, we can all agree, is a powerful instinct, for very good Darwinian reasons. But, as we also saw in the preceding chapter, some genes might do well for themselves by disposing their possessors to less self-interested endeavors, such as extending favors to relatives, friends, and other members of the community, even when such favors are costly to the self. We must now contend with the issue of *how* genes might produce these behaviors. To establish the reality of altruism, as we have defined it, it is not enough to reconcile altruistic *behavior* with natural selection; we must demonstrate that such behavior is indicative of altruistic *motivation*.[1]

In this chapter we will make the case that genuine concern for the well-being of others is natural for human beings and that such concern exists in various forms, any of which are capable of motivating action that has as its ultimate objective securing the welfare of the other. Human capacities for other-regard, we will further argue, sprang from the biological mechanisms described in the previous chapter, but their operation is nevertheless not limited to situations and recipients strictly conforming to the conditions of their evolution. This flexibility in the application of the mechanisms of altruism reflects in part the circuitous manner in which genetically rooted behavioral dispositions are actualized in human beings, a topic to which we will attend before proceeding to address specifically the psychological mechanisms of other-regard. Even more important, we will develop the idea that the biological underpinnings of altruism are but that, underpinnings, and the realization of altruism is as much a function of nurture as it is of nature. The implication of this is that although our biology provides us with certain raw materials upon which we can draw, the use we make of those raw materials is not predetermined. Our capacity for other-regard opens up possibilities for altruism that go beyond mere biology. We need only learn how to harness and expand upon the capacities with which we are already endowed. In other words, as human beings we are not subject to the constraints that chain other animals to their biology. In this chapter and the two that follow, we will explore various avenues by which nurture can expand upon and transform our natural proclivities.

The analysis presented in this chapter begins where we left off at the end of the preceding chapter, with the recognition that natural selection has favored genes that dispose individuals, in certain circumstances, to act in ways that benefit others. Again, the suggestion that genes can be said to produce behavior at all is troubling to some, but a closer look at how genes participate in the production of behavior should allay most of the common misgivings about such an analysis.[2] One such misgiving, which might be called "the fear of biological determinism," is the worry that if a proclivity to behave in a certain way is rooted in genetic programming, then behaving in accordance with that programming is both inevitable and inescapable. The supposition that genetic influence equals inevitability is unwarranted for several reasons, which, when understood, provide useful insights into the dynamics of behavior determination.

First, consider that even the *most* genetically determined characteristics can often easily be altered by the environment. Take something like the number of fingers on each hand. Do you have any doubt that the number of fingers you were born with was genetically determined? But sometimes (unfortunately in these cases), such biological determinism is overridden by environmental factors—factors such as circular saws and clogged lawnmowers. Analogously, but on a much cheerier note, medical advances may soon make it possible to cure some maladies that truly are genetically determined, such as Huntington's disease, by directly silencing the responsible genes. Admittedly, in most cases environmental circumstances do not intervene in the affairs of the genes so directly and so abruptly, but people have always managed to exercise some control over behavior through socialization, education, and the imposition of consequences. The point is that the ability of the environment to affect a behavior does not depend on that behavior being environmentally determined in the first place. Like fingers, even genetically "programmed" behavior can usually be extirpated by the environment. And, to extend the analogy, the fact that the evolved function of fingers is the manipulation of objects does not prevent us from using them for other ends, such as communicating (by pointing, gesturing, and signing) or making a fashion statement (by decorating them with nail polish and rings). Psychological capacities can likewise be co-opted for purposes other than those for which they evolved.

Second, even the most biologically determined of behaviors are also, simultaneously, under the control of environmental stimuli. Consider the sneeze reflex, for example. No one thinks of sneezing as a learned behavior or even a voluntary behavior; it is clearly a reflexive response that we all possess innately—which is to say genetically—as part of our behavioral repertoire. But what determines when the behavior of sneezing becomes manifest? Not the genes, but rather some environmental stimulus, such as a speck of dust entering the nasal passages. Although it would surely be impossible to perform such an experiment, it is conceivable that someone could spend an entire lifetime sealed in a sterile environment, so clean and free of dust, particulates, allergens, viruses, and anything else that might trigger a sneeze, that the person could live a lifetime without ever sneezing. What is a biological inevitability for the rest of us is so only because we are inevitably exposed to the environmental stimuli that trigger the innate response.

Third, the manner in which genes exert their influence over behavior is so indirect that it is wrong to characterize them as *controlling* behavior at all. Genes contain the instructions for building our nervous systems (among myriad other things), and it is our nervous systems that respond to the environment and generate our behavior. As psychologist Steven Pinker puts it, "Genes are not puppetmasters; they acted as the recipe for making the brain and the body and then they got out of the way."[3] As we shall see shortly, the idea that genes get out of the way is not quite right, but the general point that genes are not puppetmasters is correct. Moreover, and particularly it seems in the case of our own species, genes may have obtained some real advantages for themselves by specifying a recipe for a nervous system that, while sufficiently stocked with the requisite programs needed to manage the eventualities an individual will most likely face, is not so rigidly programmed that it fails to respond to experience or locks up in the face of the unexpected. In other words, selection pressures have favored genes that build brains that are good at learning and responding flexibly to the vicissitudes of an unpredictable environment. The circumstances in which an organism finds itself, after all, may differ in important respects from the environment of its ancestors, and besides that, each organism inevitably experiences a unique set of challenges in its lifetime, the specifics of which its genes could never perfectly predict. Genes can and do wire brains to respond in particular ways to particular stimulus events, but genes do not make the moment-to-moment decisions themselves. It is better for them that the brain has the executive power—that's its raison d'être, after all. In our own evolutionary history, there must have been strong selection pressures favoring the large, complicated brains that we now possess, brains that are capable of managing the extraordinary feats of learning that we routinely demonstrate. Notice that when one looks at it this way, the traditional dichotomy of nature *versus* nurture evaporates. Our capacities for learning stand not in opposition to our nature; rather, they are bequeathed to us by our nature, that is, by the genes that have done so well for themselves by building our brains.

The above argument counters another concern about evolutionary and genetic analyses of behavior, the fear that these analyses will undermine the importance of learning, socialization, and culture. Clearly, such a fear is unjustified. Among the most important capacities conferred upon us by our genes is our responsiveness to experience and culture. Still, we must be cautious not to overstate this point. The dogma of the human as a blank slate at birth is no more tenable than the caricature of the human as a genetically programmed robot. The brain provided to us has been molded by the contingencies of natural selection to give us a certain amount of flexibility, but it has also been designed with a lot of built-in functionality and specialized problem-solving strategies. The mechanisms of learning themselves are specialized biological solutions that have been crafted by natural selection to deal with the types of environmental contingencies with which our ancestors regularly dealt. The fact that genes control behavior only indirectly by building brains to execute the moment-to-moment management of behavior does not change the fact that genes, and the selection pressures that have shaped them, lie at the root of our behavioral capacities.

Nevertheless, the circuitous manner in which genes exercise their influence has an important consequence: they do not always get their way. This idea is most commonly illustrated by reference to a ubiquitous behavior that has an obvious connection to gene replication—sex. It is commonly said that we subvert the desires of our genes every time we use contraception during sex. It is important to understand, though, that the reason we are so easily able to confound our genes is that we can do so without defying the programming with which they have equipped us. Our genes have, of course, built us such that we will be very likely to engage in sexual behavior, but they did so not by providing us with the desire to replicate our genes, but rather by making us so that we desire sexual activity itself and experience it as pleasurable. When we have sex while using contraception, we are still complying with a biological imperative, but the imperative is psychological, not genetic. Of course, the psychological imperative is the consequence of the genetic imperative to reproduce, but with respect to the gene's objectives, the psychological impulses that impel our behavior are merely *heuristics*—rules of thumb that get the job done most of the time.[4] In delegating the authority to control behavior to the brain, genes take the risk that the heuristics they have embedded in our neural architecture will be misappropriated and directed toward ends other than gene replication. So the point is not only that genes do not control behavior directly, but that their ultimate purposes are sometimes subverted by the fact that they have made us so that *our* ultimate purposes are not identical to theirs. We will return to this point when we address how our biology has equipped us with the capacity for psychological altruism.

A fourth reason that the fear of biological determinism is unwarranted is that genes themselves respond flexibly to the environment. Yes, strictly speaking, bodies are tools that genes use to replicate themselves, but it turns out that one of the best things a gene can do to help its own cause is to allow the body to conscript it into its service. Genes, far from stepping aside once the brain has been built, participate actively in its operation. In particular, they play a central role in learning, through a process known as gene induction. In direct response to experience, cells in the brain turn on and off genetic switches called promoters, which have the effect of activating the expression of particular genes, the products of which may modulate other gene promoters or produce structural changes in the cells themselves, altering the strength of synaptic connections between neurons. This dynamic rewiring of the brain results in the changes in behavior and cognition that we call learning. Matt Ridley puts it this way:

> Genes themselves are implacable little determinists, churning out utterly predictable messages. But because of the way their promoters switch on and off in response to external instruction, genes are very far from being fixed in their actions. Instead, they are devices for extracting information from the environment. Every minute,

every second, the pattern of genes being expressed in your brain changes, often in direct or indirect response to events outside the body. Genes are the mechanisms of experience.[5]

Ridley's book is called *Nature via Nurture*. It could have just as easily been called *Nurture via Nature*. The point is that behavior is caused not by genes, not by the environment, and not even by genes *and* the environment. It is produced by brains that are built and continuously modified by both genes and the environment, the genes themselves having been selected by past environments and their expression being dynamically modulated by the current environment. It *is* the case that our motives, our capacities, and our inclinations are explicable in part in terms of our genetic makeup, but to say so is to assert something very different than the claim that our behavior is genetically determined.

A fifth and final reason that the fear of biological determinism is unwarranted is that even to the extent that some particularly worrisome behavior, desire, or inclination is the indirect product of genetic programming, so are innumerable other behaviors, desires, and inclinations, many of which will be incompatible with the troublesome one. Failure to recognize this seems to underlie a related objection to evolutionary explanations of behavior, the fear that our "true" nature will be revealed to be most unseemly, and moreover, that by virtue of this being our true nature, such unseemliness will become morally justifiable. Such a fear may have underlain the famous response of Bishop Samuel Wilberforce's wife upon learning of Darwin's theory: "Let us hope it is not true, but if it is, let us hope it does not become widely known." The fear is unfounded not only because facts of human nature are not the kind of things that can provide moral justifications, but also because such a view is a vast oversimplification of the facts themselves. Human nature is not a monolithic thing. In estimating the number of fundamental motives we possess, Rousseau, it seems, was closer to the truth than Hobbes, but he was still far off the mark. The basic impulses and motives provided us by nature number far beyond the two imagined by Rousseau. Indeed, we will see that altruism itself comprises a multitude of interacting psychological impulses and capacities.

To bring the discussion back to the topic at hand, the upshot of all of this is that there is no need to fear that explanations of altruism as a function of biological mechanisms, rooted in our genes, will reveal us to be self-serving automatons, even if that is precisely what our genes themselves are. To this point, we have not yet decisively ruled out such a possibility. As we suggested near the end of the preceding chapter, it could turn out that the genes that have prospered by underwriting seemingly altruistic behavior have done so by providing us with motives, possibly hidden from our conscious awareness, that have always as their ultimate object of concern our own interests. When someone helps another in need, perhaps at the most basic *psychological* level the helper is seeking the eventual payback demanded by the dynamics of the reciprocity game. In the remainder of this chapter, we will attempt to show that this is not the case. This brings us to the most basic reason that some might fear biological explanations: the fear of egoism itself, the fear that our "true" reasons are identical to our genes' reasons. As already explained, this is not *necessarily* the case, because of the indirect way in which genes implement their behavioral programs through heuristic strategies enacted by the brain. To show that it is *definitely* not the case will require us to delve into those heuristics themselves, heuristics that we experience as emotions.

KIN SELECTION AND THE EXPERIENCE OF LOVE

Those who deny the reality of genuine other-regard should ask themselves how they would feel if their own child were trapped in a burning building or helplessly stuck in the path of an onrushing train. Terrified? Yes, but that's hardly a strong enough word to capture the feeling. Panicked? Certainly, but that's still not strong enough. Perhaps there are no words strong enough to capture the abject horror that a parent would experience in that sort of situation. And, as a parent, to what lengths would you be willing to go to save your precious child? Or perhaps a better question is, What *wouldn't* you be willing to do? Would you give your life to save your child's? If so, why? Before you dash into the flames or jump onto the tracks, would you consider that this child carries your genetic legacy, and that your shared genes will stand a better chance of being propagated into the future if this child's untapped reproductive potential is preserved rather than your partly used up reproductive potential? No? Then why do it? Why do you care if your child is killed? Why not just look on with indifference? After all, it's not you in the fire or on the tracks; you're in no danger at all if you just stay put. Why don't you just shrug, go home, have a nice meal, and get a good night's sleep?

If the line of questioning has become absurd, then that leads to another line of questioning: Why is it absurd? Why is it so patently obvious that no normal human being would react with indifference to the violent death of his or her own child? One possible answer is that we have all seen enough examples of people reacting to the loss of close relatives that we simply have learned that indifference is not a typical reaction. Although it might be true that we have such episodic knowledge, that kind of answer doesn't seem to capture our immediate and visceral appreciation for the anguish of that parent. When we imagine a parent in such a circumstance, our natural reaction, like the parent's, is not one of indifferent calculation of the probabilities. No one needs to consult a database of stored memories of similar tragedies to predict the depth of the parent's horror and grief, and in imagining such circumstances, we don't merely arrive at a dispassionate assessment of the emotions involved; we vicariously feel some measure of horror ourselves. The above line of questioning is absurd because we all know what it feels like to love someone, and we can all too easily empathize with the pain of losing a loved one.

The love of a parent for a child makes a particularly compelling case for true other-regard, as it is ordinarily the strongest, purest love a person can experience. Even those who have not had children recognize the depth of parental love. But to once again pose questions about matters that seem self-evident, we must ask these questions: Why is parental love so powerful? Why do we care that our children are safe, healthy, and happy? And why are we willing to go to such great lengths and make such huge personal sacrifices to ensure our children's safety, health, and happiness? The kind of answer that seems most obvious—*because they're our children and we love them*—begs the question. A more satisfyingly synthetic (although perhaps unsatisfyingly clinical) answer is that in our species, natural selection has strongly favored an extraordinarily high degree of parental investment in children (among all species, human offspring are perhaps the most dependent on their parents for the longest time) and parental love is the psychological heuristic used to motivate that investment.

Does this demean love? Is love, even a love as devoted as that of a parent for a child, really nothing more than a self-interested attempt by genes to promote their own survival? As we have already argued, there is no call for such cynicism. Steven Pinker explains:

> People love their children not because they want to spread their genes (consciously or unconsciously) but because they can't help it. That love makes them try to keep their children warm, fed, and

safe. What is selfish is not the real motives of the person but the metaphorical motives of the genes that built the person. . . . The confusion comes from thinking of people's genes as their true self, and the motives of their genes as their deepest, truest, unconscious motives. From there it's easy to draw the cynical and incorrect moral that all love is hypocritical. That confuses the real motives of the person with the metaphorical motives of the genes.[6]

The point is that our genes have gone about achieving their selfish objectives by making *us*—human beings—*really, truly* care deeply about the welfare of our children. There is no need to be cynical about love just because it can be shown to have an evolutionary basis. From a psychological point of view, love is a genuinely other-regarding emotion. And this means that the sacrifices parents routinely make for their children, sacrifices made so routinely that it is easy to discount them as mundane and ordinary, are altruistic because they are motivated by a truly other-regarding motive. Really, what motive could be more other-regarding than love?

There are those who will object to this line of reasoning by saying, "Yes, yes, sure, all people love their children, but that's not really other-regard, not really altruism, because it's *their own children* we're talking about, after all. A parent's own well-being is so bound up in his or her children that the child's interests and welfare *are* the parent's interests and welfare, too." Somewhat paradoxically, when our feelings for another are experienced so deeply and genuinely, we feel so personally invested in the other that we are inclined to deny that what we experience is really other-regarding. A parent's love for a child is so central to the parent's sense of self and the child's welfare is so instrumental to the parent's fulfillment that parental investment feels positively self-interested. And in a sense it is self-interested, in that the parent's well-being is inextricably connected to the child's. But this is yet another example of the kind of self-interest that does not negate other-regard, but rather presupposes it and thereby substantiates it. The parent's well-being is so profoundly tied up in the well-being of the child *because* the parent cares so deeply and so genuinely for the child. The interests of the child are the ultimate concern for the parent. How could this not be an example of genuine other-regard? After all, no matter how much the parent loves the child, the parent and the child are not actually the same person!

Parental love is the most obvious example of an other-regarding emotion that results from genetic relatedness. Of course, we have relatives other than children, and we are strongly inclined to love them, too. Your parents, grand-parents, sisters, brothers, uncles, aunts, nieces, nephews, and cousins are all more closely related to you than is the average person on the street; and, if you're like most people, you probably harbor more warm feelings for these close relatives than you do for random strangers. On average, the depth of love felt toward a relative directly corresponds to the degree of relatedness. The tightest bonds are felt within the nuclear family, where the relatedness is closest. Siblings, for example, are not only genetically closer to each other than cousins; they are usually emotionally closer as well. Of course, this is not always the case, and it turns out that the heuristic constructed by the process of kin selection to impel us to assist those who share our genes (familial love) itself uses some rough-and-tumble rules of thumb for deter-mining who is a deserving recipient of our love. Cousins who are raised together like siblings will tend to love each other like siblings. Siblings raised apart may feel nothing more for each other than do strangers.

Again, then, we see that the fidelity with which the psychological mecha-nisms fulfill the genetic agenda that shaped those mechanisms in the first place is imperfect. In the same way that using contraceptive technology allows us to answer a psychological call to action while subverting its genetic basis, we can easily redirect our capacity for familial love to genetic nonrel-atives. Adoption is the most obvious example, and nothing written here should be taken to imply that adoptive parents love their children any less than any other parent, just because kin selection was the process that sculpted our propensity to love our children. The environmental triggers that elicit one's capacity to love another are not switched on and off by explicit knowledge of the actual coefficient of relatedness. They are activated by the nature of the interaction between individuals. A nurturant relation-ship between parent and child is sufficient to engender feelings of love, and while this feeling is usually accompanied by the genetic relatedness that has over evolutionary time crafted this emotional capacity, it need not be so in every case.

The idea that the very act of providing sustenance and nurturance will tend to activate feelings that foster further acts of caring suggests a way to expand the domain of altruism. Appeals to the underlying relatedness of all individuals, indeed of all life, and to the common destiny we share as inhab-itants of our world, may encourage us to think of one another as relatives. Indeed, kinship metaphors have been widely employed to encourage har-mony among unrelated groups of individuals. As Pinker points out, "The names used by groups that strive for solidarity—brethren, brotherhoods, fraternal organizations, sisterhoods, sororities, crime families, the family of man—concede in their metaphors that kinship is the paradigm to which they aspire."[7] But even when such metaphors are explicitly accepted, they are in themselves probably not sufficient to engender strong feelings of caring. A belief in the interrelatedness of humanity can probably be best internalized through action, in the same way that parental love not only is the impetus for acts of love but is itself stimulated by the performance of loving actions. So an analysis of kin selection as a basis for altruism would seem to lend support to the Aristotelian notion that love is a capacity that itself can be nurtured, embellished, and expanded through the very act of drawing on it and practicing its application. We will elaborate on this analysis in the next chapter when we discuss Aristotelian ethical thought. The point to bear in mind now is that the loving emotions we feel for those to whom we are related are psychologically harnessable. Specifically, they can potentially be redirected to motivate acts having the objective of benefiting those *other* than kin. How to achieve this expansion of the capacity for love with which we are originally endowed by nature is a question that we will explore later in this chapter, after examining the psychological consequences of the other biological mechanisms of altruism.

Reciprocal Altruism, Sympathy, Gratitude, and Other Emotions

As previously mentioned, it is easy to be cynical about cooperation and reciprocity. As David Hume put it:

> I learn to do service to another, without bearing him any real kindness: because I foresee that he will return my service, in expectation of another of the same kind, and in order to maintain the same correspondence of good offices with me or others. And accordingly, after I have serv'd him and he is in possession of the advantage arising from my action, he is induc'd to perform his part, as foreseeing the consequences of his refusal.[8]

Is it really the case that we exchange favors without any real kindness? Or did the capacity for kindness evolve precisely because it is a psychological heuristic for promoting reciprocity? Biologist Robert Trivers has developed the psychological implications of reciprocity in human beings, and the picture he paints, while not devoid of cynical implications, is more complicated and more interesting than Hume imagined.[9]

In the preceding chapter we described Axelrod's computer simulations and presented the argument that natural selection could favor the tit-for-tat strategy in ecological conditions approximating an indefinitely repeated Prisoner's Dilemma game. Humans are just the sort of species in which one should expect the dynamics of cooperation to favor implementation of the tit-for-tat strategy. We have long life spans, and through most of our ancestral history we lived in relatively small, interdependent social groups with fairly stable memberships. This created a situation in which individuals were likely to interact repeatedly over a long period of time. With large brains, well-honed abilities to recognize particular individuals, and good memories, our hominid ancestors were well equipped to take into account the past behavior of others before deciding whether or not to offer favors. Trivers suggests that a wide spectrum of emotions evolved in our species to mediate the demands of social interactions in which a tit-for-tat strategy is called for.

In the moment of encountering another in need, it might be possible, as Hume suggests, to calculate coldly a utility function that factors in the cost of helping, potential costs of not helping, and anticipated future benefits pursuant to the recipient's obligation to return the favor, weighted by the probability that the "kindness" will in fact eventually be reciprocated. But it is much more likely that this calculation has already been carried out by natural selection, which has provided us with a psychological shortcut (no math required!) that impels us to help when it is sensible to do so. The heuristic in this case is an emotion called sympathy. Sympathy is particularly likely to be elicited and in turn to elicit helping behavior when the potential recipient is in dire need of help.[10] But why does sympathy correlate with the severity of the other's plight? Wouldn't it be better (in terms of potential fitness gains) if sympathy was strictly an index of the likelihood of future reciprocation? Perhaps sympathy is just that. This would be the case if the recipient of help rated the value of the help rendered according to the benefit to himself compared to the cost to the helper. Over repeated iterations where the benefits of receiving help are great and the costs to the helper are also significant, potential recipients of help would be well advised to reciprocate with gusto in order to maintain the benefits of the relationship. Again, the cost-benefit ratio would not have to be calculated explicitly, as natural selection will have provided a psychological state to arouse the appropriate behavior in such circumstances. In this case, the heuristic is an emotion called gratitude. The bigger the favor, and the more it was needed, the deeper the gratitude. And gratitude makes one likely, even eager, to offer a favor in return. So sympathy is tuned to the gravity of the other's plight because the ensuing gratitude, and the consequent probability of reciprocation, is likewise tuned.

Of course, not all favors are of the lifesaving sort, and people exchange all kinds of goods as acts of friendship and good will. These acts may serve to cement bonds of friendship, loyalty, and trust, valuable social commodities when push does come to shove and real help is needed. The dynamics of reciprocity and cooperation should instill in us mechanisms that evaluate the fairness with which others reciprocate our favors and the likelihood that they can be counted on when the chips are down. Again, the calculations will not feel like calculations; rather, they will be experienced as emotions. We like and feel affection for those who treat us well, and because we like them, we are apt to treat them well in return, so they are apt to like us and treat us well in return—and as long as mutual acts of kindness continue, so does our friendship.

If all this sounds sweet and charming, remember that Prisoner's Dilemma games have their other side, too, and that side has its temptations. If you can get away with accepting favors from others while not enduring the cost of repaying those favors, then you will come out ahead. But you can expect that your partners will be watching you, and they will not be complacent if you show a tendency to "cheat" them by disregarding your obligations to the reciprocal relationship. Indeed, there is a psychological mechanism that is prepared to warn your partners of your ingratitude and impel them to cut off their favors and shun you, or worse, actively attempt to bring harm to you, should you fail to reciprocate adequately. That mechanism is—no surprise—an emotion, which Trivers calls moralistic aggression, more familiarly known as anger. Worse yet, moralistic aggression is not confined to those against whom one actually defects. Other members of the community can become incensed as well and join the aggrieved parties in retaliating against you. Recently, it has even been shown that people are willing to endure *further* costs, beyond those already incurred, to punish those who have failed to cooperate, a phenomenon ironically called altruistic punishment.[11] Remember that it is the nature of tit for tat always to respond in kind, and if our emotions truly are calibrated to engender tit-for-tat behavior, then a single act of defection could initiate an endless series of hostilities. Cycles of mutual recrimination and retaliation between individuals, families, or larger groups are no less a manifestation of the tit-for-tat strategy than cycles of mutual cooperation, with the important difference that retaliatory exchanges are, over the long run as well as the short, costly to both parties. The fact that people enter into destructive feuds, even though such behavior is strongly contraindicated by any self-interested rational calculus, is further evidence against the thesis that people are always self-interested rational actors. As Bishop Joseph Butler noted some 280 years ago, the impetus to "rush upon certain ruin for the destruction of an enemy" is no more self-interested than is compassion for a friend.[12]

Since the consequences of defection are likely to be unpleasant and detrimental to all involved, people should have mechanisms in place that will tend to override the temptation to defect. The emotions of guilt and shame seem well suited to perform this job. If you have failed to live up to your obligation to a benefactor, guilt might even impel you to remedy the disparity through a conspicuous act of kindness before the reciprocal relationship is permanently severed. (Trivers calls this "reparative altruism.")

More insidiously, some might try to gain the benefits provided by others without granting a full measure of reciprocation by feigning the emotions involved. A duplicitous scammer might create a false impression of need or distress in order to elicit sympathy from others, and then affect a false gratitude upon receiving help. If the acting is not thoroughly convincing and suspicions are aroused, a show of fake guilt and remorse, or even a show of fake anger at being "falsely" accused, might persuade the accusers that the faker is trustworthy after all. (We are reminded of a particular student who, caught red-handed cheating during an exam, expressed such indignant moral outrage over her character being "falsely" impugned that the instructor might have been convinced had the evidence been even slightly equivocal.) As some individuals became good at faking the emotions that guide reciprocity, natural selection responded by endowing everyone with good discriminative capacities for detecting such shams. Trust became a social currency of great value, as did the sharing of information about the trustworthiness of everyone else (i.e., gossip). To develop and protect our reputations, we became likely to engage in conspicuous displays of beneficence. Sharing food and other resources, giving gifts, and helping those in danger are ubiquitous human behaviors that demonstrate sympathy and gratitude for all to see, which engenders trust and reciprocity.

Does this all sound quite Hobbesian? Is sympathy (or pity) merely the imagination of one's future self in a similar sad circumstance? Is providing help (or charity) merely a show put on to gain the trust, friendship, and respect of others, a hedge against the possibility that one will someday need their help? Once again, we will let Pinker answer:

> The cost-benefit calculations are a metaphorical way of describing the selection of alternative genes over millennia, not a literal description of what takes place in a human brain in real time. Nothing prevents the amoral process of natural selection from evolving a brain with genuine big-hearted emotions. It is said that those who appreciate legislation and sausages should not see them being made. The same is true for human emotions.[13]

And:

> Go ahead and think the worst about the sham emotions. But the reason the real ones are felt is not that they are hoped to help the feeler; it is that they in fact helped the feeler's ancestors. And it's not just that you shouldn't visit the iniquities of the fathers upon the children; the fathers may never have been iniquitous to begin with. The first mutants who felt sympathy and gratitude may have prospered not by their own calculation but because the feelings made it worth their neighbors' while to cooperate with them. The emotions themselves may have been kind and heartfelt in every generation; indeed, once sham-emotion-detectors evolved, they would be most effective when they *are* kind and heartfelt. Of course, the genes are metaphorically selfish in endowing people with beneficent emotions, but who cares about the moral worth of deoxyribonucleic acid?[14]

IS SYMPATHY AN ALTRUISTIC EMOTION?

The question of whether sympathy is truly an other-regarding emotion is an interesting one that merits further examination. Although difficult to investigate, the question is an empirical one, and social psychologist C. Daniel Batson has made significant headway in addressing the issue. Batson prefers to refer to the motivating emotional state as empathy, so we will do likewise in this section.[15] Batson's hypothesis is that feeling empathy for another evokes altruistic motivation; that is, the ultimate objective of actions thus motivated is to secure the welfare of the other. He calls this idea "the empathy-altruism hypothesis."[16]

Batson begins his analysis by acknowledging that one might help another for purely self-interested reasons. If one perceives an opportunity to profit in some way by offering help, or if one believes that failure to help will result in punishment, and if these perceptions or beliefs form the psychological impetus that elicits the helping response, then obviously the act is ultimately self-interested, not altruistic. At first glance, this makes it seem unlikely that reciprocal altruism is ever truly altruistic because, in the first place, the very idea of reciprocity has built into it the connotation of future rewards and, second, defection is discouraged by the very real prospect of punishment at the hands of a morally outraged community. Moreover, Batson considers the possibility that these societal sanctions might be internalized as psychological states that serve as proxies for society, creating the potential for egoistic motivation to obtain self-rewards (experienced as pleasure, perhaps) or to avoid self-punishments (experienced as guilt or shame, perhaps). In this analysis, pleasure gained from helping and guilt endured from not helping do not presuppose the welfare of the other as an end in itself, so there is no reconciliation of these emotions with altruism. Further complicating the matter is the possibility that another self-interested motive other than reward-seeking and punishment-avoidance is routinely activated by an encounter with someone in distress. If the other's suffering is vicariously experienced as personal distress, then one may experience a motivational state that has as its ultimate aim the goal of eliminating this personal distress. Although this might elicit helping behavior, the good thereby provided to the recipient would be an instrumental means to the ultimate end of reducing the aversive feelings aroused by contact with the suffering other, so the act of helping would not in that case be altruistic.

Genuinely altruistic empathic arousal might itself be experienced as an aversive sensation, but as a motivational state it can be distinguished from the egoistic desire to alleviate one's own personal distress. The key is that an altruistic motive cannot be satisfied by remedies targeted directly toward reducing personal discomfort because it has as its goal the replenishment of the other whose distress elicited the reaction in the first place. This distinction suggested to Batson that it should be possible to separate experimentally the motivational effects of empathy and personal distress. If people can be made to experience personal distress without empathy, then they should be satisfied to follow a course of action that alleviates their own discomfort even if it does not lessen the pain of the other. But if empathy can be elicited along with vicarious personal distress, then people should reject that course of action as insufficient and accept only options expected to have the effect of easing the other's pain.

In one of Batson's experiments[17] female college students were taken one at a time into an observation room where they observed "Elaine," ostensibly another student participant but actually an accomplice of the experimenter, as she worked on a task while receiving periodic electric shocks. Elaine's (faked) reactions to the initial shocks indicated that she was experiencing considerable pain, and the observer was led to believe that Elaine had an unusual sensitivity to electric shock. The observer was then asked if she would be willing to switch places with Elaine and endure the remaining series of shocks. Half of the observers had already been told that they only had to watch the initial shocks, so their choice was between stepping in for Elaine and leaving. The other half had been told that they would have to remain and observe Elaine through the entire series of shocks, so their choice was to step in for Elaine or continue to observe. Within each of those two conditions, half of the observers had received information designed to elicit empathy for Elaine; the other half had received information not expected to produce empathy. All the observers were expected to experience vicarious personal distress as a result of witnessing Elaine's apparent distress. For those who couldn't just leave, they could nevertheless alleviate their distress by trading places with Elaine, which is exactly what most of them agreed to do, whether their empathy had been stoked or not. Those in the "easy escape" condition could just leave and thereby relieve their own distress without having to endure any shocks. Is that what they did? As it turned out, the decision depended on the degree of empathy: nearly all of those in the low-empathy condition took the easy escape and declined to help Elaine, but almost everyone in the high-empathy condition elected to remain and trade places with Elaine! This result seems to indicate that when empathy is aroused, the ultimate object of concern shifts from the self to the other.

In other experiments, Batson and his colleagues showed that the prospect of losing psychological self-rewards that normally would accompany helping behavior decreased the likelihood of helping among those in low-empathy conditions, but not among those in high-empathy conditions. For example, when low-empathy participants were told that they would not receive feedback about whether their efforts were successful in helping the other person, they were less likely to volunteer to help. The prospect of receiving feedback increased the likelihood of volunteering, suggesting that anticipated psychological self-rewards were a motivating factor for these individuals. But participants whose empathy had been stoked (the high-empathy condition) were no less likely to volunteer when they expected no feedback. In fact, of all the conditions, the highest rate of helping was observed among those with high empathy and no prospect of feedback. Evidently, empathic arousal is distinct from the desire to obtain psychological self-rewards, since when empathy is aroused, the psychological rewards attendant to relieving the distress of the other are not required to initiate action. It seems that securing the good of the other provides sufficient motivation. Further evidence for this conclusion is provided by findings that high-empathy participants experience enhancements of their own well-being upon discovering that the person in need was helped, even when they were prevented from providing the help themselves. This, of course, indicates that the welfare of the other was the ultimate concern, in support of the thesis that empathic motivation (i.e., sympathy) is genuinely altruistic.[18] Other experiments employing similar logic showed that low-empathy participants given a way to alleviate guilt for not helping became even less likely to help, but high-empathy participants were still likely to volunteer their assistance even when the guilt-avoidance motive was obviated. Evidently, empathy also does not reduce to the egoistic motive of escaping self-punishments.[19]

More recently, Batson has manipulated participants' empathy before placing them in a Prisoner's Dilemma situation in which points earned could possibly be redeemed for a gift certificate. Recall that in the case of indefinitely repeated Prisoner's Dilemmas, tit for tat is a robust strategy, and both players can do well by mutually cooperating. But the one-shot version of the game provides no opportunity for reciprocity to develop, and a self-interested rational calculus leads to the conclusion that defection is the best strategy no matter what the other player does. Nevertheless, close to half of the participants in Batson's version of the game played nice and cooperated in a one-shot game, even when their empathy was not aroused.[20] Batson showed that this proportion could be reduced by providing instructions portraying the exchange as an impersonal business transaction, which suggested that the moral rules that govern social exchanges are often suspended in the case of business transactions. But when empathy was stimulated, the majority of participants cooperated, whether the scenario was painted as a social exchange (80 percent cooperation) or a business transaction (70 percent cooperation). In a follow-up study,[21] participants were informed before playing their hand that the other player had defected. As predicted by both rational actor theory and Batson's empathy-altruism theory, in the absence of empathic motivation, nearly every participant (95 percent) reciprocated the defection. Among players whose empathy had been aroused, however, only 55 percent defected, which means that 45 percent intentionally threw the game for the sake of the other player! Obviously, this finding is difficult for rational actor theory to accommodate, and these results, along with Batson's earlier findings, provide powerful evidence that empathy is an other-regarding state.

The reliability of Batson's results indicates that his strategy for manipulating empathy is an effective one, so perhaps an examination of his method will reveal something important about the factors that elicit other-regarding empathic motivation. Batson claims that "two conditions are necessary and sufficient for the creation of empathy: (1) perception of another person as in need and (2) adoption of that other's perspective."[22] Accordingly, the manipulation that created the high-empathy condition in all of his experiments involved providing participants with a description of the other person that referenced some significant personal difficulty, *plus* an explicit instruction to try to understand her point of view. Those in low-empathy conditions typically heard the same sob story accompanied by instructions that led them to adopt an objective, impersonal point of view. In some cases, empathy induction was fostered by providing information that led the participant to believe that she and the other person had markedly similar personal characteristics. Presumably, this perceived similarity encouraged identification with the other, which promoted perspective-taking. The idea that perspective-taking and identification are central ingredients in altruistic motivation is an important one, and we will see later in this chapter that there are other lines of evidence to support the same conclusion. For now we are content to remark, echoing Batson, that if empathy-induced altruism can be aroused in the relatively austere circumstances of the laboratory, then it should be possible to create conditions in the real world that encourage its development.

With regard to the subject of naturally occurring reciprocal altruism, then, the experimental evidence indicates that while natural selection may have favored the evolution of sympathy because it motivated actions that led to long-term beneficial outcomes for the actor, the motivational state itself is *not* self-interested. Sympathy appears to be a genuinely other-regarding emotion, capable of eliciting behavior that should therefore be considered truly altruistic. As Pinker pointed out, this makes evolutionary sense because the system is less likely to collapse under the weight of universal suspicion if the feelings are usually genuinely caring. "Reciprocal altruism," it seems, is not an oxymoron after all.

GROUP AFFILIATION, PATRIOTISM, AND THE DARK SIDE OF ALTRUISM

As Batson's research demonstrates, perceptions of similarity can increase the likelihood of sympathetic perspective-taking. This suggests that to the extent that people aggregate on the basis of various kinds of commonalities, feelings of solidarity will tend to develop within groups so formed. We can be agnostic concerning the role that group selection has played in human evolution while maintaining that people can be expected to identify with others on the basis of group membership. Some such groups may be formed by the mechanisms previously described: kin groups and groups of mutually cooperating friends. Other groups are based on common interests or common beliefs, and some of these groups can be quite diffuse. Sports fans provide an instructive example. Put two Boston Red Sox fans together and they may instantly behave as old friends. Try the same experiment with a Red Sox fan and a New York Yankees fan, and the results might be quite different. That fans can become overzealous fanatics is attested by the frequency of riots at soccer games, riots between people who presumably all love soccer but who are divided by devotions to different teams. Other ad hoc groups comprise individuals united in their love of a particular rock band, their affinity for a certain political point of view, or even their preference for a specific breed of dog. People advertise these affiliations with bumper stickers and T-shirts. Whatever the membership criteria, people identify more readily with members of their own group than with outsiders, and they tend to extend greater courtesies to group members.

Like the other mechanisms underlying altruism, solidarity within the group is sustained by emotional states. For better or worse, the most prevalent distinctions responsible for such solidarity among those who are otherwise strangers are those based on race, ethnicity, religion, and nationality, and the emotions associated with these distinctions can be quite salient. When one's identification with the group is based on nationality, for example, the feeling is called patriotism. Like love, and like sympathy and gratitude, patriotism can impel acts of self-sacrifice for the sake of other group members, most of whom are complete strangers.

The beneficent emotions of love, sympathy, and patriotism, it behooves us to point out, are also associated with a seamier flip side. Altruism, with its connotations of selflessness, compassion, and helpfulness, is usually assumed to be an unassailable virtue; indeed, it seems on the surface a lovely centerpiece for any theory of virtue. But now we need to challenge that assumption and examine the ways in which naturally occurring altruism can actually undermine decency and morality. The mechanisms that have given us our beneficent emotions have unfortunately also contributed to the honing of other human capacities that are not so morally laudable.

This subject is closely related to an issue that is so central to any meaningful analysis of altruism that it must be adjudicated in arriving at even a definition of altruism—the issue being that of the appropriate recipient of altruism, and the problem being the tension that can arise between competing obligations to devote oneself to those close at hand versus attending to the needs of the stranger. We have already seen, in chapter one, one of the "dark sides" of altruism emerging from this tension, that being the potential for reckless neglect of self and family when one becomes too seduced by the appeal of altruistic giving, as exemplified by Zell Kravinsky, who against his wife's wishes gave away his fortune and one of his kidneys. Mr. Kravinsky's case is remarkable in part because it represents an unusual inversion of the normal priorities instilled in us by evolutionary forces. The varieties of benevolence favored by natural selection all, in some way, predispose us to prioritizations favoring the relatively near and dear. This in itself can create serious problems. By inherently limiting the recipients of altruism to certain specified individuals, these mechanisms create boundary conditions that consign most people by default to a position outside the privileged circle, thereby denying them equal consideration. Moreover, the formation of in-group and out-group categories may spawn not mere indifference to those outside the circle, but outright contempt and hostility.

All the biological mechanisms underlying the altruistic emotions have also been the sponsors of various malicious emotions and have generated much in the way of social discord, conflict, and outright suffering.[23] Kin selection leads to the nepotistic favoritism that contaminates businesses and governments, where it can undermine egalitarian and meritocratic ideals, and it fosters the sequestering of wealth and resources within family lineages, contributing to the massive economic disparities that characterize the

world. The wealthy and the middle classes in the developed world spend lav-
ishly and without remorse on all kinds of extravagances for their children,
while children in faraway lands die in droves for want of basic necessities.
Pinker describes a thought experiment "in which people can run through
the left door of a burning building to save some number of children or
through the right door to save their own child," then asks parents to consider, "Is there *any* number of children that would lead you to pick the left
door?"[24] If this seems to be only a fanciful philosophical game, consider the
number of lives that could be saved with the money that parents spend on
just one kind of indulgence for their children—say, video games or designer
jeans. Real consequences and real moral implications emanate from the
massively disparate treatment granted to our own families compared to
others.

Reciprocal altruism fares no better than kin selection when all its manifestations are considered. We have already considered the less sanguine emotions (such as suspicion, distrust, and anger) that accompany reciprocal
altruism. These emotions evolved (along with the more tender ones) largely
in response to the selective advantages of mutual cooperation, but they continue to operate even after cooperation breaks down. Neural machinery
enjoining us to play tit for tat is all well and good until someone defects and
sets off cycles of mutual recrimination and retaliation. Reciprocal exchanges
of aggression (feuds), fueled by moralistic anger, can be bloody, long lasting,
and costly to all involved. As Gandhi pointed out, "an eye for an eye makes
the whole world blind."

The greatest suffering and the most dreadful atrocities of all come from
conflicts between groups. Many discussions of altruism consider the ostensibly exemplary case of the soldier who leaps onto a hand grenade, sacrificing himself for the sake of his comrades in arms. (Indeed, we will go on to
refer to such a case ourselves in chapter seven.) We do not mean to diminish the valor and unselfishness of such an act—it is a prime example of altruism in action—but consider for a moment that the same soldier may well
have been, right up until the moment of his death, deliberately causing the
deaths of enemy combatants. The sharp contrast between within-group
munificence and between-group animosity is never more palpable than during war. Altruism is a double-edged sword, and many of the scourges of
humanity are corollaries of those parts of our nature that, on the other edge,
impel us to care about those with whom we identify. The impression that
outsiders present a danger to group insiders can motivate brave acts of self-

sacrifice in the interest of protecting the group, and it can motivate acts of extreme brutality perpetrated against outsiders. Prejudice, racism, xenophobia, intolerance, hate crimes, sectarian violence, war, terrorism, ethnic cleansing, genocide—what all these things have in common is the massive disparity in the value assigned to some human beings compared to others, all on the basis of in-group/out-group distinctions. The most reprehensible of human motives and actions stem in part from the same processes that gave us our some of our best qualities.

Lest it seem that we wish to renounce the title of this book, let's also be clear that we believe there are reasons to hope that the benevolent qualities of human nature can triumph. As history and the daily newspapers amply demonstrate, we have the capacity to be a malevolent species, too. But the point is that we have *lots* of emotional and cognitive capacities, many of which can be conscripted into service to subdue our more belligerent tendencies. Suspicion, anger, and intolerance may be rooted in the same evolutionary dynamics that gave us friendship, sympathy, and love, but that does not mean that we cannot marshal the latter against the former. As we argued in the opening section of this chapter, biology is not destiny. Or to put it more enigmatically: our biological nature has provided us with the tools to exceed our biological nature.

Catholic theologian Stephen Pope argues convincingly that an understanding of our natural altruistic priorities, or "the ordering of love," is central to the development of a workable ethics.

> [T]he "ought" of the ethically proper ordering of love must be grounded in the "is" of natural human behavioral predispositions that have evolved as adaptations to group living. . . . The ordering of love provides conditions necessary for friendship to develop and be sustained, to take root and grow. It encourages attunement to others and weighs their needs appropriately, avoiding excessive concern for others but attending with sufficient gravity to their needs and desires—and to our own needs.[25]

The mechanisms of natural selection may have been responsible for providing us with capacities for loving and caring, but, as Pope says, once created, these capacities serve needs that exist at higher "levels of existence" than the organic level.[26] Natural selection favored the evolution of other-regard because it benefited the selfish genes that invented it. But as a consequence, we have a genuine capacity to treat others as ends in themselves rather than as mere means to selfish genetic ends. Natural selection favored the evolution of sympathy and love because of the adaptive advantages they conferred. Once installed, though, those faculties are available to be co-opted for purposes other than those intended by the genes (as in the example of adoption). In this view, we do not need to repudiate our natural tendency to care most for our families and friends; we need merely to extend some measure of that caring to those less close at hand. But how can we do that? How do we go about extending our circle of compassion to include the anonymous distant stranger? For most people, radical other-regard extended beyond the customary narrow circumference of family and friends does not come easily. Interestingly, however, for a few special individuals it seems to come quite easily and naturally. It is to the bright side of altruism—personified in the exemplary altruists among us—that we now turn our attention.

THE PHENOMENOLOGY OF ALTRUISM

On January 16, 1975, during the evening rush hour, unemployed New York musician Everett Sanderson leaped onto the subway tracks mere moments before the approaching train cruised into the Eighty-sixth and Lexington station. Why did he do it? Was this intended to be the final act of a desperate, despondent man? Was he mentally ill, drunk, or on drugs? No, Mr. Sanderson was not suicidal, deranged, or intoxicated. He was a normal guy, on his way home after a visit to his mother. And he was a hero. Seconds before, four-year-old Michelle DeJesus—a stranger to Mr. Sanderson—had pulled away from her mother's grasp, ventured too close to the edge of the platform, and fallen onto the tracks. There she remained while the crowd of commuters looked on in terror. Mr. Sanderson, like the other onlookers, initially expected to see someone else leap to the girl's rescue, but no one did. Then he suddenly thought, *What if it was my child down there?* Although he was fifty feet away from Michelle, and although the approaching train was so close that onlookers could hear it rumbling through the tunnel and could even feel the rush of wind forced ahead of its bulk, this moment of personal identification jolted Mr. Sanderson into action, and he leaped onto the tracks, ran to Michelle, and heaved her up onto the platform. His heroism had saved her, but it seemed that he would now have to pay the ultimate price sometimes charged to the altruistic. Even before he reached Michelle, the train had entered the station, and despite quick braking by the alert conductor, during those brief moments that it took to rescue Michelle, the train had closed the gap significantly, narrowing Mr. Sanderson's window of opportunity for escape to a mere two seconds. He tried once to pull himself onto the platform but failed. As he leapt desperately one last time, he was seized by other onlookers and yanked to safety just in the nick of time, undamaged by the train except for a scratch on his right shoe.[27]

History has a way of repeating itself, and as we write this, news outlets are reporting on the heroism of another regular guy, Wesley Autrey, a New York construction worker, Navy veteran, and father of two young girls, who left his children looking on from a subway platform while he jumped onto the tracks to rescue a nineteen-year-old man who had fallen to the tracks after suffering a seizure. With the train bearing down on them and unable to lift the fallen man to safety quickly enough, Mr. Autrey pushed him into the trough between the rails, which, at twenty-one inches deep, had enough clearance for someone to lie safely as the train passed overhead. But Mr. Autrey was afraid that the young man, who was still jerking and disoriented from the seizure, would not be able to keep his limbs off the rails. So instead of leaping back onto the platform, Mr. Autrey leaped onto the man, pinning him down and restraining his limbs by coiling his own around them. Luckily, the trough was just deep enough, and the train cars passed above the two men, leaving them unharmed. Interviewed afterward, Mr. Autrey admitted that most people, fearing for their own lives, would not have done what he did, but he adamantly denied that he was a hero, claiming that because he acted in the way that others *should* act, his act was not morally extraordinary. "I don't feel like I did something spectacular; I just saw someone who needed help. I did what I felt was right."[28]

Much about the psychology of altruism can be discerned through the testimony of exceptional individuals like Everett Sanderson and Wesley Autrey. Fortunately, such testimonials have been gathered, analyzed, and reported in fine books such as Kristen R. Monroe's *The Heart of Altruism*,[29] Samuel and Pearl Oliner's *The Altruistic Personality*,[30] and Philip Hallie's *Lest Innocent Blood Be Shed*.[31] Despite differences in purposes and methods, distinct common themes emerge from these works. We will consider Monroe's book in the most detail, in part because she systematically uses her results to test the claims and theories of some of the disciplinary perspectives with which we deal in this book.

Monroe adopts a fairly stringent definition of altruism: not only must an altruistic act be motivated by other-regard, such that securing the welfare of the other is the ultimate end, but it must entail cost, or at least risk, and it must not set conditions or seek personal rewards. Monroe recognizes that some acts will meet some of the criteria enumerated in her definition but not others, and she calls these acts quasi-altruistic. Quasi-altruistic acts may be fairly common and may be within the normal range of behavior for most people, but genuinely altruistic behavior is, in Monroe's view, rare, and so are the people who engage in such behavior. Although it is a conceptual possibility that people's behavior varies so extensively over time and across circumstances that any label we give a person at one moment in time would quickly become obsolete, Monroe did not find this to be the case. Among the four categories of people she identified, other-regarding inclinations seemed to be stable over time and across situations. One of the categories of individuals interviewed by Monroe, those whom she called entrepreneurs, had been successful in acquiring material wealth but did not have any strong inclinations toward acts of altruism. Then there were those equally successful people, the philanthropists, who were more deeply committed to using their wealth to help others. The charity of the philanthropists is closer to genuine altruism than the limited giving of the entrepreneurs, but it still technically qualifies as merely quasi-altruistic. Closer yet to the ideal of pure altruism are those acts of heroes and heroines who risked their lives to save others during acute emergencies (Everett Sanderson and Wesley Autrey would qualify for this category). The consummate examples of altruistic conduct, though, were the dangerous and costly attempts to rescue Jews in Nazi-occupied Europe during World War II. Monroe considers these rescuers to exemplify altruism of the purest sort for several reasons, including the extended duration of the actions, the low probability of receiving any social approbation, and the enormous risks not only to self but to family. Thus, the four categories—entrepreneurs, philanthropist, heroes/heroines, and rescuers—encompass people at four points along a continuum of human behavior, from the typical person for whom self-interest is the rule to the rare person for whom altruism is the norm. Monroe's objective was to identify the variables, if any, that covary with altruism.

She found little indication that differences in altruism could be attributed to differences in sociocultural factors such as religious orientation, family structure or wealth, or closeness of the community. Egoistic approaches that attempt to reduce altruism to rational cost-benefit calculations also fared poorly in Monroe's analysis since altruists were willing to endure enormous costs with no expectation of future benefits. Evolutionary theories were likewise deemed inadequate because altruists did not preference their families, friends, or group members above strangers, as theories of kin selection, reciprocal altruism, and group selection would predict. Factors that developmental and social psychologists might expect to be pertinent, such as the presence of altruistic role models, conformity to behavior of nearby others, and familiarity and likeability of those needing rescue also did not predict helping behavior.

First-person phenomenological accounts do not obviously offer direct support for any of the standard academic interpretations of altruism, but they do allow several generalizations to be drawn about the subjective experience itself. First, altruists do not see themselves as heroes or morally special, and although they value the good that they have done for others, they do not see their actions as being outside the range of normal, reasonable human behavior. Recall Wesley Autrey's words: "I don't feel like I did something spectacular; I just saw someone who needed help. I did what I felt was right." His words echo those of one of Monroe's subjects, a Dutch rescuer named Tony, who told her, "I don't think that I did anything that special. I think what I did is what everybody normally should be doing. We all should help each other. It's common sense and common caring for people."[32] Hallie reports the same attitude among the villagers of Le Chambon, who collectively saved about five thousand Jews. Typically, the response to questions regarding moral praiseworthiness was: "How can you call us 'good'? We were doing what had to be done. Who else could help them? And what has all this to do with goodness? Things had to be done, that's all, and we happened to be there to do them. You must understand that it was the most natural thing in the world to help these people."[33]

These comments reveal another interesting point of commonality among altruists, which is the sense that they did what was required. But this feeling of necessity, whether we call it requirement, or obligation, or duty, seems to mean something in this context other than what is usually implied by those terms. Required, in this sense, does not connote that action is socially mandated or even morally dictated (although altruists might have the sense that acts of helping have some moral status), but rather it seems to imply that the course of action taken was really the only option, as though to do otherwise was not possible. One of the Chambonaisse, when asked by Hallie why she subjected herself to the difficulties and dangers of hiding Jews in her house, responded, "Look. Look. Who else would have taken care of them if we didn't? They needed our help and they needed it *then*."[34] Another of Monroe's rescuers, Margot, was not as articulate as Tony, but nevertheless captured the sentiment very well by saying, "I don't make a choice. It comes, and it's there" and "It's pretty near impossible not to help."[35] This raises the question of what is really being claimed when altruists say, as they consistently do, that they merely did what was required. Obviously, they are aware that options exist, and they are not blind to the fact that others (most others, in fact) behaved quite differently in similar circumstances. It was, as a matter of fact, quite possible to say no and close the door in the face of the fleeing Jew. Others did just that, and the rescuers were aware of that fact. The answer to this conundrum, perhaps, is that what is meant by "no choice" is "no choice for *me*." Altruists recognize that, in principle, it was possible to turn away a desperate Jew at their door, but such an option is not a *live* option for them. This reflects a further aspect of the subjective experience common to radical altruism, the experience of the directive to act as emanating not from within, but directly from the need of the other. This is an important point, as it suggests that whatever is felt in that moment, whether it is rightly called empathy or something else, is a state of mind that admits the other as the sole ultimate object of concern. If subjective accounts of altruists are to be counted as credible testimony, then we should take them as strong evidence for the existence of genuine other-regard.

Of course, interpretations of this sort are subject to the criticism that people do not have good introspective access to the motivational and cognitive processes that drive their behavior. Although this is certainly true, admitting as much can force only certain kinds of concessions. If what we seek to discover *is* the nature of subjective experience itself, then introspection is a legitimate tool. Motivational states may have deep roots, roots that extend all the way into our genetic past, but they are implemented by psychological states—heuristics, as we called them previously—of which we have conscious, subjective awareness. People may not have conscious access to all the factors that determine their wants and desires, but they have a pretty good idea of the *content* of those wants and desires. If one craves cheesecake, no amount of explication in terms of underlying genetic, metabolic, and neural mechanisms will change the fact of the subjective impression that cheesecake is the object of the craving. The same argument applies to other-regard. Although the descriptive methods used by Monroe, Oliner and Oliner, and Hallie lack the rigorous controls of the laboratory, they are no less adept in illuminating the subjective experiences that accompany altruism.

This defense of the phenomenological method can go only so far, though. First-person testimony is valuable insofar as our concern is with the subjective experiences themselves. If we want to know what the apparent *conscious* impetus for helping was, and if we assume that the interviewee answers honestly, then we can accept the answer as indicative of her perceived state of mind. But we must be much more cautious in using such answers to elucidate the action of mechanisms that operate below the level of conscious awareness, and we particularly cannot reject the involvement of nonconscious mechanisms on the basis of their lack of veridicality with conscious motives. It might be tempting, for example, wrongly to dismiss evolutionary theories of altruism on the basis that altruists do not have the subjective impression of working in the interests of their genes. But, of course, we should expect as much, since we never have the impression that we are working for the benefit of our genes. Monroe does not exactly make this mistake, but she makes a similar mistake when she dismisses evolutionary theories for the more particular reason that her altruists did not conform to the conventional ordering of other-regard, in which family and friends take precedence over strangers. But, of course, she already knew that would be the case, because that was one of the criteria she employed in defining exemplary, pure altruism and in selecting rescuers of Jews as its representatives. Rather than disregarding the evolutionary mechanisms as irrelevant to those cases, it might be more productive to ask how the psychological heuristics they have provided might vary across individuals, and what factors might lead them to vary.

In the final analysis, Monroe concludes that the distinctive feature of exemplary altruists is to be found in what she calls "perspective," a broad concept that includes cognitive and affective components. Altruists are gifted at taking the perspective of the other and empathizing with the one in need, but these capacities are not particularized or restricted to the near and dear as they are in most people. The consummate altruist does not parse people into the categories of "us" and "them." There is only one category, "us," and thus there is no basis for using such categorical distinctions to specify who is and who is not a worthy recipient of empathy and care. All are worthy. Monroe also argues that for altruists empathy is not an internalization of the other's pain or some sort of Hobbesian self-referential pity, but rather a compassionate understanding of the pain of the other; it is a productive understanding that allows corrective action to be taken. Altruists have a universalistic worldview, in which they see all humanity as interconnected, so their self-concept and canonical expectations (beliefs about what is normal and ordinary) reflect this sense of connection. "This perspective provides a feeling of being strongly linked to others through a shared humanity and constitutes such a central core to altruists' identity that it leaves them with no choice in their behavior when others are in great need."[36] We saw earlier that Batson, using the methods of laboratory experimentation, was able to generate altruistic motivation by instilling empathy in his participants. A central ingredient of the manipulation that produced a condition of empathy was identification with the sufferer, which fostered perspective-taking. Because of their universalistic orientation and sense of self as one among a common humanity, the altruists in Monroe's sample did not require any manipulation in order to take the perspective of the other. For them, the fact that the other was a human being was sufficient.

Nurturing Our Altruistic Identity

Despite the substantial methodological differences between the experimental work and the narrative approaches described above, their respective conclusions converge in some interesting and revealing ways. Both approaches support the conclusion that altruism is a real phenomenon and that people can be motivated to pursue the welfare of others as an ultimate objective. Both approaches have established a central role for empathic perspective-taking in generating altruistic motivation. The idea that the capacity for perspective-taking, or identification, lies at the core of altruism is a particularly intriguing hypothesis. It suggests that we have a fundamental capacity for other-regard, or at least other-comprehension, and that our ability to care about others is rooted in a cognitive capacity to see others as autonomous selves with needs and feelings like our own. Of course, the ability to identify with others probably is not sufficient all by itself to generate altruistic behavior, since a dispassionate identification of another's needs would not necessarily impel anyone to help fulfill those needs. Perhaps over the course of our evolutionary history, identification with others occurred primarily when those others were relatives, friends, and other members of fairly tight-knit groups, in which case it would have made sense for identification to take on a sympathetic tone (as Batson's research suggests it does). A prediction that follows from this line of reasoning is that those who have greater capacities for identification, or those who attribute agency to others more readily, will tend to be more altruistic.

Supportive evidence for this hypothesis comes from the results of a recent brain-scanning study.[37] Volunteers underwent functional magnetic resonance imaging (fMRI) while they participated in a computer game and also while they watched as the computer played the game by itself. The volunteers were then sorted according to the level of self-reported engagement in altruistic activities. Those participants who scored high on the altruism scale exhibited a greater level of brain activity in a part of the brain called the posterior superior temporal sulcus than did less altruistic volunteers, particularly while watching the computer play the game by itself. What is so interesting about this result is that the posterior superior temporal sulcus is associated with the perception of agency. Thus, individuals who were apparently more likely to perceive actions as indicative of the agency of others were also more likely to be altruistic. While hardly conclusive, the implication is that altruism is a function of our capacity to identify with others as agents like ourselves.

If identification with the suffering other is the key to altruism, then that which promotes identification should promote altruism, and that which interferes with identification should have the opposite effect. Thus, parenting techniques that encourage children to identify with others can be expected to facilitate the development of altruistic dispositions. Indeed, this is exactly what the developmental literature shows.[38] In particular, the disciplinary techniques that best promote the development of moral reasoning and prosocial behavior are those called inductive techniques. Inductive techniques are contrasted with power-assertive disciplinary techniques, which employ commands, threats, deprivation of privileges, or use of physical force, and love-withdrawal techniques, in which the parent expresses anger or withdraws emotionally from the child. Inductive techniques, on the other hand, instruct the child to consider the feelings of others, the consequences of actions and how others are affected, and ways of making amends or reparations. In general, the more encouragement children are given to consider the feelings and perspectives of others, the better able they are to identify with others and the more likely they are to pursue opportunities to help others. The Oliners also found evidence corroborating this conclusion: "Induction focuses children's attention on the consequences of their behaviors for others, drawing attention to others' feelings, thoughts, and welfare. Children are thus led to understand others cognitively—a skill known as perspective- or role-taking—and are also thus more inclined to develop empathy toward others."[39]

Conversely, those who wish to persuade people to commit atrocities against others, as the Nazis did, face the problem of countering our innate capacity for sympathy, so easily aroused by the suffering of others. As documented in several places by Jonathan Glover in *Humanity: A Moral History of the Twentieth Century*, the Nazis and other brutal regimes developed and utilized various techniques for accomplishing this.[40] One was to convince their officers and soldiers that sympathy itself was an evil, or at least a weakness to be resisted. But perhaps most effective were techniques designed to inhibit perspective-taking and identification. Jews were dehumanized by being characterized as "vermin" and carriers of disease. For those who were brought to the camps to be worked to death or slaughtered, the physical torments of shaving their heads, starving them, and forcing them to live in filth may have, ironically, made it easier to ignore their suffering by making them appear other than completely human. Glover describes how, despite the efforts made to dehumanize victims, sometimes normal compassionate human responses are triggered anyway, a phenomenon he calls "breakthrough" in recognition of the fact that the sympathetic response is natural and its suppression unnatural. The triggers consist of little things that are undeniably human, things to which anyone can relate, indeed to which one can't help but relate. George Orwell, Glover reports, while fighting in the Spanish Civil War, refrained from shooting an enemy soldier because the man was having difficulty keeping his pants in place. "I did not shoot partly because of that detail about the trousers. I had come here to shoot at 'Fascists'; but a man who is holding up his trousers isn't a 'Fascist', he is visibly a fellow creature, similar to yourself, and you don't feel like shooting at him."[41]

The argument that we are making in this chapter is this: Altruism is a capacity conferred upon human beings by evolutionary mechanisms that in our ancestral past favored various sorts of sociality. It is mediated in large part by affinitive emotions such as love and sympathy, but it entails elements of cognition as well. In particular, sympathetic emotional responses capable of motivating helping behavior are likely to be activated when one identifies with others as fellow sentient beings and engages in empathic perspective-taking. The constellation of benevolent, altruistic social dispositions described in this chapter has been characterized by some authors as an innate moral sense. While it is the case that these capacities in some cases encourage moral behavior, the psychological resources provided to us by nature should not be relied on as exclusive arbiters of morality. As we saw when we examined the "dark side" of altruism, mechanisms such as kin selection, reciprocity, and group affiliation reinforce the differentiation of in-group members from out-group members, sometimes with horrific consequences. Nurturing our capacity for altruism to the betterment of all will require us to transcend the tendency to parse humanity into moral categories on the basis of objectively arbitrary distinctions such as proximity and similarity to self. The material of this chapter indicates that one way to nurture and expand our natural benevolent impulses is through exercising our capacities for identification and perspective-taking and learning to extend those processes to those outside our normal circles of interaction. As Stephen Pope points out, this does not mean that we must diminish our attachment to our families and friends, but rather that the bonds of caring that are so natural in those relationships can be harnessed, amplified, and redirected beyond the boundaries of special relations. Everett Sanderson asked himself, "What if it was *my* child down there?" In that moment of identification, that moment of empathy, that moment of recognition of the other as a fellow being worthy of love and sympathy, he simply acted.

EVOLUTION AND MORALITY

The recognition that many of our moral judgments are rooted in our evolved nature as social beings has prompted several authors to explore the implications of having an innate moral sense.[42] Like the ideas we have covered in this chapter and the preceding chapter, these explorations of morality are primarily descriptive, explicating the psychology of moral behavior in terms of our evolutionary history and sociality. Sometimes they lapse into the prescriptive, in the same way that we have done in this chapter, identifying strategies for nurturing and expanding our benevolent capacities. Once one moves beyond the descriptive into the prescriptive, however, justifications for why these prescriptions should be followed are required, and these justifications necessarily entail more than simply specifying their utility in bringing about certain ends. In other words, the ends themselves must be justified, and it is not enough merely to call upon descriptive accounts of morality in making these justifications. To put it another way, reductionistic accounts that consider the biological and psychological sources of moral behavior are perfectly legitimate in the descriptive and explanatory realms, but the facts about how we *are* do not in themselves establish any conclusion concerning whether or not we *ought* to be that way. We need only remember that prejudice, suspicion, exclusion, and aggression are as much parts of our evolved nature as are kindness and compassion to recognize that ethics cannot be reduced to the natural sciences. If we must be selective with respect to which parts of our nature constitute our moral sense and which parts do not, as it seems we must, then it is clear that we are already imposing criteria from somewhere other than nature to make such distinctions.

The temptation to try to provide a reductive basis for normative ethics by appeal to the facts of the natural sciences has seduced some who should know better. Perhaps we can excuse Wolf Larsen for falling into this trap; after all, he was a self-schooled ship's captain, not an ethicist, and a fictional character to boot. Given the ground that we have covered in the last couple of chapters, we could easily dismiss Wolf Larsen's ethical claims on the basis that he had his facts wrong. He did not understand the genetic basis of natural selection, so he did not imagine that natural selection could actually favor genuinely altruistic behavior. But the point is not that he had his facts wrong; the point is that even if his descriptive theory—psychological egoism—had been correct, his ethical conclusion—ethical egoism—would not have followed as a logical consequence because ethics is not reducible to biology or psychology. Yes, we *are* a certain way, but that does not denote that we *ought* to be that way.

Hume was one of the first to recognize this sort of fallacy, pointing out that normative statements cannot logically be derived from factual statements.

> In every system of morality, which I have hitherto met with, I have always remark'd, that the author proceeds for some time in the ordinary way of reasoning, and establishes the being of a God, or makes observations concerning human affairs; when of a sudden I am surpriz'd to find, that instead of the usual copulations of propositions, *is*, and *is not*, I meet with no proposition that is not connected with an *ought*, or an *ought not*. This change is imperceptible; but is, however, of the last consequence. For as this *ought*, or *ought not*, expresses some new relation or affirmation, 'tis necessary that it shou'd be observ'd and explain'd; and at the same time that a reason should be given, for what seems altogether inconceivable, how this new relation can be a deduction from others, which are entirely different from it.[43]

The style of Wolf Larsen's argument is a special case of the specious reasoning identified by Hume, in which one asserts that that which is natural is that which is good. If we are by nature selfish, then that is how we ought to be; to attempt to be otherwise not only breaks the laws of nature but breaks the laws of morality, or so says Wolf Larsen. This particular violation of Hume's law, in which the good is equated with the natural, is called *the naturalistic fallacy.*[44]

The naturalistic fallacy can be shown to be a fallacy through dissection of its formal structure, which illogically attempts to derive one type of proposition (an ought) from another type (an is). But it is even easier to refute by reductio ad absurdum. Here are some examples of natural behaviors, all of which have been favored by natural selection: A male lion who successfully takes over a harem will kill the cubs of his vanquished rival, bringing their mothers back into estrus more quickly so that he can father the next generation. Pandas frequently give birth to twins, but panda mothers usually only provide for one of the twins (presumably the one that signals somehow its greater fitness), allowing the other to die. Among egrets and some other bird species, the more robust among siblings peck their weaker brothers and sisters to death in full view of the parents, who look on with apparent indifference. Some animals do not stop at merely committing infanticide when times are tough but cannibalize their young to obtain calories for themselves.[45] Rape is also common in nature, as documented by Randy Thornhill and Craig T. Palmer in their controversial book *A Natural History of Rape.*[46] In a span of about one page, Thornhill and Palmer cite ninety-one studies documenting the occurrence of rape across the animal kingdom, in species ranging from the scorpionflies studied by Thornhill himself, to guppies, mallard ducks, and orangutans.[47] Nature offers plenty of examples of infanticide, cannibalism, and rape, and it is not difficult to see, in every case, how natural selection not only permits such behavior but favors it under certain conditions. Tragically, infanticide and rape occur among humans as well (and the conditions in which they are likely to occur are those predicted by an evolutionary analysis).

So should we, on the basis of these facts of nature, begrudgingly accept infanticide and rape as morally acceptable behaviors? Of course not. To do so would be to commit the naturalistic fallacy. Whatever foundation one wishes to construct upon which to erect an ethical theory, it will have to be grounded in principles other than those that merely describe the facts of nature. This is no less true when the facts are confined to those specifically descriptive of human nature. As we observed when we addressed the "dark side" of altruism, human nature comprises all sorts of impulses, and even the moral sense is a double-edged sword. The authors of most of the recent works about our innate moral sense are aware of this and they understand the pitfalls of the naturalistic fallacy; and to the extent that their work is descriptive of the human condition they are on solid ground. But it is surprisingly easy to slip from the descriptive to the normative. Outside of academia, doing so seems to be more the rule than the exception. Geneticists, evolutionary biologists, and evolutionary psychologists who attempt to explicate the baser impulses of human nature are castigated by those who cannot, or will not, distinguish between explication and justification. The abuse directed at Thornhill and Palmer provides a good example of this, despite the care the authors took to explain that explicating rape in no way legitimizes it and that their most fervent hope is that the information and ideas presented in their book will help to eradicate rape among humans. To provide another example, which is particularly reminiscent of Wolf Larsen's failure to navigate the perils of the naturalistic fallacy, author and radio personality Laura Schlessinger condemns homosexuality on the basis that it is a "biological error," misunderstanding both the facts *and* the fact that ethical precepts cannot be derived from natural facts anyway.

Others with more respectable credentials have violated (or at least flirted with) the naturalistic fallacy, seemingly embracing this idea that we *can* derive moral principles from the operation of nature. Edward O. Wilson, one of the founding fathers of evolutionary psychology (if sociobiology is considered an early form of evolutionary psychology), is not unencumbered by an appreciation of the facts of biology as Wolf Larsen was, and he has suggested that some ethical principles follow from such understanding. In the final chapter of *On Human Nature*, Wilson proposes that advances in the social sciences and humanities will follow from an understanding of our evolved nature, and that those disciplines should root themselves in biology.[48] Wilson goes on to articulate a naturalistic normative theory in which ethical precepts are derived by consideration of what principles best correspond to the operation of the natural world. For example, preservation of a diverse human gene pool is, according to Wilson, to be considered a "cardinal virtue."[49] Human nature, he believes, disposes us to be selfish, but we can construct a naturalistic ethics that emphasizes the long-term survival of our genes and the good for our species that comes from that. Wilson further suggests that the principle of universal human rights can be upheld, not for any principled reason, but because *as mammals* we inherently value our own individual pursuit of life, liberty, and reproduction. Ants, he speculates, would demur, choosing a more collectivist ethic and taking a dim view of individualism.[50]

In fairness, there are two senses in which Wilson's apparent violations of the naturalistic fallacy can be defended. One is that in most places he seems to be offering instrumental advice rather than moral injunctions. In other words, he is saying that *if* we want to preserve our species and *if* we want the members of our species to be happy and fulfilled, then these are the policies we should adopt. If that is what he means, then he has not committed the naturalistic fallacy after all. If one takes it as a given that some end is a good to be pursued, then the facts of nature may provide insight into the instrumental means that might best achieve the desired end. Wilson is assuming that most people will agree that the perpetuation and flourishing of our species are ends worthy of pursuing—not an unreasonable assumption—and his "cardinal virtues" are meant to be those pathways through nature that will best realize those goals. The other defense of Wilson's flirtation with the naturalistic fallacy is that while "is" does not imply "ought," "ought" does imply "is." Ethical precepts, by their very nature, are prescriptive (or proscriptive) guides for conduct and, as such, need to be realizable by real people in the real world (although not necessarily *easily* realizable). Wilson's claim is that the kind of animals we are dictates the conditions under which we are most likely to flourish, so it behooves us to consider our animal nature in formulating our ethical theories.

Other theorists have been much more careful to respect the naturalistic fallacy and the is–ought gap. Philosopher Michael Ruse concurs that natural selection has provided us with an innate moral sense that disposes us to altruism in circumstances in which altruism would have been adaptive for our ancestors.[51] But, he points out, the morality thus conferred upon us, because it is a contingent product of our evolutionary history, is arbitrary and subjective. Had the circumstances of our social evolution been radically different, we would have a radically different moral sense. We have, in addition to the moral precepts themselves, the sense that our morality is objective and universal; but that sense is itself part of the inherited moral sense, evolved to serve the purpose of making us believe that our innate moral precepts wield the authority of objective, universal principles, so that we will not be inclined to disregard them. In the hypothetical case of different evolutionary circumstances and different ensuing morality, those moral precepts would no doubt seem no less objective and universal. This line of reasoning leads Ruse to a position he calls "moral nonrealism." Accepting that our values are contingent products of our evolution, he claims, entails admitting that they do not have any objective backing, that, indeed, the very idea of objective morality is an illusion. In this view, we can accept as a happy fact of life our innate moral compass, but whatever ethical theories we create to justify our morality cannot discover any universal moral truths because they do not exist.

Ruse's argument is unconvincing to most ethicists, and its weakness is immediately apparent. Ruse admits that the fact that our biology has given us the sense of something does not necessarily mean that the thing sensed is therefore an illusion. In his example, our biological capacity for vision tells us of an approaching train, the reality of which we would be foolish to deny on the basis that we know it via a biological adaptation. But Ruse thinks that a better analogy for the case of morality is provided by the practice of communicating with spirits, which when explained in naturalistic terms (wishful thinking combined with suggestion and a vivid imagination) obviates the need for any further explanation. To continue to believe that spirits speak to the living is at best unnecessary once the naturalistic explanation has been revealed. In that case, he may be right, but it is not immediately apparent why that is a better analogy for morality that the eyesight analogy. Does the fact that our innate moral sense can be accounted for by the contingencies of natural selection necessarily mean that it is not reflective of any underlying principles? Consider another analogy: The human knee, like the moral sense, is an adaptive product of natural selection designed to participate in the performance of certain jobs, such as walking, running, jumping, and kicking. A complete biological explanation of the knee in terms of the selection pressures that created it does not, however, render the principle of leverage illusory. In fact, when we understand the principle of leverage, we understand something important about the knee—as fulcrums go, it is not the best it could be. In the same way, a biological explanation of our moral sense, and even the recognition that there could be a wide variety of radically different moral systems designed to facilitate sociality (just as there are various ways to design a lever), does not necessarily mean that there are no objective ethical principles to be discerned. And, if we can discern those principles, we might discover that our innate moral sense, like the knee, falls short of the ideal. But we will not make progress toward narrowing the is–ought gap either by standing on the is-side denying that there is an ought-side or by standing on the ought-side while ignoring the is-side.

In this and the preceding two chapters, we worked primarily on the is-side of the is–ought gap, establishing the reality of altruism, describing the evolutionary dynamics and mechanisms that underlie it, and demonstrating how it is realized in human beings as genuinely other-regarding psychological states. We also acknowledged the limitations of our natural dispositions and suggested ways in which we can harness and expand our compassionate inclinations by nurturing our sense of interconnectedness with others and our capacity to engage in empathic perspective-taking and identification with others. Now it is time to move to the ought-side of the is–ought gap and consider, in the next two chapters, what the great philosophical and religious traditions have to say about how we ought to be.

5

Philosophical Perspectives
Altruism and the Role of Reason

THE POWER AND LIMITS OF REASON

IN THE LAST CHAPTER we discussed the "naturalistic fallacy": the false belief that because our nature furnishes us with certain propensities and constraints we *should* accept these conditions as (morally) good. There are, to be sure, brute facts about how we find ourselves in the world, one of which is that we are to a large degree hardwired to look after our own interests. While we are also genetically equipped for altruism, as the cases of reciprocal altruism, kin selection, and group selection demonstrate, we are thus equipped only in a limited manner. The upshot of our evolutionary biology is that we have become endowed with the capacity to display concern for those related to us or those with whom we have learned over time that it benefits us to enter into symbiotic relationships. But accepting this empirical reality at face value—accepting that this is how far our evolutionary biology has brought us—implies neither that we cannot nor that we should not try to go farther. As Hume pointed out, it is an error to move from facts about ourselves to values we should espouse. Because we discover that we have the desire or appetite for certain things (and that we lack the desire or appetite for certain others) does not necessarily mean that the best way to live is to assume that these things are what is best for us. This is particularly true with respect to our assumptions about ethics. To let inclination become our only or even our primary guide in ethical decision making is to submit to moral complacency. Moreover, it is to assume that nature has the final word over our capacity for moral development and thereby to overlook the potential we have to avail ourselves of our social environments, rational faculties, and religious traditions to build upon our already existing moral capacities. Nature may have the final word with the majority of the animal kingdom, but it does not with human beings.

Why do we make this claim? Why do we assert, in contention with some biologists, that when it comes to explaining altruism, human "nature" represents only part of the story? One way of answering the question is again to call attention to the methodological pluralism in our approach: we do not want to assume in this book that the way of understanding a particular human phenomenon can be reduced to the language and conceptual apparatus of a single discipline. Human beings are complex and arguably the least predictable organisms, drawing upon a variety of motivations for their moral and other actions. It would seem odd, given the mental capacity we are afforded by the size and makeup of our brains, if we were not distinctively positioned to do what other animals cannot. The more obvious answer to the above question, however, is that rare though they might be, there *are* instances of other-regard that cannot easily, and certainly not directly, be explained by the theories of kin selection, reciprocal altruism, and group selection. Particularly with respect to very costly altruistic sacrifices made for the sake of the complete stranger, the traditional resources identified by evolutionary biology are insufficient to explain how our love grows beyond its foreseeable dose and extends beyond its usual recipients. There are simply too many instances of unusual and substantial giving to fail to conclude that human beings rely on, or are nurtured by, their cultural, moral, and religious traditions to supplement the moral resources with which they are naturally endowed.

In this chapter, we investigate one of the most important ways in which nurture improves upon nature, namely, through human reason. Specifically, we look at how reason can enable human beings to display a deeper and broader concern for others than they would simply by utilizing the resources to which all the animals have access. Having demonstrated the various ways in which reason plays a constructive role in morality, we subsequently discuss the limitations of reason to serve as the only ground for a workable ethical framework. Put in another way, the central work to be done in this chapter is to investigate how reason serves as the bridge that moves us from "fact" to "value" while keeping in mind—respecting that "ought" implies "is"—that reason is not sufficient to deliver us entirely out of our animal, biological situation. Although reason can move us to enlarge and strengthen our scope of concern for the other, this is not necessarily the same as saying that reason contains the internal resources to spur us to *love*. Love implies a first-order desire on the part of the actor. Biologically speaking, this makes it a motive on which it is more natural and therefore easier for humans to act. Unlike the impulse to love, reason can be perceived to affect the moral actor from the outside, as an alien encumbrance, thus raising the question of just how effective reason can be by itself in motivating us to be more altruistic. On the other hand, it is precisely this feature of reason—its level of remove from our native constitution—that is hailed to be its advantage in ethics. In virtue of the distance between reason and natural impulse, our self-preferential tendencies are kept in check. This is, after all, how reason purports to offer us objective guidance in moral decision making. However, the question remains: To what extent is reason as a *motive* sufficient to prompt people disposed primarily to be self-interested to become other-regarding?

THE EXPANDING CIRCLE AND THE IMPARTIAL PERSPECTIVE

One way of asking the question with which we are primarily concerned is to pose it as the well-known and influential philosopher Peter Singer did in his groundbreaking volume *The Expanding Circle: Ethics and Sociobiology*. In this work, Singer grants the importance of acknowledging the biological basis of any ethical framework that aspires to be feasible for human beings but then subsequently wonders about the extent to which reason, too, is implied in the process of evolution.[1] If reason can be shown to stand as an upshot of our evolutionary biology, then this will lend credence to its potential effectiveness as a moral motive. Singer addresses the issue by beginning with the empirical fact that generosity toward strangers, which is implied neither by kin and group selection nor by reciprocal altruism, has not gone "under in the struggle for survival."[2] He explains:

> Evolution should have wiped out such non-rewarding traits as a broad, unselfish feeling of benevolence. If, however, we say that the expansion of the sphere of altruism is the result of the human capacity to reason, a possible solution to the mystery emerges. For the capacity to reason is not something that evolution is likely to eliminate. In finding food, in avoiding danger, in every area of life, those who reason well have an advantage over similar beings less capable of reasoning. So we can expect evolution to select strongly for a high level of reasoning ability. . . . Accordingly, if the capacity for reasoning brings with it an appreciation of reasons for extending to strangers the concern we feel for our kin and friends, evolution would not eliminate this rational appreciation of the

basis of ethics. The price would be too high. The evolutionary advantages of the capacity to reason would outweigh the disadvantages of occasional actions which benefit strangers at some cost to oneself.[3]

While there are instances in which reason commands us to undertake self-sacrifices, which would seem to be to our detriment individually, a broader view of the matter establishes that on the balance we are better off, evolutionarily speaking, with reason rather than without it. Singer goes on to cite empirical evidence for the claim that ethical reasoning has been around since nearly the dawn of humanity, along with tool use, cooperation, and problem solving.[4] Because the human capacity to reason is evolutionarily advantageous to human beings, if among the things that reason implies (along with the ability to use tools and logic to survive) is adopting an impartial perspective in matters of morality, we can come to accept the validity "of extending concern beyond [our] narrow circle of friends and relations,"[5] hence, the moral justification for adopting the impartial perspective and "expanding the circle." Acting on the basis of reason is a package proposition. To embrace it partly is at once to be governed by all of it. In this argument it only remains to be shown that reason in fact *does* imply adopting the impersonal perspective.

Much of what follows in this chapter will be devoted to explaining the ways in which the principle of impartiality works in morality (for there is more than one option), but this is already to assume that impartiality is, in fact, the linchpin of moral reasoning. What is rationally compelling about adopting the impartial perspective that grounds the expansion of ethical concern for the other to include those we do not know personally? Since Singer's answer represents one of the classic defenses not only of consequentialism, to which he himself subscribes, but also of Kantianism, as well as all other ethical frameworks that are distinguished by the refutation of our natural tendency to display favoritism toward special relations, we will quote him at length:

> In making ethical decisions I am trying to make decisions which can be defended to others. This requires me to take a perspective from which my own interests count no more, simply because they are my own, than the similar interest of others. . . . Disinterestedness within a group involves the rejection of purely egoistic

reasoning. . . . Justifying my actions to the group therefore leads me to take up a perspective from which the fact that I am I and you are you is not important. Within the group, other distinctions are similarly not ethically relevant. That someone is related to *me* rather than to you, or lives in *my* village among the dozen villages that make up our community, is not ethical justification for special favoritism; it does not allow me to do for my kin or fellow villagers any more than you may do for your kin or fellow villagers. Though ethical systems everywhere recognize special obligations to kin and neighbors, they do so within a framework of impartiality which makes me see my obligations to my kin and neighbors as no more important, from the ethical point of view, than other people's obligations to their own kin and neighbors. . . . Once I have come to see my interests and those of my kin and neighbors as no more important, from the ethical point of view, than those of others within my society, the next step is to ask why the interests of my society shall be more important than the interests of other societies. . . . Ethical reasoning, once begun, pushes against our initially limited ethical horizons, leading us always toward a more universal point of view. Where does this process end? Taking the impartial element in ethical reasoning to its logical conclusion means, first, accepting that we ought to have equal concern for all human beings.[6]

Moral reasoning, like other forms of reasoning, is based on its universal accessibility and persuasiveness. As such, it succeeds or fails on the basis of the legitimacy with which its arguments can appeal to any prospective evaluator. But the only way this will happen is if its premises are not reducible to egoistical claims; otherwise, someone will inevitably have cause to object. Since preferential treatment toward the ones we know personally usually implies some sort of self-benefit, even if one of which we are not necessarily consciously aware, favoring the special relation over the impersonal runs the risk of resulting in egoism. Therefore, moral reasoning must adopt a disinterested perspective to ensure that everyone's interests count the same. Once this much is granted, the "expanding the circle" that characterizes the growth and extension of all forms of other-regard from those for whom we have cause to care on the basis of evolutionary biology to everyone (in fact, on Singer's account, to *all* sentient beings)[7] can be justified to human beings who are otherwise disposed to favor only themselves and their loved ones. To the extent that we are *reasonable* beings in the first place, we must *rationally* be committed to expanding our "circle of concern" to include those whom we do not know personally.

Naturally, this does not mean that human beings *will*, on the basis of this argument, be moved to expand their circle of concern. Justification is not the same thing as motivation. And in this chapter, as well as the others in part II of this book, we are primarily concerned with what *motivates* altruism. Singer is not unaware of the problem: "We are capable of reasoning; but we are also the products of selective pressure on genes. We owe our existence to the ability of our ancestors to further their own interests and the interests of their kin. Can we really expect beings who have evolved in this manner to give up their narrower pursuits and adopt the universal standpoint of pure reason?"[8] This objection goes back to Hume, who in the *Treatise of Human Nature* claimed that reason is incapable of giving rise to new desires and is therefore impotent to do anything more than provide direction to desires that already exist. "Reason may help us to sort out the consequences of our choice," writes Singer, "but it cannot tell us what we most want."[9] A little later in this chapter we will consider how Singer deals with this famous Humean objection as part of our consideration of the theory of consequentialism. It might be useful here, however, to spell out the objection, which highlights the gap between justification and motivation, a little more thoroughly.

As we pointed out earlier, the naturalistic fallacy is the errant view that "fact implies value." Because as a result of our nature we have a propensity to be a certain way does not mean that we *should* be this way. This is not to say, however, that facts about ourselves do not *constrain* what we should do and how we should be. They do. As human beings we remain animals, even if we are animals who reason. Reason cannot deliver us from our biological situation entirely, and it is possible to overestimate reason's capacity to provide us with moral guidance that also results in moral action.

Michael Stocker has called this error, which lies at the other extreme of the naturalistic fallacy, the trap of "moral schizophrenia." The best moral *reasons*, Stocker argues, fall on deaf ears if they are brought forth to trump competing impetuses to action held by persons who fall under the sway of egoistic desires to a particularly large degree, i.e., most of us. Stocker's point is empirical: if evolution has turned us into animals who reason then it has done so at a faster rate than it has turned us into animals who obey what reason yields. What is more, in its promotion of the impartial perspective, reason sometimes recommends a course of action that opposes not merely self-ish but also evolutionarily beneficial desires, including, for example, the desire to form social bonds, the desire for erotic love, and the desire to enter into meaningful friendships. When this happens, reason advances one moral good at the expense of another. What is lacking in moral theories that emphasize impartiality, Stocker explains,

> is simply—or not so simply—the person. For, love, friendship, affection, fellow feeling, and community all require that the other person be an essential part of what is valued. The person—not merely the person's general values nor even the person-qua-pro-ducer-or-possessor-of-general-values—must be valued. The defect of these theories in regard to love, to take one case, is not that they do not value love (which, often, they do not) but that they do not value the beloved. . . . To embody in one's motives the values of current ethical theories is to treat people externally and to preclude love, friendship, affection, fellow feeling, and commu-nity—both with others and with oneself. To get these great goods while holding those current ethical theories requires a schizo-phrenia between reason and motive.[10]

Even if moral theories are governed by perfect rational logic, if they are to be effective we must be able to live by them, lest they strike us as some for-eign imposition, which we are unlikely to heed. If we did base morality, and by extension altruistic motives, exclusively on the impartial perspective, then we would lose something essential to the way in which we enter into first-person relationships with others, namely, the "first-person" relevance of our perspective to those actions and attitudes that represent the activities pro-moted by social interaction.

There is no doubt that evolution itself is responsible for our becoming the most rational beings among the animals, a development that has bene-fited our species by, among other things, opening up moral horizons unavailable to us through recourse to instinct alone. Without reason, moral-ity would be unduly impoverished. However, granting Singer's point that we are served by our evolutionary development into beings who reason, the outcome of which allows us to expand our circle of concern, does not ren-der null and void the other evolutionary advantages to choosing particular others with whom to interact, and to directing our love more narrowly, in ways not necessarily sanctioned by the impartial perspective. We should expect the prioritization of reason to lead to a tension of motives when we reflect upon exactly what other-regard practically implies. Both not enough and too much can be made of the is–ought or fact–value gap. Neither ethical naturalism nor a morality based totally on rational impartiality will be adequate to serve as a guide for human actions toward others.

With this very important qualification in place, it remains to be seen just what reason *can* do to improve upon nature. This is the point of the rest of the chapter, wherein we will lay out three historically significant philosophical approaches to (descriptively) understanding and (normatively) promoting altruistic conduct. In order, we will consider Kantianism, focusing primarily on the moral theory of Immanuel Kant himself; consequentialism, with reference to its greatest contemporary advocate, Peter Singer; and finally, after subjecting the first two approaches to critical scrutiny, virtue theory, where we will take a close look at Aristotelian ethics. What these three approaches have in common is their commitment to making use of human reason as a means to inspiring us to display a more robust sense of other-regard than that with which we are endowed in the state of nature. While they are not the only approaches we could consider, they are arguably the most important and are in any case generally representative of "philosophical perspectives" on altruism. How far can a morality justified by rational principles take us in terms of motivating altruism? By the chapter's end, we hope to have offered some insight into the relative possibilities for certain philosophical moral traditions to improve upon the altruistic propensities already provided by our biological constitution.

IMMANUEL KANT, FREEDOM, AND THE CATEGORICAL IMPERATIVE

The most important proponent of impartiality in ethics is the eighteenth-century philosopher Immanuel Kant (1724–1804), a thinker known for rigor and precision in his writings and so dependable in his personal habits and routines that people in the Prussian town of Königsberg used to set their watches by his three o'clock afternoon walks. Kant's ethical writings are found primarily in three major works: *Groundwork of the Metaphysics of Morals* (1785); *Critique of Practical Reason* (1787); and *The Metaphysics of Morals* (1797), consisting of two parts: *The Metaphysical Elements of Justice* and *The Doctrine of Virtue*. These works represent a progression of a profound, single idea: what we morally *ought* to do in terms of our interactions with others is discernible not through divine revelation, human authority figures, or sentimental desire, but rather through reason alone, to which human beings are distinctively privy. (Kant himself was a deeply religious thinker, but he saw God's role in human affairs as a provider of happiness. He conceived morality as completely humanly derived.) For Kant, the moral "ought"—*duty*—is a matter of autonomous self-governance. No one but we ourselves are responsible for determining what we morally ought to do. How is this determination made and in what sense does it specifically bear on altruistic conduct? The answer, in short, is that we are to conform all our action-impulses to what Kant refers to as the Moral Law, an unwavering principle through reference to which universally fair prescriptions and proscriptions can be derived in any given situation. When we do this, it will turn out that we filter out selfish impulses that we sometimes do not even recognize as selfish. As a result, a much higher percentage of the things we do will be done for others. By obeying duty consistently, in other words, we will as a matter of course become more altruistic.

Kant names the overarching ethical tenet that directs us to conform our maxims to the Moral Law the Categorical Imperative. Throughout his ethical writings, particularly the first two mentioned above, we are exposed to a variety of characterizations of the Categorical Imperative, although in essence the same point is expressed on each occasion. *Groundwork of the Metaphysics of Morals* contains its first and most succinct statement: "I ought never to act except in such a way that I can also will that my maxim should become a universal law."[11] What this means is that in any given situation having moral implications, everything we do must be something that we would direct anyone in our shoes to do. Just what this is cannot be determined in advance of the actual situation in which we find ourselves, but whatever it is, it has to be able to be prescribed for anyone who could find themselves similarly circumstanced. In this sense, the Moral Law is a kind of secular Golden Rule that is essentially procedural in nature. In any situation requiring a moral action of some sort, we are to go through the *procedure* of imagining what we would have anybody do and then act according to the course of action that that thought process, undertaken in earnest, yields.

It is important to note that in asking the central question "What ought I to do?," we are to assume no prior conception of the good. The Categorical Imperative is free of content. This has implications for how we are morally to deliberate. Take Kant's own example of someone who is called to testify and tell the truth on the witness stand. The choice not to lie to protect an

accused friend depends on bracketing the potentially corrupting consideration that it is someone the witness cares about, and not anyone as such,
whose fate hangs in the balance.[12] Bracketing these and similar details upon
engaging in moral deliberation is something most of us do not do, mostly
because it is so hard to do consistently, but also because some of us think
such details are ultimately relevant to our decisions. If we know that being
honest will hurt someone whom we care about, many of us will think twice
about the normal moral assumption that we should at all times endeavor to
tell the truth. Perhaps we would not want our friends to betray us when we
are in a tight spot, or perhaps we simply value being perceived as a good
friend. According to Kant, this kind of reasoning amounts to an evasion of
duty, one indicative of a rationalization that obscures the weighty if subtle
influence that self-interest has over us at all times. It is only in asking ourselves "What would we ideally want someone (about whom we otherwise
know nothing) to do in this instance?" that we are successfully able to undercut any existing selfish incentives we may harbor to play a role in governing
our actions.[13]

It is conceivable that in exceptional cases the application of the Categorical Imperative will justify an instance of deception (although this is unlikely
in the vast majority of cases). In this case truth-telling is not required and
may even be morally ruled out. Again, it is important always to bear in mind
that the Categorical Imperative is a procedural test, free of moral content
before the fact. The point is that the decision, whatever it is, will not have
been influenced by self-interest. Telling the truth in Kantian ethics in this
way becomes a matter of respecting all people, as does the performance of
any moral action. By taking the personal element out of the equation, we
show proper reverence for the Moral Law and ensure that we do not make
of our own case an exception when it is expedient to do so. The construction of duty is thus a matter of deriving fundamental principles that can be
adopted by all rational agents without making any assumptions about their
preferences, social statuses, specific needs, or any other concrete circumstances pertaining to them. By implication, duty implies the rejection of all
nonuniversalizable principles.

Another formulation of the Categorical Imperative involves the way in
which reason compels us to interact with other people. Kant calls this the
Formula of the End in Itself, which enjoins us to "act in such a way that you
always treat humanity, whether in your own person or in the person of any
other, never simply as a means, but always at the same time as an end."[14] We

have a duty never to use anyone (even our own self) as a means. This, again, means shunning expedience in favor of acting rationally on behalf of others' overarching interests. As with the first version of the Categorical Imperative, the Formula of the End in Itself limits what constitutes acceptable moral behavior. While pondering a course of action we must always be asking ourselves questions like: Are we promoting others' capacity to act by themselves (e.g., by giving them information to which they have a right; by nourishing them when they are incapacitated)? Are we safeguarding others' capacity to offer their consent, and by implication, dissent? Do we go out of our way to advance the standards of social justice that open up opportunities for others to flourish?

Kant helpfully employs some illustrations to demonstrate the kinds of actions ruled out by the Formula of the End in Itself. These range from suicide to failing to contribute (through charity or good works) to the general felicity of the impoverished and downtrodden. On the subject of suicide, Kant remarks: "If he does away with himself in order to escape from a painful situation, he is making use of a person merely as *a means* to maintain a tolerable state of affairs [until] the end of his life."[15] To this duty owed to the self, Kant provides a complementary injunction to maintain an other-regarding outlook:

> [A]s regards meritorious deeds to others, the natural end which all men seek is their own happiness. Now humanity could no doubt subsist if everybody contributed nothing to the happiness of others but at the same time refrained from deliberately impairing their happiness. This is, however, merely to agree negatively and not positively with *humanity as an end in itself* unless every one endeavors also, so far as in him lies, to further the ends of others.[16]

It is not enough in Kantian ethics successfully to avoid moral crimes and violations. The Moral Law also compels us to go out of our way to help others. In both the original and subsequent versions of the Categorical Imperative, we are directed to exclude self-interest as motivating any moral action, even when this pertains to the preservation of our own life. (Suicide that occurs out of self-interest fails to be self-regarding or self-respecting.) To be rational involves acting freely and autonomously, which means not being enslaved to one's appetites or inclinations and remaining vigilant against the surfacing and resurfacing of selfishness. The human capacity to reason, in other words,

implies the freedom not to give in to animal instinct and inclination by acting judiciously and fairly in any prospective course of action. It remains to
be shown, for Kant, why we would choose to act according to this "pure"
motive to the exclusion of all other incentives, given how difficult it apparently is to do so.

Here it becomes important to delve into the pivotal concept of the will.
An often underemphasized and frequently misunderstood aspect of Kantian ethics is its subjectivist (although not relativist) orientation. According
to Kant, we are "self-legislators": we ourselves are solely responsible for
determining, through availing ourselves of our capacity to reason, what the
Moral Law requires and then summoning the wherewithal to act accordingly. This requires wisdom, patience, and strength of character. To do the
right thing is to decide first what reason dictates and then summon the voli-
tion to act on it. Hence, Kant refers to moral action as the outcome of "practical reason." Reason, by virtue of the propelling force of the will, leads to
practical action. It is important for Kant that we exercise our moral responsibility by enacting the "good will," that is, the will that acts only according
to what reason dictates without regard either for the goodness of the results
it produces or the impulse to act according to any nonrational guide, such
as inclination.[17] In other words, to act for the sake of duty is to do the *right*
thing without regard for consequences or appetites.

Kant is insistent that the good, pure will not be "heteronomous," or a will
that is motivated to respond to anything other than that which the Moral
Law makes imperative. In this judgment, Kant seems to contrast "nature"
and "reason" as strongly as does any thinker. Only by being motivated by the
latter do we know for sure that the good that comes from our action is a dignified kindness rather than a "pathological" love contaminated by hedonistic impulse. Good action resides only "in the will and not in the propensities
of feeling, in principles of action and not of melting compassion."[18] To be
free, on this account, is to distinguish ourselves from the animals who have
no choice but to act according to their nature. One rises above one's animal
nature because of the capacity one possesses to enact the good will, a capacity which allows the enactor

> nothing less than the *share* which it affords to a rational being *in
> the making of universal law*, and which therefore fits him to be a
> member in a possible kingdom of ends. For this he was already
> marked out in virtue of his own proper nature as an end in him-

self and consequently as a maker of laws in the kingdom of ends—
as free in respect of all laws of nature, obeying only those laws he
makes himself in virtue of which his maxims can have their part
in the making of universal law (to which he at the same time subjects himself). . . . *Autonomy* is therefore the ground of the dignity
of human nature and of every rational nature.[19]

In the Kantian view, we are the "altruistic species" because reason enables us
to transcend a nature too often marred by hedonistic, immediate desires.
Exhibiting "willpower," to borrow a contemporary idiom, requires work.
Freedom, ever our capacity, is not easy to maintain. It involves remaining
watchful and suspicious of the inclinations to which we routinely become
susceptible, and, more important, acting, actually *doing* the right thing that
is hard to do. That right thing, on most occasions, will be contravened by
self-interest, so it has to be overridden by the will. This overriding is what
Kant calls *freedom*. The good will is good in itself. It is intrinsically worthy,
for it alone gives independence to our agency. The intrinsic value of the good
will precipitates human *dignity*. Goodness is not merely a matter of doing
the right thing, but of choosing to do it for the right reason, namely, because
reason demands it. Conversely, we forego our distinctive opportunity to be
dignified when we cede our freedom back to nature and enslave ourselves to
inclination.

The idea of goodness as right action has implications for how to conceive
of altruism in Kantian ethics. The upshot of right conduct will be other-
regard. When we actually manage to see a moral situation clearly, we will
come to realize just how many occasions there are for us to help others when
we should, in fact, be doing so. As such, right action becomes more a matter
of proactive beneficence than of prudential nonmaleficence.[20] Kantian
ethics, which is based on seeing reasonably what any situation requires,
places an emphasis on positive duty. Seen in this light, altruism is not to be
understood as something romantic, something to which we are moved by
appeal to sympathy. It is the outcome of logical, human thought, followed
by action consistent with that thought. Here it is important to note that
"love" is not the Kantian's term of choice to characterize what is actually
going on when other-regard takes place. There is nothing sentimental about
right action in Kantian ethics. Duty is not an obligation to feel warmth
toward the ones we help, but one to promote their welfare and happiness
because both our and their humanity demands as much.[21]

In the Kantian view, altruism can therefore be accurately characterized as the result of acting on reason, which is bound to require other-regard in instances where inclination does not. To apply the Categorical Imperative in earnest will reveal daily responsibilities toward others that we might have been inclined to overlook. The actual performance of altruistic deeds assumes, of course, that human beings will be motivated to follow reason once reason has issued its verdict. Acting according to the motive of duty implies few if any moral options and frequently implies demanding, other-regarding acts. Living life, in the Kantian view, becomes a rather serious endeavor, for we are always called to keep in the forefront of our minds the overriding ambition of keeping ourselves in check for the sake of the others whom, if we take a good look around, we are in a position to help.

This does not mean that we are to see ourselves as human automatons. Kantian ethics does not lead us mindlessly and ceaselessly to devote our lives to alleviating suffering everywhere it is found in the world. To the contrary, Kant insists that as human beings we should use our heads and think. Doing so, however, may come to imply an overwhelming reprioritization of what we aim for, invest in, and value. Inclination tends to lead where we are naturally already inclined to go. If we are hungry and fast food is available, the likelihood is that we will eat it. If we are in a rush, we may not be so quick to help our elderly neighbors shovel their driveway after a snowstorm or so eager to pick up old candy wrappers we encounter in a nature reserve. Reason gives a different answer to the question "What ought I to do?" than does inclination. That different answer is often psychologically disconcerting, for it demands a way of looking at the world that does not put the self first, and, moreover, implies that there are many more occasions than we realize to intervene proactively on behalf of someone who needs our help. Is it realistic to expect to monitor ourselves the way Kant's approach to right action suggests we should? Before we answer this question, it might be useful to address another ethical theory that construes goodness as right action. Thus, we will withhold our critical response to Kant's ethics until we have examined the theory of consequentialism, which is even more logically constraining and morally demanding than Kantianism.

Altruism and Consequentialism

While Kantians require us to make reason our primary guide in decisions leading to moral action, consequentialists contend even more strongly that we must engage in a rational calculation of the overall good before undertaking any action at all. Strictly speaking, consequentialists maintain that moral action comprises the entirety of human action. Everything we do, even when seemingly trivial, potentially has morally significant consequences. In introducing the theory of consequentialism to our students, we sometimes like to read aloud this provocative passage, which opens Shelly Kagan's *The Limits of Morality*:

> When I go to the movies I may spend a few dollars and enjoy myself for an hour or two. The pleasure I get is genuine, and it seems absurd to say that I have done anything *wrong*. Yet this is exactly what the [consequentialist] claim entails, for both my time and money could be better spent: the pleasure one could bring in an evening visiting the elderly or sick quite outweighs the mild entertainment I find in the movies; and the money itself would have done much more good if it were sent to famine relief—for even a few dollars is sufficient to enable another human being to survive a temporary food shortage brought on by drought. If the claim is right, then in going to the movies I do what is morally *forbidden*. This strikes us as wildly implausible; we agree that it would be *meritorious* to visit the elderly and donate the money to charity—but no more than that. If the claim is right, however, it is not merely nice for me to forgo my slight pleasure: it is morally *required*.[22]

Every time we choose to go to the movies, we decide to withhold eight to ten dollars from one of the many worthy charities to which that sum of money could otherwise be devoted, and, according to the consequentialist perspective, we do something immoral. This is because in going to the movies we do not make the optimal use of our time and resources. The consequentialist claim is that on the basis of reason, through which we have the ability at least to try our best to calculate the overall good, there may be no limit to what morality may come to require of us. We act irrationally and immorally if we act so as to favor the things we care about at the expense of some greater good we could have achieved. Because the promotion of the overall good qualitatively and quantitatively outweighs what it is in our own interests to do, the performance of altruistic deeds counts among the most basic of moral requirements. Conseqentialists are naïve neither about the counterintuitive nature of this proposal nor about our natural psychological resistance to it.

That something strikes us as hard to do, however, in no way excuses us from doing it. Commonsensical notions of what qualifies as "overly burdensome" or "excessively self-sacrificial" do not excuse any failure on our part to promote the overall good.

The case for consequentialism is perhaps most sympathetically made in connection with world hunger, and it is with this example that Peter Singer, one of the best-known consequentialists, proceeds to argue that altruism ought rightly to be seen as morally compulsory. In "Famine, Affluence, and Morality," an article just as controversial as it was influential, Singer begins by throwing down a gauntlet: "As I write this, in November 1971, people are dying in East Bengal from lack of food, shelter, and medical care. The suffering and death that are occurring there now are not inevitable, not unavoidable in any fatalistic sense of the term."[23] Singer goes on in this article to call upon every citizen of well-to-do countries to donate a small sum, roughly five to ten dollars, to relief funds across the world. Since we in fact *can* do something about people starving and afflicted with disease in underprivileged parts of the world—since efforts to alleviate their suffering would not be exerted in vain—we are not merely negligent but morally derelict for not doing so. All other things being equal, there is no moral difference between killing and letting die. Our positive duty to help others is no weaker than the negative duty not to hurt them. Any rational assessment of how bad it is for the needy to be deprived of basic goods warrants that those in positions of relative wealth and security must give to the needy up to a point at which they themselves begin to bear the same level of cost as their beneficiaries.

Those skeptical of this view often raise a practical objection associated with a policy of donating money to strangers abroad. They point out that in the real world charities are ineffective, or worse, corrupt. Donated funds rarely reach their intended recipients. The objection, however, is misguided for, current problems of implementation notwithstanding, it remains beyond dispute that we (i.e., nations of the first world) do have the available technology and administrative capability to put into practice regular and effective institutions of social justice that will meet their stated objectives. If it mattered enough to us, we could make sure that the most important and best-known charities in our society never, or rarely, strayed from their missions. That some charitable organizations fail in this regard does not bear on the rightness or wrongness of the moral theory under consideration, for such organizations *could* become successful with due attention. Moreover, the fact that some charities, like CARE, *do* have a very good record undercuts the skeptic's objection even further, for there are at least some organizations where we can be confident *now* that our prospective donation will be put to good use.

Because it is empirically true that current technology enables us to become a more altruistic society than we are currently, those who doubt the pragmatic implications of the consequentialist's position about world hunger will have to come up with a better argument. The burden is on them to demonstrate that there is something intrinsically problematic about the theory of consequentialism itself. Is there or isn't there a difference between killing and letting die when, for example, it comes to the issue of world hunger? If there is no difference, is it also true that we ought to be expected to attempt to share an equal portion of the burden experienced by all the world's inhabitants who go without on a daily basis? What are the limits to what morality may demand of us in pursuit of the overall good?

In his article, Singer essentially backs two propositions. The first, relatively straightforward, is that suffering and death from lack of food, shelter, or medical assistance are bad things. It is important to note that in making this claim, Singer joins the majority of ethicists in assuming, contra nihilists, that something can be morally bad and that it is epitomized by the suffering and sorrow experienced by others. The second proposition, much less widely held, is that if it is "within our power to prevent something bad from happening, without thereby sacrificing something of comparable moral importance, we ought, morally, to do it."[24] "Sacrificing something of comparable moral importance" delineates two sorts of constraints. As a result of our good action, we should not additionally cause something comparably bad to happen nor should we fail to do something comparably better. In the consequentialist view there are absolutely no moral options. Absent appeal to one of these two exceptions, we *must* perform the action that alleviates the moral badness identified in others' suffering and sorrow.

These two propositions lead to some major implications for how we are to think about the scope and centrality of altruism in our day-to-day activities. Among the most significant of these is that in the consequentialist view, no account is taken of proximity or distance. Impartialist ethical theories do not allow us to discriminate between the close-by and the faraway. While there may be valid practical reasons for deciding to be concerned initially with the poor and sick in our own region or country (e.g., we are best positioned to help them first), psychological reasons for favoring those

geographically closest to us have no moral standing. And in any case, in a
world of instant communication in which the majority of homes and nearly
every business is wired for the Internet, it is now appropriate to look at all
the societies we inhabit as but one "global village," whereby we have the
means to bring the distant closer to home. Only the depth and scope of the
need can morally dictate the recipients of our aid.

Another implication of the propositions enumerated above is that we are
not allowed to refer to the inaction of others to justify our own inaction.
Although we may feel less guilty about our own shortcomings when we point
to the fact that others are morally negligent when they do not carry their
other-regarding loads, the consequentialist view mandates that when this
happens our load increases, not decreases.[25] Reason compels us to examine
each situation in light of whatever empirical realities exist in the world,
including the reality that many will ignore what reason dictates. We must
then act according to what will bring about the best consequences in terms
of procuring the overall good.

Finally, and perhaps most drastically from the commonsense perspective,
there is no distinction to be drawn between duty and charity. The category
of "supererogation," which refers to meritorious good deeds that are nonetheless not morally required, dissolves in a consequentialist account (just as
it does in Kantian ethics). One implication of this is that the demarcation
normally asserted between public morality and private entitlements breaks
down. There are simply too many things that we could do, and would want
to do in the freedom of our own privacy, whose investments in terms of time
and money according to any rational assessment take away from more important activities. There are activities we enjoy doing that are admittedly not
wrong in themselves. Nevertheless, these activities almost certainly lead to
not doing other things, the result of which will lead to otherwise preventable
calamites. It is fair to say that a life lived within consequentialist parameters
contains far fewer hedonistic experiences and many more altruistic ones.

This leads to the central and controversial consequentialist position that
there is no moral difference between killing someone and failing to save
someone from dying. We customarily think that performing a bad action is
worse than failing to perform a good one. One reason for this is that while
there is an identifiable guilt directly associated with going out of our way to
harm someone, there is only an indirect connection between our inaction
and anyone's suffering that ensues, suffering that we presumably do not
intend. When we fail to rescue or aid someone who lacks basic resources, we

at least leave open the possibility that someone else will. But looking at the situation in this way represents an error in thinking according to consequentialist reasoning. The philosopher James Rachels explains the rationale behind the fallacy:

> The importance of "optionality" in any particular case depends on the actual chances of someone else's saving the person we do not save. Perhaps it is not so bad not to save someone if we know that someone else *will* save him. (Although even here, we do not behave as we ought; for we ought not simply to leave what needs doing to others.) And perhaps it even gets us off the hook a little if there is a *strong chance* that someone else will step in. But in the case of the world's starving, we know very well that no person or group of persons is going to come along tomorrow and save all of them. We know that there are at least some people who will *not* be saved, if we do not save them. So, as an excuse for not giving aid to the starving, the "optionality" argument is clearly in bad faith.[26]

In other words, we know enough through earnest empirical observation combined with accurate rational assessment to understand that the inaction of failing to save is tantamount to the action of letting someone die. The one who resists drawing an equivalence between killing and letting die, according to this line of thinking, errs not by overestimating the wrongness of killing, but by underestimating the wrongness of letting die.[27] All lives are of equal worth. Once we grant that the value of preserving a life is a good that outweighs other, lesser competing goods, including pleasures that we individually experience, any honest process of reasoning morally condemns us when we subsequently fail to include the performance of lifesaving altruistic deeds among our most pressing priorities.

Does placing altruism at the top of the priority list represent too drastic a modification of the way in which we normally think about our responsibilities toward others? To those who say it does, consequentialists have a response: we are setting our moral expectations too low. That we frequently do not act on reason is not the failing of the moral theory that is based on it, but our own. Consequentialists wager that if we lived up to our human capacity to exercise reason, which also entails utilizing reason as our primary source of moral guidance, then what we call "drastic" would not in actuality seem so drastic. Like Kantians, consequentialists hold that we are most human, most essentially ourselves, when we listen to reason, which is distinctively our capacity to harness. When we see ourselves in this light, recognizing the rational justification for making the overall good a higher priority becomes at once a motivation for doing so. Knowing ourselves as we truly are, i.e., as beings of reason, we will want to act as reasonably as possible. This (rational) desire will, in turn, prompt us to work very hard at eschewing selfish impulse, which, without reason, we may be slow to recognize as selfish. Just like the Kantian, the consequentialist believes that our nature ironically provides us with the capacity to transcend our nature. Acknowledging ourselves for who we truly are—beings of reason—furnishes us with all the motivation we need to become primarily altruistic rather than selfish beings. Conversely, the selfish among us are to be regarded as "lesser," as beings ignorant (hopefully temporarily) of their own nature and purpose in this world.

Altruism, then, is the by-product of reason. Properly understood, it is the upshot of our rational nature. When we come to recognize ourselves as rational beings, we will want to be as altruistic as possible, not out of an emotive compassion, but because by being this way we most faithfully realize the potential latent in all of us. Critics of the consequentialist view stress that it is by virtue of our deciding to be altruistic of our own accord—and not being forced in that direction by a moral theory—that altruism retains its special quality. The consequentialist reply to this objection is similar to the Kantian reply: human beings truly exercise freedom by attuning themselves to their higher, rational selves. As human beings, we have the liberty to choose enslavement by ignoring reason and acting on impulse or to live up to our humanity. But genuine freedom is moving past the limitations that determine the conduct of other animals. Those in favor of the existence of options in ethics contend that options enable us to cultivate a desire that has not been coerced to help others in need. Moral options, in other words, are tantamount to moral motivation. Consequentialists demur. Moral options are not necessary to motivate altruistic conduct if we exercise our rational faculties. What is more, they insist, the highest sort of motivation is the motivation of reason, which enjoys its exalted place in the hierarchy of motivations precisely because human beings distinctively, if not uniquely, have the capacity to possess it. Moral options allow us the space to come to desire affectively the betterment of others, but the sort of ad hoc altruism that ensues as a result of this process is not sufficient to meet our moral demands. Affective, emotional responses are ephemeral and too discriminating. They valuably serve as a precondition for acts of giving only in lieu of self-governance through appeal to human reason.

Is the consequentialist commitment to maintaining faith in our capacity to act on reason realistic? And if it were, if reason were sufficient for us to become motivated to meet our moral demands, would we want to be such creatures? That is, beyond being possible or efficacious, is consequentialism morally desirable? Is Kantianism? Finally, how accurate is it to characterize altruism as the result of logical thinking? Can there be altruism without love? The time has come to examine more critically Kantianism and consequentialism, both of which rely on the notion of reason as motivating altruism.

KANTIANISM AND CONSEQUENTIALISM UNDER SCRUTINY

Kantians and consequentialists conceive of human beings as self-sufficient deliberators. Because of reason, we are not morally limited in a way that the other animals are. We have the means to see clearly our responsibility to the stranger in need, to understand that that stranger could be anyone, and to perceive that he or she, depending on the circumstances, could require a great deal from us. Further, because of reason, we do not just have the means to be privy to this knowledge; we can also act on it. Seeing ourselves as reasonable beings, we acquire the wherewithal to want to become our best selves, i.e., selves who choose to do what is right as opposed to what feels good, which often is not right or at best is only incidentally right.

There is a difference between Kantians and consequentialists, to be sure. For Kantians, what is "right" pertains to what is right in itself, as determined by the Categorical Imperative. This means that we are never to act preferentially toward ourselves or those we care about. Instead, we should do what (as an onlooking third party) we would rationally have anyone do who finds him- or herself in our shoes. Altruism is implied in this process because we are commanded by the Moral Law to replenish others as we would want to be replenished ourselves, which amounts to acting less selfishly than we would otherwise act. For consequentialists, what is right corresponds to our best attempts to calculate what will lead to the overall good. We must act to advance the best interests of everyone, everywhere, at all times. Thus, like Kantianism, consequentialism implies significant altruistic activity on the part of the agent. According to both theories, we need only reason to be successful moral agents. Reason fills in where our biological resources dry up.

The matter that needs to be raised with Kantians and consequentialists, in terms of the topic at hand, concerns whether altruism is really a command of reason. The philosophical approaches so far considered assume that by virtue of their humanity, human beings possess equally the ability to act according to what reason dictates. From this it follows that what qualifies as a "right" action can be enumerated regardless of who is performing it. This assumption gives rise to at least three issues. First, it is possible that human beings are not actually or even latently motivated by reason to the same degree. Second, reason itself may not even be the most desirable sort of motivation for the would-be altruist to try to cultivate. Finally, it is questionable whether an impartialist approach to morality is adequate to the kinds of beings we are, as a result of which there may be grounds for favoring the special relation over the impersonal other. We will consider these three issues in the order just mentioned.

The first criticism asks if there may be cause for skepticism about the Kantian and consequentialist faith in reason to supplant impulsive desire and emotional affectation as a motivation for acting. Kantians understand human "freedom" in contrast to animal instinct. The former is considered to be a higher, more rational, more appropriate state for human beings to be in. Once we know ourselves as beings for whom such an existence is possible, we will want to live our lives accordingly and act on the direction of the pure will in order to escape enslavement. Consequentialists advocate the same stance toward adopting a rational orientation. Since acting to advance the overall good represents the most evolved and sophisticated kind of human life, it is one, upon discovery of this fact, that we will naturally become determined to embrace for ourselves. However, it is far from clear that in actuality we operate so logically, and certainly unlikely that we are all equally capable of doing so. Momentarily granting for the sake of argument the supremacy of rational thinking to other grounds for acting, what is important in terms of the ethical payoff is how we act. Good *reasons* do not necessarily amount to good *actions*. It is possible for one to affirm the rightness of impartialist ethics theoretically without acquiring the motivation to act on behalf of it. When it comes to actions, it is essential to consider what matters most to us. These tend to be things like personal projects and ambitions, loved ones, family and friends, ideals, and religious convictions. Becoming persons who behave rationally also counts as something that does and should motivate us, but the process of realizing ourselves as such is slow going. We have to dispose ourselves to changing our routines and habits in concert with the other things that naturally motivate us.

The problem with Kantian and consequentialist ethics is that they are psychologically unrealistic insofar as both assume that by discovering our capacity for reason we will thereby want to become more reasonable. Desire, ambition, and love are too enmeshed in the way in which we evolutionarily have come to form incentives for us to be able to dispense with these motivations when they clash with reason. Indeed, the way people become more reasonable is by *desiring* to be, which means that reason is not independent unto itself, at least in terms of human motivation. This leads to a second aspect of the first objection: people are just too different for all individuals to dispose themselves to be reasonable to the same degree. As human beings, we are psychologically constituted in distinct ways. The manner in which our selfish and selfless proclivities compete with one another has to be determined case by case. In assuming that reason provides a "best" answer to certain quandaries, applicable to all moral agents, both Kantianism and consequentialism do not adequately take into account that people have different moral capabilities, and are even capable of different moral feats at different stages of their lives. In other words, Kantianism and consequentialism overlook the importance of *moral development* in ethics, the idea that over time we can work on ourselves to become better equipped to perform other-regarding actions, including those other-regarding actions that are recommended by rational analysis.

Part of the problem is the implied distinction on the part of both theories between "altruism" and "love," where the former is identified with other-regard while the latter is seen as a product of self-induced, affective desire. Impartialists of the sort we have been examining are worried that if we rely on notions of love to motivate altruism, the needs of the most desperate will go unaddressed. Exclusive dependence on reason, by contrast, ensures the most equitable distribution of resources. But what if it is love, and not a command of reason, that primarily, or at least significantly, precipitates giving? Hagiographical studies and first-person narrative accounts of some of the world's greatest saints meticulously chronicle the passion for the other that such exemplars routinely display.[28] These accounts reveal that passion is not an incidental saintly trait. It is the driving force behind saintly altruistic activity. Even small altruistic gestures, such as donating a modest amount to charity or being late for an important meeting to give directions to someone who is lost, are triggered and nurtured by one's loving nature and the good feedback one enjoys from knowing oneself as loving.

This is not to dismiss the importance of reason in the process of motivation. It is, rather, to suggest that reason and desire both seem to be essential
components in forming an altruistic character. It is reason that tells us that
the welfare of the starving Ethiopian is just as worth promoting as our next-
door neighbor's, or our own. But it is seeing an image of this suffering one
on a television infomercial, or coming to know the saga of this individual
through some personal investment, that most often leads us to act on reason. When we act, including when we morally act, we act in the concrete,
with an image in mind of the one for whose sake we are acting. Kantian ethics
insists that we undergo a sophisticated thought experiment on the basis of
which we are moved to respond altruistically. In similar fashion, consequentialists would have human beings respond as automatic promoters of the
good who consistently enact whatever the moral calculus yields. Passion and
desire are not a necessary part of the picture. But human beings are designed
to be most motivated in these states. This is not to say that love, in consul-
tation with reason's guiding light, cannot come to be a more just love. But it
is to aver that love is an essential biological resource of ours, particularly in
terms of promoting altruistic activity. As Hume and many of his successors
have pointed out, if passion without reason is blind, then reason without
passion is impotent. Thus, there is a lingering question about how *capable*
human beings are of acting on reason alone.

The first objection just considered is descriptive in nature. It addresses
whether it is possible to act morally on reason alone, as Kantians and consequentialists would have us do. The second objection is normative. If we
were beings capable of acting solely on reason, would we want to be? Part of
what is at stake in asking this question is the question of the normativity of
altruism itself: if we could swallow a pill and choose to become the sort of
person who did the "right" thing all the time, would we want to be that person? Granting for the moment that reason always tells us what is right, and
further granting that we have the ability always to act on reason, would we
want to *be* this sort of person for whom reason alone served as our guiding
light?

In a famous article, the philosopher Susan Wolf calls such a person the
"rational saint."[29] The rational saint, according to Wolf, is an almost flawless,
bland do-gooder who prizes moral virtues like benevolence, compassion,
and generosity over other, perhaps more colorful virtues like poise and wit.
Moral activities, she argues, need to be balanced against other valuable activities like playing the oboe or reading Victorian novels for one to participate

in a fully flourishing human life. In a telling footnote, Wolf quotes George Orwell: "[S]ainthood is . . . a thing that human beings must avoid. . . . It is too readily assumed that . . . the ordinary man only rejects it because it is too difficult; in other words, that the average human being is a failed saint. It is doubtful whether this is true. Many people genuinely do not wish to be saints, and it is possible that some who achieve or aspire to sainthood have never felt much temptation to be human beings."[30] Wolf's point is another appeal to the "commonsense" way of thinking: too much of anything is a bad thing. Making altruism a way of life on purely rational and theoretical criteria, which we are directed to do when we adhere to demanding philosophical systems like Kantianism and consequentialism, requires us to forego other important, separately demanding desires and ambitions, desires and ambitions without which, Wolf argues, we cannot fully realize our human potential. Moral excellence does not necessarily equal altruistic perfection. Otherwise, morality becomes a kind of idolatry, and an important kind of liberty aside from Kantian "freedom" gets lost.

Moreover, even if altruistic perfection *is* what we should aim for if we are to participate in the best kind of human life, it is unclear that we would want the motivation for that to be reason alone. Recent studies show that human beings are happier, healthier, and live longer lives when they learn to enjoy the act of giving on a regular basis.[31] In other words, assuming for the moment that we could be equally motivated by reason or by loving desire to perform altruistic deeds, there is cause to believe that independent of the value of altruistic acts to those who benefit from them, it is better to be motivated by loving desire than by reason. For, in being motivated in this way, we replenish an important biological need, just as we do when we consume essential nutrients. Benefactors, on this account, need to give just as their suffering recipients need to receive. Since we are already biologically constituted to flourish under conditions of reciprocal giving, it is perhaps not a stretch to imagine that we are creatures not merely capable of altruistic activity, but, to a certain degree, in need of it.

Now, in response to this line of reasoning, the Kantian or consequentialist would naturally be led to ask: Isn't the consideration of what is healthier or more rewarding for me a selfish one? If we are to be our best moral selves, shouldn't the predicament of those in need be the only thing that it is legitimate to consider? In response to these objections, we can note that if the recent studies just cited are correct, then people genuinely need to become giving sorts of people, in which case *accepting* generosity itself becomes a kind of altruism! To state as much is not to commit the naturalistic fallacy, which, it will be recalled, is to infer value from natural propensity in virtue of natural propensity alone. We are not suggesting that just because it is easier or more natural for human beings to give from the motivation of desire than from the motivation of reason, that sort of giving is better. The counterproposal under consideration is more subtle. Human beings have needs beyond material needs, including the need to be giving sorts of people. And if this so, then it is misleading to think of altruism narrowly, as an action or series of actions that flow exclusively in one direction. To the contrary, altruism is better construed as an organic, holistic process in which different people help one another differently, sometimes materially, sometimes more spiritually or psychologically, depending on the circumstances. One assumption that runs throughout the writings of most Kantians and consequentialists is that the demand of reason to be altruistic is not something that is likely to strike the prospective altruist as a pleasant burden to bear. Altruism, for them, is a process of *overcoming* human nature, of having the strength of will to obey reason over and against nature. They assume that altruism is generally onerous, almost invariably involving a sacrifice that outweighs any benefits that the altruist stands to accrue by being altruistic. However, if this assumption is not borne out—and recent research suggests the claim is overstated—it may not be such a stretch to imagine that loving desire, in addition to reason, is a critical motivator of altruistic activity.

Finally, there is the matter of impartiality. At the beginning of this chapter we discussed the assumption held by many philosophers that only the perspective that takes everyone's welfare and well-being into account can be considered the *moral* point of view. Reason dictates that no one person's interests count more than another's. As such, reason recommends a "cosmopolitan altruism," which encompasses the whole human race, over a personal altruism directed toward the near and dear.[32] This claim raises two subissues that need to be examined. The first is whether impartiality is necessarily, or even likely, the upshot of reason. Do impartiality and reason go hand in hand, as Kantians and consequentialists hold? The second calls into question the supposed superiority of impartiality itself, which favors impersonal altruism to more conventional displays of care and concern to the other already known. Does a more enlightened, or morally advanced, ethical system correspond to the one that does not distinguish among kinds of recipients? Conversely, does giving preferential treatment to loved ones imply a moral failing of some sort?

The first of these two considerations gets to the heart of the motivation for altruistic deeds. Kantians and consequentialists believe that the human capacity for reason inspires impartialist thinking. This capacity for reason is what distinguishes us from the other animals, whose propensities for self-less conduct are limited to their genetically programmed capacities for reciprocity and kin preference. In service of this conviction, they sometimes call attention to the fact that many of the world's historically prominent moral exemplars were impartial in their moral outlook. Gandhi and Martin Luther King Jr., for example, favored universal fellowship over preference of individuals belonging to particular groups and with specific statuses. Gandhi, a Hindu, called for the overthrow of the caste system for the sake of those most hurt by it, the untouchable class, and also urged a brotherhood to be forged with Muslims as part of a "greater India," ultimately giving his life for these convictions at the hands of a Hindu nationalist. Martin Luther King Jr., accused by Malcolm X and other black leaders of selling out his own people by including whites in his "American dream," was legendary for his risky and counterintuitive gestures of outreach to racist klansmen.[33] As political activists committed to procuring conditions of peace and social justice, both Gandhi and King invited criticism throughout their lives by crossing boundaries to cultivate broader, cross-cultural communities of mutual support. They bucked convention and chose to forego the natural urge to respond out of kinship in favor of their enlightened vision of a united, interdependent global community. For them, anyone suffering anywhere counted as a legitimate target for relief. Their kindness toward others represents a moral advance beyond the sort of giving expected in kin, group, or reciprocal altruism. Kantians and consequentialists sometimes call attention to the indiscriminate kindness of Gandhi, King, and others as evidence of the superiority of an impartialist morality based on reason.

This raises an important empirical question. Is the egalitarian approach adopted by altruists like Gandhi and King inspired by a *rational* thought-analysis of the sort we have been considering so far in this chapter? It does not seem likely. Gandhi's championing of the untouchable class was rooted in the sympathy he felt for all of God's children, or "harijan," the name he deliberately gave to them. This sympathy, as Gandhi himself frequently stated, was awakened as he became familiar with the life circumstances of the less fortunate, not by a rational, deliberative process. Martin Luther King Jr. traveled long distances to try to spur unlikely moments of reconciliation between whites and blacks, managing to do so, it must be pointed out, by basing his hopes for success on his faith in agape, an unconditional love of the other for the other's sake that first and foremost instructs the giver to become acquainted with the plight of the sufferer. In neither case were these two figures prompted by a strictly intellectual notion of altruism that could be separated out from the real-world process of intimately familiarizing themselves with the predicaments of the ones they helped.

For altruists with an impartialist orientation such as Gandhi and King, the actual *caring* for someone takes place in two phases. The first phase is quite possibly a rational derivation of the common respect owed to all human beings by virtue of their humanity, the discovery of which makes them worthy of care and attention. The second phase, however, is the "getting to know" the other in his or her otherness so as to be able to supply an appropriate response. It is in this second phase that the motivation for altruism takes effect and reason gives way to a more immediate sentiment. Here, in phase two, the impersonal is made personal and the altruist is able to act on what reason recommends. Although reason gets the ball rolling, the other moral sentiments are required to get the job (i.e., the altruistic deed) done. Thus, even for those who are clearly impartial in their moral outlook, like King and Gandhi, it is not at all clear either that reason is what exclusively motivates their impartiality, or that endeavoring to acquaint themselves personally with their recipients is not ultimately required en route to the performance of the altruistic deed.[34]

The second, more serious question to consider is whether impartiality ought to take precedence over special relations in the first place. In chapter one we considered the example offered by Bernard Williams of whether it is morally incumbent on the man poised to rescue his wife from a potentially fatal accident to reason judiciously that she is a human being among other human beings in need of his help, who, for *this* reason, stands as a legitimate object of his aid and assistance. Williams calls the thought that in addition to being the man's wife she is a human being as such, "one thought too many." His point is that the person in need of help is *not* just anybody, but the man's wife, and that there is something a little inappropriate about his being motivated to rescue her for any more pressing consideration than that she is his wife. It is the nature of special relations to confer upon the one involved in such a relationship special duties. If Williams is right, then we must wonder why preferential treatment would not be considered a legitimate criterion to weigh in discussions about altruism.

As we discussed in chapter one, it is nearly impossible to present a knock-down argument normatively prioritizing one type of recipient over another. The debate provoked by impartialist versus partialist approaches to identifying the recipient of other-regard goes back to the ancient philosophers. In the *Republic*, Plato mounts a case for the eradication of all family relationships among the Guardians for the sake of the pursuit of a higher good, only to have the moral good of family life philosophically retrieved by his successor, Aristotle, in books one and two of the *Politics*.[35] For Aristotle, the bonds formed in family and friendship were constitutive models of virtue, and not merely in the sense that particular relations in themselves were tantamount to the good life. Aristotle argued that it is a psychological if not a biological truism that human connection in general begins with caring for the ones we already know, either because we were bound to know them in the course of our lives or because we know them accidentally. We learn to give to the stranger, in other words, by first giving to our loved ones and friends. In the *Nicomachean Ethics*, Aristotle emphasizes this phenomenological point: goodwill alone is at best "inactive" and does not yet imply altruism, for altruistic deeds must be based in a genuine, loving relationship.[36] William Galston elaborates upon this Aristotelian point:

> Acting on behalf of others requires effective identification with them, which requires in turn that we be able to experience their feelings as our own. . . . Aristotle is arguing, in effect, that rational altruism provides at most a motive for desiring the good of others, but not for acting on that desire. The movement from desire to action is mediated by sympathy, but sympathy is inherently limited in scope. Full-blown altruism is necessarily particular altruism; full-blown cosmopolitan altruism is virtually inconceivable.[37]

Altruism that remains entirely in the abstract is ineffective. To act on the desire to help others, one must, to a certain extent, identify with them. This is not to deny the existence of an impartialist orientation on the part of noteworthy altruists. Clearly Gandhi and Martin Luther King Jr. were cosmopolitan altruists, as were, for example, the rescuers of Holocaust victims who over a period of years saved scores of strangers while putting themselves and their own families at great risk. However, their giving was made possible by a concrete orientation to the particular situations of their recipients. Whether or not impartiality is a normatively superior value on the basis of reason's recommendation, it remains lexically ancillary to the personal bonds that enable it.

Of course, there are those whose gifts reach beyond their capacity to get to know their recipients personally. Gandhi and Martin Luther King Jr. did not personally know everyone they helped over the course of their lives. But in these cases there is a sense in which the altruists have made an effort to learn about the socioeconomic environments and hardships of their beneficiaries as well as to place themselves in relative proximity to them. In other words, the altruists in these cases have genuinely attempted to empathize with the predicament of those they helped, and in a surprisingly large number of instances, in spite of logistical limitations, have even managed to walk the proverbial mile in their shoes.[38] At least a good-faith effort in the direction of personal knowledge seems necessary for cosmopolitan altruism.

This is not even yet to bring up the supporting point that moral universality of the sort recommended by Kantians and consequentialists, in the form of cosmopolitan altruism, might be procured at the *cost* of moral particularity.[39] In Camus' *The Plague*, Dr. Rieux stays behind to care for the victims of Oran at the expense of being with his wife. We have already discussed the example of Holocaust rescuers, whose noble heroics put not just themselves but also their families in jeopardy. Certain types of grand moral heroism, as both Susan Wolf and William Galston point out, imply a sentimental unresponsiveness that would make mundane yet crucial forms of caring remote possibilities. The sentiments keep the internal pilot light of compassion lit.

Also central to the issue of impartiality is the related matter of self-flourishing and its compatibility with other-regard. Our capacity to give to others is tied to our self-worth and ability to determine for ourselves our aims, ambitions, and objects of value. As Jean Hampton writes:

> To love another deeply should not mean to lose all sense of oneself in another's personhood and to be unable to make any independent claims of one's own. Self-sacrifice cannot be commendable if it springs from self-abnegation.... If we are so "altruistic" that we become unable to develop and express ourselves properly, we become unable to give to others what they may want more than anything else.[40]

If altruism is a part of our development into flourishing human beings, then it benefits us to characterize ourselves as self-affirming rather than self-denying givers whenever we assume altruistic burdens. But this, in turn, entails embracing rather than eschewing the natural motivation we sometimes feel to act on behalf of those with whom we have formed special bonds, undergone memorable and life-building experiences, and made plans, for these experiences are also central to one's development into a flourishing self. Our human worth and self-authorship cannot be determined apart from our own particularity and that of those with whom we interact.

There is a connection between caregiving itself and the particular relationship that exists between the caregiver and the beneficiary. This connection is tied to the concept of self-flourishing. Altruism is a shared activity, an organic process through which the participants refine their identity by virtue of their interaction with one another. An other-regard that is motivated purely by reason, and thus takes no account of the relationship between the parties involved in the altruistic activity, can neither accommodate the variety of demands that recipients place on givers nor equip givers with sufficient incentive to be effective responders for their recipients. We have arrived at the central constructive question of this chapter: what positive, psychologically realistic role can reason play in human altruism? We conclude chapter five by examining what might be characterized as a philosophical *via media* between the naturalistic view that altruism is made possible only through the biological resources made available by our nature as animals and the Kantian or consequentialist view that reason alone ought to govern our other-regarding activities. How do our animality and our distinctively human capacity for reason combine to make us the "altruistic species"? In answering, we turn our attention to Aristotle.

ARISTOTLE, HUMAN BIOLOGY, AND PRACTICAL REASON

Late in his career, Alasdair MacIntyre, perhaps the most famous of all the contemporary neo-Aristotelians, wrote a book entitled *Dependent Rational Animals* in which he traced our psychological and moral development from its beginning stages of infancy and childhood, when we are most reliant on the nurturing of our elders, to our moral maturity as "independent practical reasoners."[41] MacIntyre argues that our dependence on others and ultimate independence as beings capable of practical reason are inexorably linked. Early on, we learn the significance of kindness and love as each of us benefits from these affections or suffers from their absence. Over time our exposure to kindness and love makes us eligible to become virtuous actors. This happens as we morally develop, learning how to apply judiciously the sentimental capacities with which we are biologically endowed. MacIntyre's title deliberately evokes two seemingly contradictory features of human experience that in actuality complement each other: our vulnerability as beings in need of care and our self-sufficiency as beings independently able, through reason, to know and understand why care is a moral necessity. We need others to survive and prosper and so have evolved to exist in mutually supportive relationships with people we encounter on a regular basis. The self-awareness of this ongoing experience, however, feeds into a broader moral horizon governed by our place as human beings among other human beings (and other living creatures as well).

Thus, in the Aristotelian view, affection and reason are not moral resources that cancel each other out. They work together to prompt the expansion of our virtuous character. How, exactly, does this happen? This is really to ask two questions: How do the affections, rooted in our biological experience and manifested in our childhood development, enable our capacity for reasoning and equip us for a "wider" sort of altruism? And, conversely, how does human reason represent an added value to the sentiments and ensure that our relationships do not remain tied to egoistic motives?

The first question asks about the scope of other-regard. How do grounding experiences with the affections, which typically involve a caretaker and a cared-for, feed into universal morality? Aristotle's response reveals his sensitivity to the biological conditions that initially govern the contours of human care and concern. It entails what might be labeled a thesis of "building up,"[42] wherein the virtues of sympathy and benevolence are learned traits refined through the practice of cultivating familiar relationships first, and, over time, less familiar relationships. Aristotle writes:

> [A] parent would seem to have a natural friendship for a child, and a child for a parent, not only among human beings but also among birds and most kinds of animals. Members of the same race, and human beings most of all, have a natural friendship for each other; that is why we praise friends of humanity. And in our travels we can see how every human being is akin and beloved to a human being.[43]

In speaking of "friendship" Aristotle refers broadly to the *philial*, relational love displayed in an altruistic sharing of a common good. Two people are friends if each wants the other to flourish for the other's sake and if they each know and rejoice in this fact.[44] The other-regard being expressed in Aristotle's description is admittedly limited to community, if not family. It extends out in concentric circles only on the condition that the giver and receiver stand in a mutually acceptable relationship to each other. In other words, the altruism that such a process implies remains reciprocal. It is neither ultimately self-serving nor asymmetrically focused in one direction, from giver to receiver. Still, according to Aristotle, "belovedness" is genuine other-regard. It is vibrant, self-sustaining, and without egoistic motive even if it simultaneously involves the self-love of desiring to see oneself existing and flourishing in the context of such relationships. Moreover, for Aristotle it is indeed not only possible but normal to move from one level of special relation to the next, more diffuse one. Our rudimentary situations of dependency and formed bonds of concern endow us with the opportunity to become more skilled givers and receivers. That is, through the *practice* of loving and being loved, in the Aristotelian account, we prepare to love and be loved in wider, less obviously self-serving environments. Just as any skill is harnessed, through experiencing caring and being cared for in familiar, repetitive environments, we get better at the activity. This is how our biological proclivities for kin-selected behavior, group-selected behavior, and reciprocity give way to less conditional, partial, and self-protecting forms of other-regard.

It is at this point that reason steps in to refine moral development further. Aristotle is clear that, in the case of human beings, ethics must not be guided by feeling alone but rather by practical reason—deliberate and reflective scrutiny resulting in "fine" action—through recourse to which the raw resource of feeling can be honed into virtue. Virtue is a character state apropos to both self-flourishing and other-regard. Like feeling sometimes does, virtue involves a self-regarding desire to care for others and experience joy when their condition improves. However, it is more stable than feeling because it is the result of a self-conscious effort to sustain the good. In this sense, virtue remains more within human control than does feeling.

In the Aristotelian account, virtue corresponds to objective[45] standards of moral betterment for which the virtuous agent should always be striving. In contrast, the ethical naturalist believes that ethical "striving" is akin to pushing too hard against our nature. According to the ethical naturalist, what we *should* do is what we *would* (naturally) do. Like Kantians and consequentialists, Aristotelians are not satisfied with the naturalist's answer to the ethical question "What should I do?" As human beings, we are works in progress who, because of our ability to direct and realize our aims intelligently, should aspire to be better than we currently are. Unlike the Kantian and consequentialist view, however, the Aristotelian approach to acquiring virtue emphasizes that we are particular persons who stand in particular relationships with others. As a result, morality will demand different things from different people at different times as well as different things from the same person at different times. Virtue is a function of the character development of particular agents over time. This is something that does not happen in isolation but in relation to others.

In Aristotelian ethics, then, there is a distinctive emphasis on being over doing, on *becoming* virtuous people over *performing* right actions. Precisely what morality demands of us in terms of our obligations to others and in terms of our own self-flourishing depends on the circumstances and particular pace at which we each advance, in our own lives, toward moral betterment.[46] This is a matter of practical reason. As we reflect on the good, which crucially involves the good of others, and orient ourselves toward its pursuit, we become more virtuous. In acquiring more virtue, we in turn become better at seeing what our responsibilities for others are, and become more adept at exercising the courage and perseverance required to act responsibly.[47] In this way our character develops and we become better equipped to serve others and flourish ourselves. In this process, reason does not provide us with an abstract prescription for what any agent in our shoes would do or for what will mathematically lead to an increase in the overall good. Rather, it directs us to distinguish between pleasure and the good, between appetite and what is nourishing. Reason leads us to introspect, to know ourselves as beings who flourish when others are flourishing alongside us, and to use without overusing the sentimental resources with which we are biologically endowed to seek this end.

This analysis has implications for how we are to understand altruism. Other-regard and self-regard are connected to each other and are together jointly opposed to naked self-interest. In this vein, Aristotle speaks of a "good form" of self-love that is conducive to altruism and in opposition to a life of self-gratification supported by feeling only. Aristotle explains:

> Those who are unusually eager to do fine actions are welcome and praised by everyone. And when everyone competes to achieve what is fine and strains to do the finest actions, everything that is

right will be done for the common good, and each person individually will receive the greatest of goods, since that is the character of virtue. Hence, the good person must be a self-lover, since he will both help himself and benefit others by doing fine actions.[48]

Practical reason helps us to craft our virtuous character by showing us how to modify instinct in order to promote the good of others, and in turn make room for our own participation in the good. Character improvement is in this sense a matter of self-education in tandem with education at the hands of mentors whose advice can be trusted because they are more virtuous than we are. Moral education results in the transformation of unrefined inclinations into virtuous norms and, as MacIntyre puts it, turns us into "neither self-rather-than-other-regarding nor other-rather-than-self-regarding [individuals], but [into] those whose passions and inclinations are [now] directed to what is *both* our good and the good of others."[49] Altruism is a shared activity. It is the counterpart to the good sense of self-regard, but this in no way implies that in desiring the betterment of the other, we do not also do so for his or her sake. This coincidence of self- and other-regarding aims is comparable, in the Aristotelian view, to the compromise that is drawn between biological inclination and reason in terms of what provides the incentive for moral conduct. We ought to strive against the self-interested limitations with which we are naturally endowed to the greatest degree possible, without attempting to transcend human nature altogether.

Sometimes being virtuous will involve the sort of self-sacrifice that only reason can reveal. For example, Aristotle remarks that the virtuous person "labors" for those for whom he or she cares, will forego money, honors, and other cherished possessions for their sake, "and will die for them" if he or she must.[50] The motivation for self-sacrifice is not the narrow biological incentive of survival but the more complicated and distinctively human ambition, made accessible through practical reason, of realizing the good. Through reason we become informed that the path of self-sacrifice can sometimes lead more quickly to flourishing than do its pleasurable or even instinctively efficacious alternatives. This is one way in which an Aristotelian ethic improves upon an ethical naturalism that recognizes only the biological resources provided by kin selection, reciprocity, and group dynamics as realistic or legitimate displays of altruism. At the same time, reason is not the whole story in the Aristotelian account, for it always remains subject to the particularity of the moral agent exercising it. Kantianism and consequentialism, in relying exclusively on reason to dictate action, allow little space for moral options that afford different agents the ability to flourish at the pace at which they are able to flourish. As such, those moral frameworks are not as psychologically realistic as Aristotelian ethics. In acknowledging the role that our biological tendency toward partiality plays in our decision making and action, Aristotelian ethics does a better job of accounting for what spurs us to be moral beings than do its impartialist alternatives.

The Kantian and consequentialist ambition for us to become immediately and radically more altruistic than we are in nature exists at the expense of the viability of these moral theories for the kinds of animals we actually are, namely, beings who locate meaning in our identity and in the relationships that our identity allows us to cultivate. In taking into account what human beings care most deeply about, including self-projects and particular attachments, the Aristotelian alternative advances altruistic norms more realistically than these two other alternatives. It does this, moreover, while managing not to succumb to ethical naturalism. Thus, whereas the Aristotelian prescription for altruism is not as demanding or as far-reaching as that in Kantianism and consequentialism, it is more sensitive to what actually motivates human beings to engage in other-regarding behaviors. As such, it represents, on balance, the more feasible moral framework. Like the rival theories, the Aristotelian approach to ethics relies on the human recourse to reason, but as a supplement to rather than as a replacement for the proclivities we naturally possess. Reason works to refine our desires, desires that by themselves only partly inform us of what we need to do to participate in the good. Without the human capacity for reason, ethical naturalism would be the best we could do (morally speaking).

By availing ourselves of our rational faculties, there is only so much we can do. Such is the prognosis, in any case, from within the point of view of the philosophical approaches that we have considered in this chapter. Many whose worldviews are governed by religious ways of life heartily concur. For them, morality as a whole is unrealistic without a religious motivation behind it. It is to an understanding of altruism from the perspective of the religious mindset that we now turn.

6

Religious Perspectives
Altruism, Saints, and Believers

WITH GOD'S HELP

"God bids us to do what we cannot, that we may know what we ought to seek from him,"[1] St. Augustine once famously remarked. Augustine's sentiment is not defeatist. Nor does he endorse a whimsical God bent on asserting his power, or one who wishes to frustrate the human being made in his image. Rather, the statement reflects Augustine's deep conviction about the centrality of God to everything we do, including everything we do morally. Although the utterance may seem to refute the maxim "ought implies can," it does not, for what is being affirmed as impossible is not our attempting to meet our moral demands but our attempting to do so without God's help.[2] By ourselves, we are capable of little more than ephemeral achievements. With a divine relationship and influence, by contrast, we have the capacity to distinguish ourselves within the animal kingdom.

Understood in this light, Augustine's remark functions to affirm conventional assumptions about human nature as well as corresponding naturalist concerns about the limits confronting us when we try to be responsible for others needing our help. Augustinians, along with other religious thinkers of a variety of stripes, share the commonsense theorist's skepticism about the capacity for philosophical ethical systems based on reason to deliver us from our predominantly selfish predicament. As we saw in the preceding chapter, good reasons do not necessarily result in effective motivation for moral action. Augustine, preoccupied with the inconstancy of all things man-made, certainly shares this doubt about a goodness inherent in human nature. We do not have the resources to solve our problems by ourselves, including the moral ones. We are not that self-sufficient. Contra Kantians and consequentialists, and with the majority of ethicists who insist that feasible ethical frameworks must also be psychologically realistic, Augustine maintains that our natural moral abilities are insufficient for us to act altruistically on more than an exceptional basis. Unlike naturalists, however, Augustine sees this as an unacceptable state of affairs. Just because, due to finitude, we have limitations, morally and otherwise, it is not *all right* to settle for a less than demanding standard of other-regard. His solution to the problem is classically religious in orientation: with the grace of God's intervention, the otherwise morally impossible becomes possible. Himself among those quick to point out the unwelcome moral implications of committing the "naturalistic fallacy," Augustine proposes that we need not be satisfied with the way we are in the state of nature. There are resources from within religion to make us otherwise.

The purpose of chapter six is to examine this claim more thoroughly and in a broader context. How might we describe *religious* motivations to meet our moral demands, and to what extent does ethics, and altruism in particular, depend in the first place on religion? What motivation can religion offer that reason cannot to move us beyond the biological limitations of our moral development?

To address these questions, we must first bring some clarity to the notion of "religious motivations." Just as there is no such thing as "religion" in the abstract, independent of the particular religious traditions that give the concept its content, so it is disingenuous to speak of a single "religious" motivation for altruism, as if it were one thing. Some religious traditions, such as Buddhism, are nontheistic and so do not refer to a deity that could intervene in human affairs. The commandment to love the neighbor inherent in the various articulations of the Golden Rule ("Love thy neighbor as thyself . . ."), well known in Western traditions such as Judaism, Christianity, and Islam, is absent in Buddhism. Nevertheless, there are ethical concepts in disparate traditions that it does make sense to compare cross-culturally. For example, whereas Christians speak of agape, an unconditional love of the other for the other's sake, one of the fundamental tenets of both Theravada and Mahayana Buddhists is *karuna*, or compassion for all sentient beings, the cultivation of which is understood as a crucial element of the key doctrine of Anatta ("no-self").

Agape and *karuna* are surely similar concepts, in terms of their function if not their specific content. Analogous concepts that refer to other-regard are not merely present, but emphasized, in all of the world's major religious traditions. And, to continue with our example, although agape and *karuna* are notions that manifest differently in Christianity and Buddhism, both constitute a powerful impetus for their practitioners to move beyond the limited other-regarding capabilities available to them without religion. Jacob Neusner and Bruce Chilton, editors of a recent volume called *Altruism in World Religions*, argue that this claim applies to all of the world's traditions, not just Christianity and Buddhism. On the first page of the book they write:

> All world religions concur that altruism—unrewarded action for the sake of another person—is virtuous. All world religions encourage sacrifice of one's own interests for those of another— a stranger, an outsider. Each religious tradition frames altruism in its own context, however.[3]

Although Neusner and Chilton's definition of altruism is perhaps too restrictive,[4] their larger point, that altruism is centrally present in a cross-cultural context, is well taken. Although inevitably different—and sometime even untranslatable from one to another—disparate religious traditions arguably do have in common the capacity to enable their adherents to bridge the gap between the moral capabilities with which nature endows them and their actual moral demands. In other words, religious traditions provide believers with a motivation to be altruistic that those persuaded by reason's reasons could well lack.

Since constraints of space prohibit us from examining how all the world's major religious traditions, or even several of them, provide their constituents with moral motivation, we will focus here on the two examples of Christianity and Buddhism, recognizing that we could just as easily have chosen to focus on others. We pretend to do descriptive justice neither to the theological ethics that correspond to all denominations under the general heading of "Christianity" nor to the many normative systems implied by the various nontheistic subtraditions of Buddhism. Our analysis of Christianity and Buddhism will be basic and broad enough to cover the subdivisions to which both traditions have given rise, although in-depth enough to give the reader a general understanding of the religious motivation for other-regard that pervades each. We hope to show that there is a distinctive ethos that attaches to a religious worldview, an ethos that has implications for human altruism.[5] If nothing else, Christianity, Buddhism, and the other religious traditions of the world are similarly functional *human* derivations, which have historically been enormously influential in helping large numbers of people to alleviate suffering everywhere.

Exemplars of these traditions, whom we may call "saints," transform the religious imperatives to alleviate suffering into a vocation. In one language or another, they attribute their good works to a "love" they have come to possess for their beneficiaries. The rationale and nature of this love cry out for explanation. After our discussion of Christianity and Buddhism, we will inquire into "sainthood" as a concept and its relation to altruism. In that section we will delve into hagiographical accounts of benevolence, in the process looking at some figures who have been proposed as world "saints," for example, Gandhi, Martin Luther King Jr., and the Dalai Lama. These figures maintained throughout their lives that they were to be emulated rather than admired. Thus, we examine the "saintly claim" that altruism is something both accessible to and morally required of ordinary mortals and assess the arguments of one moral theorist who wishes to normalize saintly "excessivity." This is a move that, in turn, raises an issue that perennially preoccupies those working in ethics: namely, to what extent is morality dependent on religion? To what extent must we *be* Hindu, Christian, or Buddhist in order to act upon the convictions that govern saintly figures such as Gandhi, Martin Luther King Jr., and the Dalai Lama? If we fail to embrace a particular religious worldview and undertake the religious commitments to which they correspond, will the normative imperatives that emerge from these worldviews fall on deaf ears?

One advantage of philosophical ethical systems based on reason is that their aspirations are by definition universal. The appeal they make is independent of our beliefs. The problem with such approaches, as we discovered in the last chapter, is that people are different and are therefore understandably motivated differently. The particularity of religious traditions allows for flexibility among different moral agents. Yet, it is hardly a requirement of religious traditions that they be rational, and, as world events all too frequently confirm, religions often strike the global mindset as irrational, sometimes even destructive. The upshot of this reality about the nature of religions is that we cannot unconditionally rely on them to solve all our ethical problems. Some people will not be swayed by religious worldviews to begin with, and religious worldviews are not guaranteed to lead to altruistic outcomes. Thus, just as we discovered (in chapter five) limits to how far approaches based on reason can take us in terms of widening and deepening our circle of concern, so we must consider in this chapter worries about whether religious motivations for morality can influence nonbelievers.

At the same time, our conclusion is not pessimistic. Along with the psychological heuristics discussed in chapter four and the philosophical ethical frameworks considered in chapter five, religion represents a distinctively human resource through recourse to which "nature can be nurtured." Acknowledging that an appeal to religion will not result in a morally positive outcome for everyone, we nonetheless think it noteworthy that religious traditions in cultures across the globe give rise to the motivation to be altruistic. If *some* points of intersection (e.g., agape/*karuna*) can be gleaned through a comparative analysis of discrete religious traditions, as we hope to show in this chapter, then it follows that the religious motivation to be altruistic is in principle applicable to anyone. What this means is that there is at least one respect in which religion and science are compatible with each other. Religious traditions, which make similar claims about the human condition and our capacity to transform ourselves, stand, in their own particular ways, to improve upon and expand the limited biological capacities for other-regard with which most human beings are born.

CHRISTIANITY, ALTRUISM, AND THE SECOND LOVE COMMANDMENT

One way of contrasting reason-based and faith-based models for the duty to become more other-regarding is to characterize the former as "horizontal" and the latter as "vertical" in orientation. The imperative to widen and deepen the circle of concern in reason-based ethical theories issues from the self and is directed toward others. Reason alone is what morally binds human beings qua human beings to one another. Everyone has the same moral status. To express this state of affairs, we may imagine the two-dimensional image of a bicycle wheel in which the commandment to be other-regarding travels outward from the center, along the spokes, in all directions. The center of the wheel is the prospective altruist; the one in need can reside anywhere and at any distance on one of the spokes that radiate from the center around a 360-degree circumference. By contrast, in many religious traditions, and particularly Western theistic ones, the apt geometric model is a three-dimensional cone at the apex of which sits God. In this model, the motivation to be altruistic comes from God. The altruist's love of God is necessary because it supplies him or her with the ability to respond to others in need. Thus, in the religious model, whether directly (between human being and God) or indirectly (between God and the recipient of altruism, via the giver), love travels vertically rather than horizontally. Each act of altruism forms a three-dimensional, right-angled triangle between God, giver, and recipient. The simultaneous performance of altruistic deeds by several human beings, by implication, invokes the image of the cone, described above.

In the Christian tradition, the vertical component of the altruistic act can be inferred from the two "love commandments." The first of these commandments is to love God with all one's heart (Matt. 22:37–38; Mark 12:28–30; Luke 10:26–27). Through God's grace we become equipped to fulfill the second of the great injunctions, to love the neighbor just as we would love ourselves (Mark 12:31; Luke 10:27ff.). The second love commandment, we immediately notice, is made possible in virtue of the first. God is ultimately the source of all the love we display toward one another. Standing in vertical relation to his devotees, who rest at all points on the plane below, God awakens in them both the knowledge that they should love one another and the capacity to act accordingly. For Christians, each instance in which one obeys the second love commandment entails this triangulation.

At this point, it will be helpful to take a closer look at the Gospels in which the second love commandment is announced, most famously, in the Good Samaritan parable. Perhaps its clearest rendering comes from Luke 10:

> "You shall love ... your neighbor as yourself." ... "And who is my
> neighbor?" Jesus replied, "A man was going down from Jerusalem
> to Jericho, and he fell among the robbers, who stripped him and
> beat him, and departed, leaving him half dead. Now by chance a
> priest was going down the road; and when he saw him he passed
> by on the other side. So likewise a Levite, when he came to the
> place and saw him, passed by on the other side. But a Samaritan,
> as he journeyed, came to where he was; and when he saw him, he
> had compassion, and went to him and bound up his wounds,
> pouring on oil and wine; then he set him on his own beast and
> brought him to an inn, and took care of him. And the next day he
> took out two denarii and gave them to the innkeeper, saying, 'Take
> care of him; and whatever more you spend, I will repay you when
> I come back.' Which of these three, do you think, proved neigh-
> bor to the man who fell among the robbers?" He said, "The one
> who showed mercy on him." And Jesus said to him, "Go and do
> likewise." (Luke 10:27–37)

At least four things in this parable give us an indication of the nature and motivation of altruism as traditionally understood within the Christian tra-

dition. First, and most obviously, altruism is commanded. It is not merely a
virtue but also a duty (Luke 10:27). The faithful disciple of Jesus has no
option but to love the neighbor as him- or herself. Second, the neighbor can
be anyone, including a stranger walking down any well-traveled road (Luke
10:29). As with Kantianism and consequentialism, the Good Samaritan parable endorses an impartialist ethic. There is not even a morally relevant distinction to be made between the friend and the enemy. This is one of the
reasons that Martin Luther King Jr., a devout Christian, insisted on resisting
the oppressors of African Americans nonviolently. The second commandment, which does not insist that we like anyone, does require us to love everyone, even a white racist. Third, loving the neighbor is based on *compassion*
and, as such, has no restrictions on what it may come to demand of the altruist (Luke 10:33). The appeal to cost is explicitly disallowed. The nature of
compassion is that it responds to the needs of the one suffering, without
regard for what, prudentially, is a "just" or "fair" response on the part of the
giver. Agape can be demanding. Unlike characterizations of altruism found
in evolutionary biology, Kantianism, and consequentialism, altruism is construed in this parable as asymmetric rather than reciprocal. In this sense,
"other" is hierarchically superior to "self." Finally, there is the famous, and
perhaps most controversial, phrase "Go and do likewise" (Luke 10:37). The
Good Samaritan parable makes no allowances for Christians who think
themselves incapable of loving the neighbor or poorly equipped to do so.
Put another way, the parable makes no distinction between the ordinary person and the saint; both are equally to be on the lookout, always in their lives,
for the needy traveler along the Jericho road.

The standard conception of altruism according to the Christian tradition
is therefore exceedingly demanding in four respects. It is not optional; its
scope is maximally broad and can come to include even the enemy; there are
no limits to what sacrifices it may require of us; and there are no dispensa-
tions for ordinary mortals who may not consider themselves up to the
apparently morally strenuous nature of the duty to love the neighbor. This
point is reinforced in the Gospel of John, where the obligation to emulate
Jesus could not be made more explicit: "You call me Teacher and Lord, and
you are right, for so I am. If I then, your Lord and Teacher, have washed your
feet, you also ought to wash one another's feet. For I have given you an example, that you should do as I have done to you" (John 13:13–15). Jesus' example is valuable to the extent that it is taken up by his followers. *Everyone* is
the Good Samaritan. Moreover, everyone has the chance to be the Good

Samaritan. As Jesus observes, since we always have the poor among us, we always have the opportunity to do them good (Mark 14:7). The traditional understanding of altruism in the Christian tradition is so demanding that it beckons us to raise some of the same questions about psychological realism that we considered in chapter five.

In particular, two sorts of issues arise in connection with the Christian's attempt to incorporate the second love commandment into his or her own life on a regular basis. The first has to do with interpreting the commandment itself. Is the Good Samaritan parable meant to be taken literally or rhetorically? Are Christians *really* meant to love the neighbor in the way and to the extent that Jesus implies in the Good Samaritan parable (and in the Sermon on the Mount), or are they merely exhorted to do so as a recommendation? That is, are Christians to take the injunction to love the neighbor with a grain of salt, taking into account real-world concerns, not the least of which is their own self-assessments of what they are, in fact, capable of doing in the first place? In asking this question, we are really asking about the religious motivation to be altruistic. How strong must one's faith be, from within a religious context, to motivate one to love the neighbor for religious reasons? If one must be a devout believer to love the neighbor, does not this state of affairs significantly restrict the number of Christians who are realistically positioned to obey the second love commandment?

The second issue follows from the first. We have seen that to "go and do likewise" poses a significant moral burden. There is a risk that the altruist will become overextended in the process of trying to fulfill it. It is an empirical fact that the needs of the suffering always exceed the resources of those trying to attend to that suffering. But this makes altruism an all-consuming and never-ending task. Is the upshot of the second love commandment, then, to turn us all into moral saints? This is a serious problem for the adherent of Jesus to consider. If the adherent chooses not to "water down" the second love commandment by modifying or ignoring some of the demanding impositions discussed above, then what guarantee is there that it will not also come to comprise the entirety of his or her life? How does the faithful disciple of Jesus fend off the danger of self-exploitation?

The first issue pertains to the interpretation of the second love commandment. Is it to be obeyed, word for word, or is it an ideal more to be admired? We may look to the prominent nineteenth-century Christian theologian Ernst Troeltsch for guidance. In *The Christian Faith*, Troeltsch notes that we have no choice in the present day but to "look through the glass darkly" (1

Cor. 13:12).[6] Human beings are flawed and stained by their necessary place-
ment within history and outside eternity. Since we are not perfect, and most
of us are far from perfect, the attainment of the ideal of Jesus is not realizable in its pure form in this life. For a few Christians whose faith is especially
strong, the religious motivation to be altruistic will be sufficient to close the
gap between what Jesus instructs and what the follower of Jesus will do. For
most Christians, however, what is expected is not perfection itself but that
one try one's best. This distinction has a bearing on how to interpret the second love commandment.

If Troeltsch is right, and there is a difference between being perfect and
striving toward perfection, then perhaps the second love commandment is
to be understood neither as strictly requiring unblemished emulation of
Jesus nor as a mere ideal, meant to be inspirational in a rhetorical sense only.
Rather, it can be seen as a worthy moral objective whose earnest approximation, but not complete fulfillment, is the expected outcome. There are only
a few who can love everyone in the same measure, but everyone has the
capacity to turn his or her heart toward the stranger in need. Whereas believers will vary in the conviction of their belief, which differently equips them
to "go and do likewise," all serious Christians must exert the greatest effort
possible to dispose themselves to become like Jesus. In this way, the power
of the religious motivation to be altruistic is revealed. When the religious
and moral objectives coincide, when the first and second love commandments become one, Christians are best positioned to expand upon the proclivities to love with which nature has endowed them. What makes this
coincidence possible? What separates the convicted believer from the struggling aspirant? A common answer within the Christian tradition refers to
the notion of "grace," the gift of a loving God, which is partly up to the individual and partly beyond the individual's control. Grace determines the
strength of one's faith. In Christianity, grace is measured in terms of one's
surrender to the divine presence that inspires moral conduct. Since this
occurrence is not completely up to the believer, people's response to the "religious motivation" will vary sharply.

This leads us to ask what role Christian ethics, or religious ethics of any
sort, ought to play in setting our moral standards in society. If the capacity
to be religiously motivated to participate in altruistic activity is dependent
on a notion like grace, how applicable can the injunction to "go and do likewise" be to the one not graced, such as the struggling Christian, or to the
nonbeliever? In responding, it is important to bear in mind that the purpose

of this chapter is to explore religion as a *possible* nurturing resource for our natural moral abilities. Even if some Christians claim that there is no other path but through Christ (John 14:6), we have not. Rather, we see religion as but one powerful route for improving upon the morally limited options afforded by human nature. We acknowledge that the religious route is not available for all travelers, although it is a route that in one form or another appears as an option in all the world's religions for helping the practitioner to become more altruistic.

In light of this clarification, it becomes easier to see how world leaders whose roots are religious come to spread a message that extends beyond their immediate flock. There are enough Christians in the world, as well as practitioners of other religious traditions for whom compassion is a highly prized value, that it is at the very least not foolish to endorse the moral of the Good Samaritan parable as prescriptive for all of society. The message will, of course, be most welcomed by those whose faith is strong. But since it is a message that is cross-culturally persuasive, it will potentially be meaningful to all sorts of people, perhaps awakening in them an impulse to help the neighbor that would otherwise have remained dormant. When religious figures enjoin us on the basis of their religious convictions to give to the poor, the success of their appeal depends more on the universal value they suppose to reside within all of us than on the number of already devout believers they hope to reach. Seen in this light, the moral leadership and political activism in society with which some noteworthy religious figures are characteristically identified are not undertaken in vain. Their efforts on behalf of the suffering and impoverished are compelling to believers *and* nonbelievers and sometimes influential on the latter.

There is thus at least something to the ambitions of ubiquity assumed by devout Christians when they urge society to embrace notions of "voluntary poverty" or "turning the other cheek." Their appeal by example will strike some clearly and others faintly, and the religious motivation to be altruistic will vary depending on how strong one's faith is. But this fact alone does not make the believer's normative vision restrictive in scope. When St. Francis, for example, announced his devotion to "Lady Poverty" in the early thirteenth century, it was not merely an individual vocational choice that he was articulating but a time-tested, proven path to righteousness, if one that his own convictions permitted him to see more clearly than most people did. What is being suggested here is consistent with a point we made when we considered Aristotle's view of other-regard in chapter five: altruism is a matter of practice and repetition, a capacity in principle available to everyone but the realization of which depends on the particularity of the altruist-in-training. The Christian tradition (as well as other religious traditions) taps into a fundamental propensity of human beings to flourish in the act of giving. Christianity, and religion generally, is neither necessary for other-regard nor accessible to all who stand to extend their other-regarding capacities. At the same time, there are enough Christians—and other religious practitioners—among us that it behooves us to take seriously the aspirations of broadness in scope intended in the phrase "go and do likewise." Indeed, there is never a shortage of opportunities for anyone to be altruistic, and we never know in advance just who will turn out to resonate with "the strategy of the cross."

This practical qualification, which justifies the aspirations of universality inherent in the Christian ideal to love the neighbor, is countered, however, by another sort of practical consideration that raises questions about the authority of the ideal even for Christians themselves. This is the concern of exploitation. Jesus' exhortation to "resist not evil" (Matt. 5:39), a direct corollary to the second love commandment, prompts the cynic to invoke Jack London's Wolf Larsen, whose life philosophy is that the strong prey upon the weak. When we turn the other cheek, what is to prevent the egoist who rejects the principles of neighbor-love from becoming a freeloader in society, from prudentially applying cost-benefit analysis to gain as much as possible from society's givers? If human beings have the capacity both to be selfless and to be selfish, and religious and nonreligious for that matter, then we should anticipate that there will be some opportunistic, callous members of society among us who will take advantage of the believer's trusting and giving disposition. What is more, in addition to those who aim to benefit quietly from society's do-gooders, there will be a significant portion of the population that makes no excuses about the rejection of conventional Judeo-Christian morality in the first place. The twentieth-century German philosopher Friedrich Nietzsche, perhaps the most famous of all the atheists, avers that altruism is based on the hegemonic and demeaning assumption that others are more important than oneself, a falsehood he believes to be perpetuated by Western religious traditions bent on enslaving the weak. Nietzsche argues that altruism is a scam, society's way of keeping the powerful in power and preventing the masses from achieving self-realization. Those who buy into the scam do so at their own peril. "In Christianity neither morality nor religion come into contact with reality at any point," Nietzsche writes in *The*

Antichrist.[7] If enough of us take Nietzsche's declaration to heart, then there is cause to worry that neighbor-love will result in a distortion of justice. For, those of us who do embrace conventional notions about the supposed good-ness of attending to the needs of others are bound unwittingly to suppress our own prospects for survival and success in the real world.

Faced with this cynical objection, thoroughgoing altruists, particularly those acting out of religious motivation, remain undeterred. Their faith in humanity and the corresponding obligation to better it derives from the worldview to which they have committed. There is no objective reason for them to abandon this worldview when they consider that the cynical, alter-native hypothesis represents merely a different understanding of the human condition, which itself requires a leap of faith. As William James once noted of religious belief, one's commitment to the "truth" or "falsehood" of the goodness of altruistic activity inevitably involves backing one sort of horse rather than another.[8] Since both claims are matters of faith, there is no rea-son to presume that the burden of proof should fall on the believer's shoul-ders. Objectively, there is as little evidence available to the defender of Nietzsche to convince the one who values altruistic activity that he or she is misinformed as there is available to the altruist to persuade the cynic of the normative rightness of being good toward others first. Thus, the allegation of "exploitation" cannot plausibly be characterized as exploitation to the one who believes in the fundamental worthiness of other-regard. The clash of assertions and denials of the necessity of other-regard to self-flourishing puts the altruist and the Nietzschean at an impasse and manages to convince neither.

Refusing the cynical view and accepting that helping others is a morally good thing does not, however, completely obviate the risk of exploitation that one incurs in choosing to be altruistic, for there is also a risk of exploita-tion internal to the altruistic activity itself. Even if we reject Nietzsche's argu-ment and accept that altruism is a "good" thing, in the very act of being altruistic one always assumes the risk of exhausting one's resources in attending to the other. In this life, to repeat, the needs of the suffering inev-itably exceed the resources and abilities of those who replenish. To obey the second love commandment without watering it down entails putting one-self "out there" for the sake of someone else. It is a daunting task even for the one who thoroughly rejects the Nietzschean hermeneutic of suspicion. Let us recall what it means in the Christian tradition to live by the second love commandment. Other-regard, as we specified earlier, (1) is not optional; (2) refers to a neighbor who could be anyone; (3) involves sacrifices in which there are no limits to the costs that one might have to incur; and (4) allows for no excuses for those who claim their talents do not easily lend themselves to altruistic activity. To be Christianly motivated to be altruistic, this means, is to gird oneself for a lifetime task, a task bound to fatigue the performer. Moreover, it is to commit to a lifestyle not readily compatible with many other ambitions, even those as basic as making a living, being a good spouse or parent, or pursuing other nonaltruistic but worthwhile activities. It would seem that one who authentically abides by the second love commandment becomes a full-blown saint. But almost none of us is or will become full-blown saints. And trying to be a saint, when one is not, is potentially dangerous. In *Saints and Postmodernism*, Edith Wyschogrod dubs the saintly ethos an "ethic of excess."[9] To devote oneself to alleviating the physical suffering and psychological sorrow of others is to participate in an activity that is by definition "excessive." As we have thus far interpreted it, the second love commandment would make such activity normal. Is Christian ethics intrinsically exploitative in this manner?

We are back to the issue of the close relation of religion and morality. Must the person who even attempts to follow the example of Jesus already be very religious, and, if so, how can the duty of neighbor-love meaningfully be recommended as a broad societal norm? In responding, we must again note that there is a difference between realizing an ideal perfectly and striving for that ideal in earnest by acting *as if* its realization is possible. Sharing one's possessions with the impoverished and loving the enemy are counterintuitive notions, and their adoption has never been tested on a large scale in society. Thus, we simply do not know the extent to which it is possible to eschew violence, or care for the poor, without first seriously attempting to enact policies intended to achieve those ends. There is, to repeat, a difference between perfectly following Jesus' example, by managing to act exactly as he did, and following it perfectly, by fulfilling our potential to act as he did within real-world constraints. We know that we will not perfectly hit the mark. There is no concept of agape that resides outside the sphere of history. This concession, however, does not imply the futility of *trying* to achieve the ideal of agape. There is a middle ground between insisting on an ideal that it is simply unrealistic to adhere to in this life and complacently settling for an ethic that misses the spirit of the ideal altogether.

In *Christ and Culture,* Richard Niebuhr elucidates five models for understanding how Christians can incorporate their religious convictions into the
constraints of the worldly societies they inhabit.[10] Three of these models bear
mentioning here: (1) Christ *against* culture; (2) Christ *of* culture; and (3)
Christ *transforming* culture. The first model, "Christ against culture," pertains to an otherworldly pietism in which the scope of Christian love cannot under any circumstances be limited by pragmatic considerations. In this
model, Christians are construed as "resident aliens"[11] on this contaminated
earth. It is a Christian's duty to love only, even if this occurs at the expense
of procuring justice or protecting one's well-being. (Loving the neighbor, for
example, precludes violence, even when violence is necessary to quell the
tyrant.) Since this life is not the one for which the Christian is ultimately destined, there is no good reason for failing to follow the second love commandment exactly, that is, according to Christ's articulation of it in the Gospels.
In the second model, "Christ of culture," there is a presumed "gospel glow"
over society that is compatible with a liberal, wide-ranging interpretation of
agape. In contrast to the first model, the second allows engaging in violence
as a last resort for the sake of restoring the beloved community or attending
to one's own needs first in order to be available for others. In the "Christ of
culture" model, Christian mores are sensitive to standard convention. The
second love commandment is interpreted rhetorically so as to avoid a dangerous idealism. Finally, in the third model, "Christ transforming culture,"
the kingdom is at once presumed to be both "here" and "not yet." This model
is a *via media* between the first two according to which it is possible for ordinary Christians to meet the demands of the second love commandment in
glimpses. These ethical moments increase in number and duration as Christians dispose themselves to become more compassionate throughout the
course of their lives. In this approach, as Martin Luther King Jr. once put it,
Christians are akin to thermostats that set society's norms rather than ther-
mometers that merely reflect them.[12] The third model grants that in society
we cannot immediately sustain Christian ideals. We are flawed and too
trapped in and contaminated by our own human history to do that. However, this does not mean that society cannot be transformed, "little by little,"[13] over the long haul.

The "Christ transforming culture" perspective allows us to understand how
an ethical ideal that is unrealizable in itself can still compel its adherents to
raise their overall standards. Acting *as if* the second love commandment is a
legitimate governing ethos can be an enterprise that is psychologically real-

istic, even while morally demanding. The Christian who attempts to live literally by Christ's example is neither naïve nor impractical. Self-reflective
Christians, the Catholic theologian Stephen Pope observes, see the imperative to emulate Christ as a means of improving upon the not yet fully developed "emotional constitution" to love with which evolution furnishes us.[14]
The implication of this observation is that the commandment to love the
neighbor is not some foreign imposition but rather an organic spur to refining existing capacities. Human beings, and by extension human societies, are
malleable. However "unnatural" it may be to insist that everyone become
maximally loving to the neighbor in the immediate present, it is perfectly
natural to regard love itself as a reasonable norm for society to pursue. The
process theologian Thomas Oord concurs with the constructive normative
thrust of the "Christ transforming culture" model. He suggests that we ought
to be neither overly optimistic nor unduly pessimistic about the human
capacity for love to grow. As he puts it, love is "progressional," a relational
activity that feeds off its own momentum once it is taken seriously both by
the one who loves and by the one who is loved.[15] Oord's view is consistent
with Pope's claim that religious traditions can awaken in us the ability to act
on other-regarding (and other-receiving) traits with which we are latently
endowed. Christianity, as Pope puts it, is a matter of "grace improving upon
nature" *within* the context of our historical, embodied, social existence.[16]

BUDDHISM, ALTRUISM, AND *KARUNA*

It takes more than one dot to construct a line. To have any hope of establishing an "altruistic" component to religion, we must show its presence in more
than one tradition. While constraints of space limit us to examining only one
additional tradition, we believe that we could have selected just about any
religion for this purpose, for other-regard represents a central part of the
ethos of all the major traditions. We chose Christianity and Buddhism as our
case studies in this chapter not only because one is "Western" and the other
"Eastern," but also because the worldviews of these two traditions differ so
considerably, in spite of their common endorsement of the norm of other-
regard. Whereas for Christians the process of becoming more loving involves
a self-transformation that hinges on the harnessing of other-regarding
(agapic) traits already in part provided for us by the process of evolution, for
Buddhists loving one another assumes a self-transcendence that implies the
dissolution of self-interest—and, in fact, the idea of the self—altogether.

Karuna, or "compassion," denotes the virtue to which Buddhists begin to have access once they take seriously the Anatta doctrine and relinquish illusory notions about selfhood. As with Christianity, we understand Buddhist ethics as a resource for improving upon that with which nature has endowed us, a resource available only to a percentage of the world's occupants. And as with Christianity, concerns arise in Buddhism with respect to the problems of idealism and exploitation associated with the norm of unchecked other-regard. In this section, as in the preceding one, we investigate the degree to which the Buddhist norm of *karuna* can realistically be adopted by society at large.

Just as one must go to Jesus' own words to extract the ethical gist of Christianity, so it is imperative to examine the message of Siddhartha Gautama, the Buddha, in order to speak intelligibly about Buddhist ethics. Born into royalty in North India during the sixth century B.C., the Buddha decided to forsake his claim to the throne at the age of twenty-nine and left his young wife, Yasodharā, in order to search for a way out of universal human suffering, suffering to which he himself was no less susceptible despite having been brought up with access to every imaginable luxury. These were not gestures of rebelliousness but the beginning of a concerted effort to experiment with a life of meditation and the renunciation of ephemeral, worldly comforts. At the age of thirty-five, the Buddha experienced nirvana while sitting under a Bodhi tree (tree of "enlightenment"), after which he devoted the rest of his life to teaching men and women, brahmins and outcasts alike, about the path that led him out of the cycle of suffering to which all human beings are susceptible at the outset of their lives.[17]

To comprehend how ethical concepts function in the Buddhist traditions,[18] one must first elucidate the Four Noble Truths, which encapsulate the Buddha's message and spell out the worldview of Buddhism generally. The Four Noble Truths, which were first announced in the Buddha's original sermon, are: (1) *dukkha* (all human beings suffer); (2) *samudya* (we suffer because of our attachments, which we crave and to which we cling); (3) *nirodha* (in order to flourish, we must exert effort to stop our suffering); and (4) *magga* (there is a path, called the Eightfold Path, that represents the way out of suffering).[19] The Eightfold Path clarifies correct conduct, correct concentration, and correct wisdom for the practitioner of Buddhism. These categories refer to the actions and states of mind available to us as we begin to take seriously the idea that the attachment to things is a debilitating ailment.

Substantively, the Eightfold Path requires the cultivation of certain virtues and the overcoming of certain vices. For example, correct conduct entails eschewing deception, slander, rudeness, and useless gossip; promoting life-affirming and honorable endeavors; and abstaining from activities that bring harm to others.[20] Correct concentration involves the "energetic will" to prevent whatever is recognized as evil and welcome conditions of warmth and nourishing of all sentient beings, all the while shedding oneself of one's craving for the self-centered distractions with which we are usually preoccupied.[21] This also requires the purging of unwholesome thoughts like envy, self-absorbed anguish, and anger in favor of equanimity and the joy of others. Finally, correct wisdom pertains to the trademark Buddhist virtues of selfless renunciation and peaceful coexistence among all creatures.[22] Violence is ruled out unconditionally, as we would expect it to be in a worldview in which the notions of competition, might, and self-assertion are falsehoods to begin with. The practitioner of Buddhism manages to achieve wisdom through deep meditation, the goal of which is to achieve a state of sober, available presence for all beings by transcending the idea of selfhood entirely. The end of the Eightfold Path coincides with the dissolution of the self and a corresponding condition of "co-arising" according to which no distinctions are made, even on a conceptual level, between one's welfare and that of another. The doctrine of co-arising avers that there is no difference between individual and social betterment; both are fundamentally related and interdependent.[23]

The norms we have just described epitomize altruistic conduct and character. Together these norms form the ethos of complete dissolution of selfish impulses reflected in the state of enlightenment toward which the self-actualized Buddhist traveling down the Eightfold Path is headed. Nirvana literally means the "cessation of suffering." The Buddhist worldview may seem radical to Westerners for whom it is difficult to understand that all misery a by-product of the human struggle with finitude. The Buddha is reported to have said on his deathbed, "Decay is inherent in all component things! Work out your salvation with diligence!"[24] What he meant is that we cause our own suffering by remaining attached to what we should realize is always changing: our material possessions, our projects and ambitions, even our most important relationships with others. Instability is inherent in human existence. We search for permanence in all things impermanent. We all constantly exist in a state of flux. We just don't realize it.

The problem is therefore not with the world; it is with us. To curb our craving for the things to which we are attached, we must exercise self-control.

This we do through following a recipe of self-reliance, meditation, and detached, calm control over our passions. The recipe amounts to love, but a very specific kind of love, one of "indifference" rather than eros. Buddhist ethics does not imply ascetic withdrawal—according to the doctrine of co-arising, the advanced practitioner is expected always to help the novice along—but it does alter the way in which we are normally to think about our-selves in relation to others. For, once we accept the Four Noble Truths and accept that the notion of individuality (and all it implies) is the cause of our suffering, the whole idea of "should," as in what we *should*, as selves, do for others, dissipates. Not seeing ourselves *as* selves, we no longer have to strug-gle to overcome what we normally self-consciously identify as selfishness.

Under these circumstances, we will, as a matter of course, simply do for others. This is in part because those who practice the Anatta doctrine immu-nize themselves to the effects of competitiveness. As the well-known Bud-dhologist Peter Harvey explains, the Anatta doctrine

> undermines the attachment to self—that "I" am a positive, self-identical entity that should be gratified, and should be able to brush aside others if they get in "*my*" way—which is the basis of lack of respect for others. It undercuts selfishness by undercutting the very notion of a substantial self. Anger, for example, feeds off the notion that "I" have been offended. The idea of not-Self does not deny that each person has an individual history and charac-ter, but it emphasizes that these are compounds of universal fac-tors. In particular, it means that "your" suffering and "my" suffering are not inherently different. They are just suffering and so the barrier which usually keeps us within our own "self-inter-est" should be dissolved, or widened in scope till it includes all beings.[25]

To embrace a Buddhist worldview is at once to commit oneself to an ethos of total ego-detachment. In this process, the self paradoxically seeks the relinquishing of its ability to identify its ambitions as its own. The upshot of this process, Harvey suggests, is a kind of virtue ethic in which the aspiring Buddhist cultivates the character states of clear-mindedness (i.e., freedom from distraction), other-awareness, and modesty, buttressed by occasional moments of self-reproach.[26] In this respect, Buddhist and Christian ethics share common ground. While Buddhism does not place an emphasis on the value of individual persons, it does, like Christianity, imply a developmental approach to moral maturity wherein (true) self-flourishing and other-regard coincide. Through training and practice, the Buddhist learns to free him- or herself from the unwholesome grip of shallow dispositions such as neglectfulness, greed, and hatred.[27] With enough training, the very objective of self-dissolution dissolves along with attachment, thereby resolving the paradox mentioned above. (This is sometimes referred to as "the ladder which is to be kicked away.") The advanced practitioner ultimately no longer needs to deliberate about acting in the "right" sorts of ways; he or she will simply see the suffering of another as if it were his or her own and respond immediately to the one in need.[28]

Thus, whereas the Christian is introduced to the concept of agape by command, directed to cultivate this state in response to the central imperatives found in Christianity, in the Buddhist tradition one discovers oneself as compassionate as a *result* of undertaking the spiritual exercises with which a Buddhist worldview is associated. In other words, in Buddhism altruism is the logical extension of a worldview that sees the universe as an interlocking web of interdependent links among all the living things that reside within it.[29] In the case of human beings, compassion, or *karuna*, is the unavoidable consequence of taking the Anatta doctrine seriously. An "expanding circle" of concern, not just beyond kin but beyond one's native species, is the outward effect of the inward movement of self-transcendence. The *Samyutta Nikāya*, one of the earliest Pali texts of the Theravada subtradition, praises the disappearing distinction between kin and stranger for the Buddhist traveling down the Eightfold Path:

> Thus a mother with her life
> Will guard her son, her only child,
> Let him extend unboundedly,
> His heart to every living being.
> And so with loving-kindness for all the world
> Let him extend unboundedly
> His heart above, below, around,
> Unchecked, with no ill will or hate.[30]

Complementing this text in the Mahayana subtradition is the bodhisattva commitment of the highly advanced practitioner, poised on the edge of enlightenment, who elects to forego nirvana and stay in the world of samsara in order to attend to the spiritual (and therefore physical) well-being of every sentient being. Having satisfied the criteria to escape the cycle of suffering, the near-saint resolves nonetheless to "dwell in each state of misfortune through countless ages" for the sake of the salvation of all others.[31] As with the Theravada canon, the Mahayana ideal maintains complementary if seemingly contrasting dual aims of cultivating mental purity through self-transcendence and "returning to the world" to assist others less far along the same path. The more advanced one is in one's contemplative, meditative endeavors, the more likely one is to participate in the furtherance of another's goals. The novice practitioner, by contrast, is directed in both the Theravada and the Mahayana subtraditions first and foremost to begin to look inward and attempt to embrace the Four Noble Truths.

This raises a question that also surfaced in our examination of Christianity: to what extent is universal compassion an ethic that we can realistically expect of the laity within Buddhist communities? In the world of samsara, where suffering because of attachment to worldly things remains an inescapable reality, what are the prospects for those who have only just "entered the stream"[32] to exert a concerted effort into much more than their own spiritual advancement? This is all to ask, How normative is altruism within the Buddhist tradition? Until recently, Western scholars of Eastern traditions have tended to depict religious "others" as exotic ascetics, preoccupied with mystical techniques and practices for the purpose of transporting themselves out of the mundane existence to which most human beings engaged in normal forms of social interaction are thought to be susceptible. Such an impression leads to the charge of escapism, as it implies a characterization of practitioners more concerned with individual withdrawal than communal contribution. Winston King and Melford Spiro, for example, have characterized the ethos of Theravada Buddhism as one of reclusive isolation and the shunning of social and political discourse.[33] The extent to which this picture is accurate bears on the issue of whether or not a Buddhist practitioner can realistically be said to have other-regarding aims. The very term "self-transcendence" makes problematic the notion of a self that maintains the capacity to give to others. How can one who is trying to cultivate detachment make use of the particular knowledge one is arguably required to possess of others in order to love them properly?

The answer has to do with the way in which love and compassion are cultivated within the Buddhist tradition in the first place. While enlightenment and freedom from suffering naturally follow from self-transcendence, the point of undertaking the meditative and spiritual practices that lead to enlightenment is to acquire the successive states of compassion that position the Buddhist practitioner to focus *more* clearly on the precise needs of those in distress. In other words, the ultimate aim of the Buddhist practitioner is not to procure the self-serving reward of escaping the cycle of samsara—although this is the upshot of enlightenment—but rather to develop his or her good character. To be sure, the Eightfold Path is all about instructing the traveler to cultivate a virtuous disposition through right thought and action. Immediately, though, and not just in the case of the enlightened one, the Buddhist is enjoined to give back to his or her community by cultivating a loving attitude toward others that begins with conventional sympathizing and proceeds to the literal substitution of one's own happiness and suffering with those of another.

This progression is evidenced in four specific other-regarding virtues in the Theravada tradition: *metta* (love), *karuna* (compassion), *mudita* (sympathetic joy), and *upekkha* (equanimity). These four cardinal virtues, which supersede one another in terms of the practitioner's accomplishment, correspond to intensifying "levels of absorption." They are defined in the following passage, taken from the classic Theravada text *The Ultimate Light*:

> *Love* is the state of desiring to offer happiness and welfare with the thought, "May all beings be happy," and so forth. *Compassion* is the state of desiring to remove suffering and misfortune, with the thought, "May they be liberated from these sufferings," and so forth. *Sympathetic joy* is the state of desiring the continuity of (others') happiness and welfare, with the thought, "You beings are rejoicing; it is very good," and so forth. *Equanimity* is the state of observing (another's) suffering or happiness and thinking, "These appear because of that individual's own past activities."[34]

Does the dissolution of the concept of selfhood impede altruistic action, or even the requisite ability on the part of prospective altruists to identify with the suffering of others, whoever they may be? Clearly not. It is significant that at the first, rudimentary level, love already minimally entails a wish for everyone's happiness. The Buddha discusses the connection between *metta* and the "mental peace" of all sentient beings in the Smaller Discourse on the Snap of the Fingers, where it is written that one who sustains a loving mind for even the brief duration of a snap is monk-worthy and breathes easier.[35] Since love is the outgrowth of one's own character and not motivated by affective desire, it will have the quality of being in all ways the same with regard to oneself, a dear friend, a neutral person, and an enemy.[36] As love

matures and becomes compassion, sympathetic joy, and, ultimately, equanimity, the practice of other-regard is transformed from a skill in need of
harnessing and refinement to a virtue naturally displayed. The culmination
of the loving virtues, equanimity, endows the practitioner with the quality
of being able to confront life in all its vicissitudes with a tranquil, even mind,
one that best positions him to respond to the other in need.[37] We may conclude that freedom from suffering, while dependent on cultivating detachment from the debilitating notion of selfhood, decisively does not commit
the practitioner to a stance of neutrality about others' misery and happiness.
On the contrary, the Anatta doctrine goes hand in hand with an ethos of
compassionate engagement for the novice just as much as for the master. In
the Buddhist tradition, suffering is as universal as the illusion of selfhood
from which all must wrest themselves. It follows that altruistic action, which
is the consequence of taking the path that leads to the overcoming of suffering, is in principle accessible to any aspiring Buddhist.

Saints

Not only is altruistic conduct thus constitutive of both Christian and Buddhist ethics, as well as of other religious traditions, but it is expected conduct from the ordinary adherent no less than from the especially pious or
advanced practitioner. This is significant. It means that although it may not
initially seem so, the capacity to be altruistic is built into normal human
experience to a greater degree than we might predict given the resources to
be altruistic with which we our provided by our "human nature." In Christianity, the second love commandment is as basic an imperative to try to live
by as there is for the Christian disciple. Likewise, the aspiring Buddhist,
enjoined to accept the wisdom of the Four Noble Truths, must immediately
dispose him- or herself to become loving toward others when embarking on
the journey toward enlightenment. Indeed, if we have interpreted the traditions correctly in this chapter, one cannot successfully practice Christianity
or Buddhism (or, we suspect, any religious tradition that we might have
examined) *without*, at the same time, becoming altruistic.

This qualification has a bearing on how we are to distinguish the exemplars of these traditions, sometimes known as "saints," from the rest of us. If
altruistic activity is part of what is considered to be normative conduct,
appropriate for saints and nonsaints alike, then we must move beyond the
conventional way of clarifying the difference between the saints and our-

selves. It will not do, for example, simply to call attention to a special class of people whose spiritual qualities equip them to be more than minimally altruistic, the presumed limitation for the rest of us. The problem with such an account is that it belies what saints themselves claim in their own voice. "Whether one believes in a religion or not, and whether one believes in rebirth or not, there isn't anyone who doesn't appreciate kindness and compassion," declared the Dalai Lama in his acceptance speech for the 1989 Nobel Peace Prize.[38] Other major "saintly" figures from a variety of religious traditions, such as Hillel, St. Francis of Assisi, Gandhi, and Martin Luther King Jr., concur: there is nothing in their view that is particularly special about them; it is just that they see sooner and perhaps more clearly that our responsibility to ourselves and to others coincides. They are not a different sort of people, meant to be traveling along a different path; they are the same as we, but farther along a path meant for all of us.[39]

According to this understanding, saints are mentors for the rest of us, exemplifiers of virtue without whom we would be slower to get in touch with our better selves. As William James characterizes them, they are "impregnators of the world, vivifiers and animators of potentialities of goodness which but for them would lie forever dormant."[40] Saints, in this view, are quicker than the rest of us to bridge our existence and our essence, our actual, lived experience and the purpose of our being here. But this purpose, certainly according to the religious traditions we have been exploring, is one we all share. In the course of our lives, most of us will not be nearly as successful as saints in closing the gap between existence and essence. As such, a saintly standard of other-regard will *appear* to us as excessive. But this descriptive reality does not let us off the hook normatively.

In this light consider the response of those closest to Dorothy Day, founder of the Catholic Worker movement, when she was officially nominated for canonization by the Claretian Fathers of Chicago. In one letter of protest, Father Daniel Berrigan, S.J., pleaded with the Calertians that this woman's soul "ought not to be stolen from her people," while in another, a fellow Catholic Worker invoked Day's own words—"Don't dismiss me so easily!"—when talk surfaced of her special sanctity.[41] Robert Inchausti echoes this sentiment in his characterization of perhaps the best-known and most inspirational contemporary saint in the Western world. Writing of Mother Teresa, the founder of the order of Missionaries of Charity, he notes that her "life . . . connect[s] us to truths, spiritual sensibilities, and a sense of sacred obligation *that already exist inside us* but are not yet fully realized."[42] The point being developed here is not that we are already "religious" but do not yet know it. It is, rather, that saints do not veer from but epitomize humanity insofar as their tremendous sacrifice and boundless devotion to others is concerned. Their religious traditions help them to actualize this propensity, but it is a propensity that is alive and well, if dormant, in all of us. No doubt, saints develop motivations that can be distinguished one from another, acquired in the context of their diverging religious worldviews, but they are nevertheless uniformly identified by their unusually noteworthy altruistic conduct and orientation. Moreover, these traits by which they are identified distinguish them from the rest of us only by their actuality. The moral potential of saints is something we all share.

The proposal under consideration here, then, is that saints are extraordinary not because they are somehow born different from the rest of us but because they are better than we are at recognizing and acting upon their humanity, the destiny of which (if not the starting point) is to display care and concern for all others. Edith Wyschogrod helpfully clarifies what separates saintliness from ordinary human conduct in the following manner. While a "rudimentary sensitivity" to others exists for everyone, writes Wyschogrod,

> not everyone yields to the pressure of the primordial [self–other] encounter. . . . Saints . . . like gifted composers or musicians are exceptional individuals, virtuosi of the moral life. Almost everyone can reproduce a simple melodic line upon hearing it, but not all are able to perform a Bach cello suite, improvise jazz harmony, or sing lieder. This analogy can be misleading if it is taken to imply that saintliness is something "natural," an inborn talent, rather than the result of copious self-exertion and self-sacrifice.[43]

The distinction Wyschogrod makes between talent and exertion is significant because it implies that altruism is a skill upon which we can improve with sufficient effort, just as we can with respect to other skills. Although in the end only a few will be accurately described as "virtuosi," who those few are is not a foregone conclusion. Anyone could be among them. The self's "primordial" moral event, which takes place as an other confronts us with his or her needs, is universal even though the response to this event will be different for each of us. For most of us, progress will take place in increments, "little by little," as Dorothy Day was fond of saying. Such an account is consistent with the situation of the novice in the Christian and Buddhist traditions, aspiring to harness the virtues of agape and detachment, respectively. They are in *essence* no different than the mentors they emulate. Only their actual, lived *existence* is different.

Wyschogrod maintains that altruism is inherently excessive, always requiring more risk and material divestment in its basic moral demand than the self is in almost all cases likely to be able to give.[44] At the same time, she identifies saints, those few who are able to live consistently according to what she aptly calls an "ethic of excess," as the potentially realizable ideal for all of us. This poses a problem. If the demands of those in need always exceed the giver's ability to replenish, and if the ethic of so giving is by definition "excessive," how can we expect anyone to become a saint? Wyschogrod defines the saint as an "extreme sumptuary, a subject that spends more than she/he has to the point of expending her/his own substance."[45] Invoking Martin Luther King Jr.'s aphorism—insofar as our obligation to the stranger anywhere is concerned, we are born "in the red"—Wyschogrod refers to the "responsible" self as one aware of its default indebtedness to others everywhere, an indebtedness that, upon genuine attempts at repayment, leads to the total consumption of the giver's psychological and corporeal resources.[46] How is this state of affairs, laced, as Wyschogrod acknowledges, with such robust "self-negation," realistically supposed to depict not merely "saintly" but all human moral "essence"? By calling an ethic intended for normative adoption by the majority of society "excessive," Wyschogrod seems to undercut her larger pedagogical objective of shaking from their complacency those who subscribe to widespread, conventional notions of responsibility.

Wyschogrod would respond that she is trying to reclaim the term "excessive"—it is a term not meant to convey any negative connotation but rather to highlight the radical asymmetry to be posited between "self" and "other" in the self–other encounter. "Normal," a term usually cast in contrast to "excessive," is here understood to reflect the presumably healthy balance we customarily strike upon considering how much attention to pay ourselves and how much to pay others when pondering a course of action in any given ethical quandary. According to Wyschogrod, true altruism must move beyond the "normal" assumptions that govern reciprocal relations, which are inadequate. Wyschogrod believes that the "Golden Rule" is neither a guide for how saintly exemplars understand their moral responsibilities nor one to which *we* should turn for our own guidance. She is worried that if one understands the other as a "second self," one's concern for the other has a tendency not to be genuinely other-regarding. It is rather an expression of self-love, more broadly construed. For altruism to occur, the other must remain purely "other," one whose needs and resultant demands cannot be predicted before the face-to-face encounter.

The main point of "radical alterity" altruism is that any conceptualization of the other that understands the other in relation to ourselves is a reduction to "sameness" and therefore, in the end, really selfishness, not other-regard. (As we saw in chapter two, the psychological egoist has claimed this all along!) In Wyschogrod's view, saints are "saintly" insofar as they successfully substitute the concerns of the "other" for their own, without, at the same time, falling into the trap of doing so as part of some other interest of the self. Since the needs of the other are unpredictable in advance of our proximity to the other, displaying other-regard becomes an all-encompassing proposition. To be altruistic, in this understanding, is to devote oneself diligently to altruistic objectives, with little room to do much else. Further, it is to do so not out of some rational, utilitarian motivation, or emotional, affective desire for that matter, but as a kind of religious command that issues from the "trace"[47] of the Divine that resides in the face of the other. Altruism is not represented in isolated activity but in holistic narrative. The dignity in being altruistic is linked to the moral expectation of being altruistic. And this is how what we might conventionally define as "excessive" becomes "normal."

Here, while applauding Edith Wyschogrod's endorsement of the default responsibility we inherit for "everyone, everywhere," we must take issue with the phenomenology of her overall approach. One of the points we made in chapter three is that we *are* interconnected and interdependent, genetically and socially. The "reduction to sameness" about which Wyschogrod is so concerned extends to diminishing the phenomenological effect and importance of sympathy and empathy in equipping one to attend to the needs of another. Wyschogrod argues that to think about the self and the other as alike in fundamental respects entails not desiring the good of the other for his or her sake. But does one really imply the other?[48] Empathy is the identification with the other who faces trouble we have seen ourselves or could easily imagine ourselves facing. Sympathy refers to the trait of compassion, cultivated in response to recognizing the suffering of the individual in need of help, regardless of our familiarity with that individual. Both of these traits do not preclude but enable us to ameliorate the other's suffering and advocate for his or her welfare and well-being, and most important, to do so *for the other's sake*. Yes, as we explained in chapter two, both empathy and sympathy technically represent interests of the self in the sense that we want to act on the motives precipitated by such traits. However, although genuine altruistic motivation may engage psychological mechanisms and motivations that entail ambitions of the self, we are still capable of pursuing the welfare of another for its own sake. The true test of whether our actions or motives are altruistic, in other words, is not whether they are motivated by an interest of the self, but whether the amelioration and betterment of the other represents their ultimate objective. To be sure, this much must be true if altruistic exemplars flourish as selves who strive to bring about the flourishing of others. Hence, the Dalai Lama, Gandhi, and Martin Luther King Jr., rebellious and maladjusted to convention as they were, were capable of experiencing moments of profound happiness, particularly when they were immersed in activities designed to make life better for their beneficiaries.

If we are right, then there is an important, qualified sense in which saints, just like the rest of us, can be said to be individuals in pursuit of their own interests, though not any less altruistic for it. In this case, saints would better be noted for their virtue than for their sacrifice, for although they do make large and frequent sacrifices, those sacrifices are undertaken in the service of a larger, deliberate objective. In their wisdom, saints come to identify themselves with humanity as a whole. This, and not the neglect of themselves, is what motivates them "excessively" to take risks and, if necessary, to stand in harm's way to prevent another from being harmed. What is "excessive" is not the denigration of saints' self-worth but the thoroughness with which saints come to bind their fates to others. Through love, they are able maximally to expand their circle of concern, but not at the expense of finding themselves outside the circle. Indeed, it is by virtue of their inclusion within it that expansion remains a possibility in the first place. Saints are extraordinary and different from the rest of us in the ability and ease with which they avail themselves of the best resources in their religious traditions to propel them to develop their altruistic character. However, their message about the centrality of other-regard to the flourishing of human life is universal. One key aspect of that message is that in relation to them, we remain works in progress. Of saints' encounter with ordinary men and women William James writes: "Treating those whom they meet, in spite of the past, in spite of all appearances, as worthy, they have stimulated them *to be* worthy, miraculously transformed them by their radiant example and by the challenge of their expectation."[49] James implies that altruism is contagious.

Wyschogrod puts the same point a little differently: "The effort to relieve suffering that is *constitutive* of saintly existence may fulfill or fall short of its aim. But even when this effort does not entirely succeed, saintly power can still be *effective* and its results may go deeper: saintly effort, even when it misfires, can morally transfigure other lives."[50] Few of us are realized saints, but we are all saints in the making.

We acknowledge how controversial this conclusion is. Many will object that it is the possession of an otherworldly orientation that allows saints to proceed from a different set of moral assumptions than the rest of us.[51] Some suggest, even more strongly, that sainthood is not even primarily about goodness, moral development, or the cultivation of virtue, but rather reflective of "an aspect of a thrust toward union with God," from which virtue, to the extent that it is part of the story at all, flashes forth.[52] The implication of this objection calls attention both to the particularity of religious motivation and, even more distinctively, to the particularity of holy figures within religious traditions to avail themselves successfully of the resources within those traditions. There is no such thing as "world saints," according to this objection. "Saintly audience" is at its broadest restricted to the flock of disciples whose worldview coincides with that of their saint. The very term "saints" only makes sense in the context of the faith communities that set the stage for the emergence of saintly personalities.

The best response to this objection comes from saints' own testimony, specifically their insistence that their message, decidedly altruistic, is not confined to the environment in which it originates.[53] Consider Martin Luther King Jr.'s account of a love that extends to the enemy, explained in the language of redemptive suffering and agape, ideas he no doubt could not expound upon without also embracing the long tradition of martyrdom as understood in connection with the struggle of the early church. King wrote:

> In the final analysis, *agape* means a recognition of the fact that all life is interrelated. All humanity is involved in a single process, and all men are brothers. To the degree that I harm my brother, no matter what he is doing to me, to that extent I am harming myself. For example, white men often refuse federal aid to education in order to avoid giving the Negro his rights: but because all men are brothers they cannot deny Negro children without harming their own. They end, all efforts to the contrary, by hurting themselves. Why is this? Because all men are brothers.[54]

King is here speaking of the interdependence and interrelatedness of "all men," not just Christians, even though he is speaking *as* a Christian. The passage is reminiscent of the utterance cited earlier in which the Dalai Lama clarifies that Buddhism does not have to be universal for the ethical truths of Buddhism to be so regarded. How, if this is the case, is the nonreligious person who nevertheless wants to become more virtuous to benefit from saintly influence? How can an atheist morally benefit from Christians such as Dorothy Day and Martin Luther King Jr., or a Hindu such as Gandhi, or a Buddhist such as the Dalai Lama?

The answer depends on whether the saintly message of interdependence and universal fellowship truly *is* universal. This we can never know for sure. If the message is not universal, then it is likely that the "fruits" of a specific religious tradition will not taste the same to those outside it. However, if it is universal—and a cross-cultural consensus among those who come from various religious backgrounds supports such a conclusion—then there is something to be said just for standing in proximity to saints, who have the capacity to inspire us even if we do not share their worldview. Saints have been known to be prophetic with respect to their conviction in the wide applicability of their message. As William James notes of saintly influence: "So many who seemed irretrievably hardened have in point of fact been softened, converted, regenerated, in ways that amazed the subjects even more than they surprised the spectators, that we never can be sure in advance of any man that his salvation by the way of love is hopeless."[55] James thinks that while trying to be like saints is a risky proposition, it is, on balance, worth it to try. Attempting to emulate the saint is admittedly a wager on the part of the nonsaint. The endeavor could be futile or, worse, demoralizing when we find ourselves woefully wanting in comparison. At the same time, the one disposed to adopt an overly cautious attitude in this matter must address the more-than-a-few documented cases in which saintly emulation has resulted in widespread social betterment. We are inclined to agree with William James. For all that saints have going for them individually, the most important saintly trait is arguably their charisma, without which they could transform relatively few of their intentions into realities. Gandhi, Martin Luther King Jr., Dorothy Day, the Dalai Lama, as well as other saints, rarely act alone; their individual ideas become large-scale movements as others begin to act on their message.

None of us knows in advance the degree to which we can successfully emulate saints, or even be positively influenced by them, and in any case we have made only the modest claim in this chapter that religious motivation represents one possible impetus for altruistic action. We hope that at the very least we have shown how religious motivations for altruism, like the psychological and philosophical motivations presented in the two preceding chapters, contain vital resources upon which we, as animals already endowed with rudimentary predilections for altruistic conduct, can build.

Part III

How Does Altruism Work?

7

Cultivating Our Altruistic Identity

"Happiness [is] only real when shared."
—*Chris McCandless, dying of exhaustion and starvation, three and
a half months after voluntarily venturing into the Alaskan wilderness
north of Mt. McKinley in search of a more authentic existence.*[1]

WHAT AYN RAND MISSED

IN AYN RAND's *Atlas Shrugged*, one of the most illustrative titles ever conceived, a civilization is kept afloat by a distinctive group of thinkers who go largely unappreciated despite the public's enormous dependence on their contributions.[2] These "individuals of the mind" are responsible for every known technological invention, medical advance, and innovative breakthrough. Without them society will stagnate and possibly die away. The title, an allusion to the mythical Greek titan who carries the world upon his shoulders, is invoked during a key exchange between two of the novel's protagonists, Francisco d'Anconia and Hank Rearden. They reflect upon what would happen if Atlas ever decided to forsake his unwitting freeloaders by insisting that they begin to participate in their progress and take responsibility for their own well-being. At a critical juncture in the story, the "individuals of the mind" go on strike, a plot device shrewdly employed by Rand to pave the way for the novel's critical normative thrust: a polemic against socialism and the notion of collective responsibility. To allow any circumstance to arise in which the weak rely upon the strong for their sustenance is to do the weak no favors. By implication, the implementation of a system of welfare through the imposition of governmental sanctions hurts rather than helps society on the whole. Flourishing is best understood as a private affair, capable of being fully appreciated only when people are directly involved in its advent. Altruism is fine, even commendable, as an exception, but it represents no basis for sensible social policy. In Rand's vision, the human spirit soars when one pries oneself free from the yoke of convention and creates an opportunity to become enduringly self-sufficient. It languishes under conditions of dependence. The goal of human life is to become genuine selves through our own, individual investments.

No doubt influenced by Friedrich Nietzsche, Herman Hesse, and other thinkers who in the late nineteenth and early twentieth centuries began to question the oppressive hegemony they believed to be inherent in "Judeo-Christian" morality, Ayn Rand has become a seminal thinker in her own right, arguably the one most responsible for the growing appeal of the idea of libertarianism in contemporary American culture. In libertarianism, decision making is unconditionally voluntary, particularly when it comes to choosing with whom one associates and cares about. Life proceeds in crowning moments that occur when one takes one's shot, so to speak. These moments cannot be handed out. They must be earned. In *Atlas Shrugged*, the leader of the strikers, John Galt, presses this point into service in a famous literary vow: "I swear by my life and my love of it that I will never live for the sake of another man, nor ask another man to live for mine."[3] Underlying the romantic bravado of this sentiment is a psychological postulate about the human condition. It is advanced as a serious proposal: in the end, we can depend only on ourselves for happiness.

The merits of this proposal are weighed in John Krakauer's *Into the Wild*, a riveting nonfiction account of a college graduate's bid to sustain himself in the heart of the Alaskan wilderness. In his book Krakauer endeavors to piece together what Chris McCandless might have been thinking when he decided to relinquish his possessions and endanger his life by trekking into terrain for which he was clearly undermatched. In an illuminating chapter, Krakauer likens McCandless' venture to one from his own past, an ill-advised attempt to forge a new route up the Devil's Thumb, a treacherous peak that demarcates the Alaska–British Columbia border east of St. Petersburg. Before embarking, Krakauer befriended a woman who lived in a town near the peak. Spending a night on her floor just before embarking, the author describes a glimpse of the wisdom that would occur to him fully only afterward:

> Kai invited me home for dinner. Later I unrolled my sleeping bag on the floor. Long after she fell asleep, I lay awake in the next room, listening to her peaceful exhalations. I had convinced myself for many months that I didn't really mind the absence of intimacy in

my life, the lack of any real human connection, but the pleasure I'd felt in this woman's company—the ring of her laughter; the innocent touch of a hand on my arm—exposed my self-deceit and left me hollow and aching.[4]

As he was supposed to be mentally preparing for his upcoming solo ascent, it had unexpectedly dawned on John Krakauer that he had misled himself. He writes:

> I was twenty-three, a year younger than Chris McCandless when he walked into the Alaska bush. My reasoning, if one can call it that, was inflamed by the scattershot passions of youth and a literary diet overly rich in the works of Nietzsche, Kerouac, and John Menlove Edwards, the latter a deeply troubled writer and psychiatrist who, before putting an end to his life with a cyanide capsule in 1958, had been one of the preeminent British rock climbers of his day. Edwards regarded climbing as a "psycho-neurotic tendency"; he climbed not for sport but to find refuge from the inner torment that framed his existence.[5]

Mountain climbing may be thrilling, and on that basis worth doing, but it does not represent the answer to life's deeper questions. What Krakauer realized is that to think one is either capable of or would benefit from total self-sufficiency is to lie to oneself, in spite of the rhetorical appeal of such thinking. As human beings we are embodied creatures, dependent on others for our survival and happiness. We are by default a vulnerable species, constantly threatened by the prospect of becoming more vulnerable. Moreover, we are emotionally constituted to crave the formation of connections with other individuals, to care about them and the story that represents how they came to be who they are, and to know that they similarly care about us. According to Krakauer, Chris McCandless misled himself when he decided to renounce human society and venture into the wild, a renunciation partly spurred by an (arguably justified) disappointment in those who inhabited the social world in which he had formerly found himself.

From what Krakauer was able to reconstruct during his investigation into McCandless' past, the young adventurer was motivated by a strong desire to flee the hypocrisy surrounding his well-to-do background by reinventing for himself a new standard of fulfillment. In itself this is a noble objective. At their worst, human beings have a tendency to use one another and lose themselves in the process. It was in reaction to this observation that *Atlas Shrugged* was written. But, as Krakauer realized before it was too late in his life, and as the ailing McCandless realized as he lay dying, to put off a problem is not to solve it. Solitude and self-actualization are therapeutic but do not by themselves attend to our human need for positive interaction with one another. At some point, we must again leave ourselves in search of others. This is what Ayn Rand misses. She fundamentally misconstrues our nature, taking us to be monads rather than interconnected beings. This is the intuition to which John Krakauer came in his investigation of the life of Chris McCandless, combined with his own earnest self-reflection.

If this intuition is correct, perhaps there is another reason the mythical Atlas carries the world upon his shoulders, a reason besides resigning himself, out of duty, to assume the burdens of others. Atlas needs the world too. Just as recipients need givers, givers need receivers. According to this hypothesis, thoroughgoing solipsism is neither morally efficacious nor particularly healthy.

As it turns out, there is scientific evidence to support this conclusion. Stephen Post, a bioethicist and director of the Institute for Research on Unlimited Love, has recently published a volume called *Altruism and Health* containing essays by various health researchers and medical practitioners, several of which are devoted to showing that interaction with others, particularly interaction characterized by kindness and helpfulness, is associated with health and longevity. *Altruism and Health* offers a comprehensive treatment of the scientific evidence that has to date been brought to bear on the causation (not just correlation) between altruism and good health.[6] One notable chapter presents the results of scores of experiments tracking ailing patients whose symptoms markedly improved following stints in which they provided some service for others in their community.[7] In an extensive study reported in another chapter, we learn that elderly patients who volunteered their services in their communities for one hundred hours or more were 30 percent less likely to experience physical functioning limitations than those who did not.[8] Several of the contributing authors argue that the physical signs of aging are noticeably retarded for those regularly engaged in voluntary altruistic enterprises.[9] In a 2003 study cited by Post, the researchers concluded that giving help was more conspicuously associated with better mental and physical health than was receiving help.[10] Other studies reported in the volume establish that the benefits of altruistic behavior are neither limited to older adults nor restricted to any specific culture.

The essays in *Altruism and Health* do not claim that altruism is the most important thing in which a person concerned with his or her health should take part. Altruism is not presented as a guarantee against the affliction of disease. It is merely given its due alongside other activities known to be valuable for a healthy life, such as fitness, low blood pressure, a good diet, no smoking and little drinking, and a good family history.[11] That altruism is not distinguished is part of the point: it makes good physical and mental sense to build altruistic activities into one's life roughly to the same extent that one adopts these other listed habits (insofar as it is within our power to do so). In other words, we should *stop* regarding altruism as special, as something either supererogatorily gracious or unreasonably costly. This is not to say that there will not be occasions on which particular acts of altruism are rightly to be characterized as "above and beyond" or entailing great sacrifices. It is to claim that, in general, altruism is something we can and should weave into our daily routines, something we should regard in the same vein, perhaps, as going to the gym. Altruism, appropriately appreciated, is a normal occurrence in life, a phenomenon that need not be deemed quite so phenomenal.

If we think about the regularity with which squirrels signal an alarm to their relatives that a predator is approaching or vampire bats regurgitate blood for other bats unrelated to them, or if we think about what human altruists consistently report when questioned about their motives—"I did nothing out of the ordinary"—then this conclusion appears less striking. One of the things we hope to have shown in this book is that each of the disciplines we have discussed lends support to the idea of altruism as existing "within the norm." Altruism is in part the natural outgrowth of an organic human need to interact with and have a positive influence on others. In this chapter, we aim to highlight this as well as some of the other conclusions about altruism to which, we believe, the insights of these disparate disciplines independently lead. That is, having discussed the various approaches available to the scholar investigating the question of what motivates altruistic conduct, we will now call attention to some of their points of commonality. In so doing, we will be methodologically "constructive": our inquiry into the nature of and motivation for altruistic conduct gives us an occasion to piece together the various disciplines into a coherent whole.

Thus, rather than construing them as rival theories, we see the approaches we have considered in the last four chapters as partial explanations that, viewed alongside one another, can give us descriptive clarity and normative guidance. In what follows, we will emphasize some conclusions about the phenomenon of altruism, calling attention to the insights that emerge from particular disciplines where appropriate. Out of this will emerge our own interdisciplinary account of the phenomenon. We wrap up the chapter with some closing reflections about what our approach reveals about the relationship between the concepts of "is" and "ought" in morality. As we hope to have shown in preceding chapters and by the end of this chapter, in the human situation there always remains a distance between what we should do and what nature by itself renders us capable of doing at any particular moment in time. This gap is arguably a good thing, for it distinguishes us as the species most capable over the long haul of deepening and expanding our circle of concern for others, both individually and as a group. At the same time, the moral gap makes us creatures with unique responsibilities in the animal kingdom, and, by implication, creatures distinctively able to incur moral culpability should we choose to neglect these responsibilities.

SEVEN CONCLUSIONS ABOUT ALTRUISM

In light of our discussion of the major methodological approaches employed by various scholars trying to understand altruism, we are now ready to defend the characterization of the phenomenon that we tentatively introduced in chapter one. To this end, it may be helpful to recall our definition. We claimed that altruism occurs when *one acts for the sake of another or others and their well-being and welfare become the ultimate object of one's concern. Altruism will usually, but not always, entail a cost borne by the actor and a benefit to the recipient(s). It will also often be an activity in which the actor deliberately intends to bring about the good of his beneficiary, although it can sometimes occur at an instinctive or prereflective level. The object of other-regard in altruistic activity can be the stranger or it can be the personal relation. Altruism is one's moral duty or it is supererogatory, depending on the context and on who is performing the altruistic deed. Finally, altruism is an activity that is fundamental to the human experience, an activity in which the vast majority of us can and should participate, and, as such, more resembles a learnable skill than a God-given talent, even though there are a few extraordinary persons for whom the aptitude for altruism comes much easier than for the rest of us.* Our definition is flexible in that it does not insist in all cases that altruism come at a cost to the actor, be undertaken with a good (or even self-conscious) intent, or bring about good consequences to the recipient, although we do acknowledge that these factors are highly indicative of altruistic conduct. We have taken no strong stance on the question of who exemplifies the recipient of altruism (stranger or kin) and have presented contexts in which altruism could be deemed required or above-and-beyond. At the same time, we have identified one key feature—that the well-being and welfare of others represent one's ultimate object of concern—as constitutive of altruistic activity as well as suggested that altruism is more appropriately understood as a learnable skill rather than an extraordinary talent.

We believe that the preceding chapters advance arguments consistent with this definition and encourage the reader, now familiar with the various disciplinary approaches explored in this book, to test it against the examples and arguments laid out in each chapter. What are some of the implications of the understanding of altruism we have offered? We are now in a position to elaborate upon our definition and present some conclusions for which, again, we believe there is support from biological, psychological, philosophical, and religious approaches to understanding altruism. None of these conclusions would have been obvious at the outset of this book; they have emerged as a result of scrutinizing a single phenomenon from various disciplinary angles. Here are seven claims that are consistent with our definition, but take us a bit beyond it:

1. Self-regard and other-regard are not diametrical opposites, but the completion of each other.

2. Altruism is a fundamental human activity that nourishes both the giver and the recipient.

3. Nature and nurture represent complementary rather than competing explanations for our existing and potential moral abilities.

4. Altruists are not all alike and are not distinguished by any one trait. They employ different means for arriving at the same end.

5. Altruism is neither a given nor an impossibility for human beings, but rather an ongoing opportunity in which to participate. Being more a matter of skill than talent, and therefore largely the result of hard work, it is something we should regard as contingent on our moral development.

6. Altruism should neither be reduced explanatorily to any one discipline nor be regarded as an irreducible phenomenon, understandable only to altruists themselves.

7. We are an "altruistic species"—or at least we can be—because we have at our disposal the resources, through nature and nurture, to cultivate our benevolent identity.

It will be useful to elaborate on these conclusions.

Self-regard and other-regard are not diametrical opposites, but the completion of each other.

In chapter two we suggested that it might be possible to reconcile psychological hedonism with altruism. Psychological hedonism, it will be recalled, is a subset of psychological egoism that holds that self-interest is measured by the pleasure we manage to attain and the pain we manage to avoid. Psychological hedonism makes no assertions about what we should (morally) do; it is a descriptive claim about our psychological makeup. We are, as human beings, ultimately constituted to pursue outcomes that will make us happy. Consider the claim of psychological hedonism alongside the first part of our definition of altruism, which states that for altruism to occur an altruist must make the well-being and welfare of others the ultimate object of his or her concern. If it is true that there is a social component to human flourishing—ultimate happiness—that involves *genuinely* giving of oneself (i.e., not giving as a means of replenishing oneself farther down the line), then it follows that these two "ultimate" concerns could be satisfied at once. Is this in fact true? Let us examine what we have discovered in previous chapters.

As we saw in chapter three, we have evolved into organisms for whom it makes sense in terms of our survival from a gene's-eye point of view to act in altruistic ways. Kin selection, reciprocal altruism, and group selection, although theories that narrowly designate the recipients of altruistic action, all specify circumstances under which the beneficiary's well-being and welfare are to be prioritized, considered by the acting agent as an end in itself. The perpetuation of our species depends on us, as survival machines, successfully sacrificing ourselves, when appropriate, for our genes' perpetuation. In other words, to *be* a human individual organism that behaves the way it is supposed to behave (again, from a gene's perspective) is to be one that does not in all cases make its own individual survival paramount. By implication, authentic other-regard (i.e., not other-regard in instrumental service of self-regard) paradoxically becomes a primary interest of the self. This insight from the field of biology was backed up in chapter four, where we discussed the psychological mechanisms that human beings have developed over time to pattern their governing attitudes and motivations after this evolutionarily successful strategy. Already disposed to be altruistic in light of our biological makeup, we internalize other-regarding impulses, the overall effect of which is further to refine the instincts for sympathy and compassion that nature has given us. Our minds, themselves the result of evolution, are powerful and complex enough to be able to propel a process already under way.

Not surprisingly, human beings have constructed moral traditions to reflect their biological proclivities and psychological capacities. In chapter five we made the case for Aristotelianism over Kantianism and consequentialism as the moral theory that moves beyond the naturalistic fallacy without at the same time subscribing to an unduly demanding moral framework based on reason alone. According to Aristotle, the goal, or telos, of the good life is to participate in human flourishing, a central component of which is cultivating an other-regarding character. Reason, in this view, alerts us to what we are morally lacking without at the same time being the sole force that compels us to try to become better. An Aristotelian normative outlook self-reflectively takes account of our own animality. It locates the resources for altruism within human biology and then avails itself of practical reason to supply us with the supplemental motivation we need to care about more people and more deeply about them than we normally would. We *want* to reason practically not only because, as human beings, it is within our nature to do so, but also because *with* reason, we acquire an awareness of an important fact about ourselves, namely, that as human beings we are not meant to languish in stasis. In other words, as human beings, we are particular kinds of animals: ones that, while finite, are meant to reach beyond themselves. Aristotle characterizes this trait by using the term "striving." Knowing ourselves as we do, as striving creatures with the capacity to build upon our capacities, including our moral capacities, it becomes in our best interests to act prudentially to acquire and develop a virtuous character. It is in this sense that the acquisition of virtue is accurately characterized as a self-regarding activity.

Aristotle's account of the importance of linking human nature to moral responsibility is substantiated by the testimony of the world's most devout and devoted. Saints perceive quickly what all eventually flourishing human beings are on the path to perceiving: that, in the words of Martin Luther King Jr., "we are our brother's keepers because we are our brother's brothers."[12] The individual sacrifices that come along with replenishing the one in need, according to a saintly worldview, are underwritten by the self-fulfillment that reflects the culmination of such replenishing. Saints, insistent on their status as "merely human," press us to reconsider our assumptions about the applicability of the normative message of other-regard inherent in religious traditions around the globe. Compassion, in the form of "agape," "*karuna*," or the countless other names for this cardinal moral virtue, is not only appropriate for but able to be summoned by greater and lesser practitioners of their respective traditions. These norms, as we argued, are best seen not as unrealizable ideals, but as viable standards that at first can be acted upon in glimpses but ultimately can be sustained over longer lengths of time. We did not argue that religion is a necessity for morality, but we did suggest that to the extent that one identifies oneself as religious, it is within one's capacity not only to admire but also to emulate the exemplars of one's tradition. The religious motivation to be altruistic is consistent with the motivational accounts previously presented: a (moral) prescription for human beings that is sensitive to human nature, including human beings' ability to extend without transcending their limitations. Religious traditions, notwithstanding their susceptibility to being politicized for violent ends, can thus bring out the best in us. They simultaneously serve as blueprints for attending to others' needs and for procuring our own happiness.

Altruism is a fundamental human activity that nourishes both the giver and the recipient.

If other-regard and self-regard are simultaneously satisfied in the process of human flourishing, then it follows that receiving is not the only component of altruistic giving wherein the participant benefits. The standard literature takes for granted that to be altruistic is to bear a burden and that altruism is as rare as it is because of the costs typically associated with altruistic behavior. In this book we have resisted the standard view, suggesting instead that human beings have needs to be both givers and receivers. As mentioned earlier in this chapter, there is accumulating medical evidence for the health advantages of living altruistically. But aside from that, we are at a prereflective level naturally sympathetic beings.

There are now studies showing that as early as eighteen months of age, toddlers exhibit a desire to cooperate with those whom they perceive to have suffered in some way. In one significant series of recent experiments, the psychologist Felix Warneken of the Max Planck Institute for Evolutionary Anthropology performed a number of "tasks," such as stacking books and hanging up towels, in front of twenty-four eighteen-month-olds, at times deliberately struggling with the tasks to see if that would elicit a response from the toddlers.[13] With remarkable consistency, the toddlers gestured to offer assistance when Warneken seemed to need help. Conversely, they withheld their assistance when Warneken intentionally took a book from the stack or let a towel fall by throwing a clothespin to the floor. According to Warneken, in addition to having the cognitive ability to grasp people's goals and intentions at an early age, something we have long known, human beings have a "pro-social motivation" that spurs them to feel connected to others by helping them when help appears needed. Warneken concludes that only sophisticated primates such as chimpanzees and gorillas are similarly hardwired, though not to the same degree even as eighteen-month-old humans.

The observation being made here is not Hobbes' classic interpretation of pity and compassion according to which we want to help others either because it is painful for us to see them struggle or because we (selfishly) imagine what it would be like one day to find ourselves in a similar predicament. The point is that we are, at the start, beings whose happiness depends on making others happier. Were we to inhabit a very different world, one in which no one suffered or had material or emotional needs, we would be importantly impoverished. It would, of course, be implausible and maybe a little offensive to contend that we are *better off* in a world that contains evil than one bereft of it, particularly given the fact that the world in which we actually live contains such drastic and cruel instances of suffering that result from evil. While acknowledging this, it is at the same time hard not to reflect upon the silver lining of catastrophic events like September 11 and Hurricane Katrina. These occasions bring out our better angels, shaking us from our lingering complacency and reminding us of the humanity that connects us all to one another.

One might wonder why, on the other hand, if altruism is so fundamental to the human experience, we become complacent in the first place. That human beings are complacent is beyond a doubt. One need merely turn on the television or look at the front page of a newspaper to learn about the suffering who are ignored. Everyday experience seems filled with encounters in which someone tries to procure an advantage at somebody else's expense. Defenders of the standard view—which regards altruism as the exception and not the rule—are hardly surprised by human complacency. If they do not embrace Wolf Larsen's ruthlessly naturalistic might-is-right view of human nature, they at least remain cynical about our prospects for becoming people who *desire* to put aside our material needs for the sake of others on a regular basis. It is easy for them to understand why people would want to *see* themselves as givers, and how this would motivate the activity of giving, but, they would point out, the claim that we desire to give and receive with equal intensity does not seem to jibe with everyday experience. How can the Aristotelian view of altruism as a "shared practice" be explained in light of the frequency of complacency and the rarity of courage and selflessness?

The response we have provided in this book emphasizes human capacity *and* human potential. Each of the disciplines we have examined attempts to shed light on the motivations for altruism when it does occur, motivations of which, we have learned, we are not always aware and are sometimes only faintly aware. It is our hope that in looking at the research from various fields, the reader will discover not only that human beings in fact have the resources to be altruistic to a much greater degree than they expect, but also that altruistic activity is not on the periphery of human experience but right in the center of it, despite the fact that the majority of us do not tend to live our lives as if this were the case. The emerging scientific and medical research on the benefits of altruism helps us to know ourselves better as human beings. The fact that it may not yet be obvious that we are beings who need to give as well as receive does not imply that human flourishing does not centrally require both. The Delphic oracle prophesied "Know thyself" for our benefit: knowing ourselves as we actually are, we are more likely to be fulfilled. Who are we with regard to the question of altruism? Complicated beings, to be sure. We are beings who have evolved in such a way that acting altruistically provides for us certain advantages, but we are also beings who (also due to evolution) reason, by virtue of which we can act upon the awareness that we are, as humans, unfinished. Human potential is the counterpart to human finitude. Nature has endowed us with the capacity to give to others on a limited basis but in such a way that these limitations are not fixed in stone. We *can* become more giving, and, as the current medical research suggests, when we come to do so regularly, we will discover that activity to be central to our flourishing and fulfillment. Moral complacency can thus be explained as the result of a pervasive ignorance about what is *truly* in our best interests. As we become better acquainted with how we function as a species, as we learn more about our nature and destiny, we will choose more extensively and frequently to give of ourselves to others.

Nature and nurture represent complementary rather than competing
explanations for our existing and potential moral abilities.

To be constrained, we have just concluded, is not to be static. Human ability, including moral ability, can to a significant extent be predicted by nature,
but it is at the same time part of our nature to move beyond this predictable
measurement in the case of particular individuals. The latter has sometimes
been referred to as the "second level of human nature."[14] This second level of
nature goes by another name: "nurture." Nurture—the psychological resources, moral theories, and religious resources of which we can avail ourselves to move beyond the constraints predicted by our nature—is already
part of nature. In *The Moral Animal*, Robert Wright uses the metaphor of an
instrument with several knobs to clarify how many of the behaviors that
nature predicts are more fluid than they may initially seem. Evolutionary
psychologists, explains Wright,

> are trying to discern . . . a deeper unity within the species. First,
> the anthropologist notes recurring themes in culture after cul-
> ture: a thirst for social approval, a capacity for guilt. You might
> call these, and many such other universals, "the knobs of human
> nature." Then the psychologist notes that the exact tunings of the
> knobs seem to differ from person to person. One person's "thirst
> for approval" knob is set in the comfort zone, down around (rel-
> atively) "self-assured," and another person's is up in the excruci-
> ating "massively insecure" zone; one person's guilt knob is set low
> and another person's is painfully high. So the psychologist asks:
> How do these knobs get set? Genetic differences among individ-
> uals surely play a role, but perhaps a larger role is played by genetic
> commonalities: by a genetic, species-wide developmental pro-
> gram that absorbs information from the social environment and
> adjusts the maturing mind accordingly. Oddly, future progress in
> grasping the importance of environment will probably come
> from thinking about genes. . . . Human nature consists of knobs
> and of mechanisms for tuning the knobs, and both are invisible
> in their own way.[15]

The way in which we develop in response to environmental factors is an act
of calibration of nurture upon nature, which is at the same time also part of
our nature. The first "level" of human nature, determined by what the knobs
are for, so to speak, places our physical abilities, emotional tendencies, and

moral propensities within a general range. The parameters that delineate this range are universal for our species; there are certain limitations we cannot transcend. Within this range, however, individuals vary depending on environmental circumstances. These exert an external influence over our development, but they also have a triggering effect on our genetic disposition to display certain traits more or less than do other individuals with very similar blueprints. That nearly everyone is subject to this kind of "fine-tuning," moreover, is *also* part of human nature, hence the phrase "second level of human nature." The fact that nature sets in motion these two sorts of processes indicates that, in terms of our moral capabilities, some of us will tend toward selfishness and others of us will tend toward selflessness. No one human being possesses the ability, through nurture, to *transcend* his or her nature altogether. But every human being is eligible to experience a *tweaking* of his or her nature, which in part explains how human beings turn out to be so different from one another in their adult lives.

This understanding of the relationship between nature and nurture is entirely consistent with the Aristotelian insight that it is not the purview of reason to lift us out of our human situation; reason should not be regarded as a desperately needed corrective to a biologically flawed existence. Likewise, it is consistent with the understanding of religious traditions that we have presented in this book, namely, that they are best understood as offering normative guidelines to be heeded now, in this life, rather than as offering an alternative to human existence. Reason and religion represent two examples of what Wright identifies as our "mechanisms for tuning the knobs," which occur at the second level of human nature, i.e., the one responsible for fine-tuning. The tuning of a knob is dependent on an interaction between what the knob is for, the first level (which is universal), and the cumulative impacts of nurture, the second level (variable according to individual circumstances). How we internalize norms, our experience of socialization, the way in which we learn to reason, our experience as religious practitioners—these are the ways in which we undergo character development and fine-tune the capacities with which nature endows us. They also in part account for why we are different from one another even though we are members of the same species. Of all the species, human beings display the most range with respect to the second level of nature.

The metaphor of the knobs is one way of explaining why, in contrast to the other animals, at any given time our existing moral capacities are not the same as our potential ones. The idea of nurture as both a part of nature and a matter of harnessing nature is consistent with another feature of how we undergo character developments in Aristotelian ethics, namely, habituation. Through the praxis of participating in our social, moral, and religious traditions—through repetition—we heighten our capacity for the traits with which nature originally equips us. The more encounters we have in situations that call for altruistic conduct, the less likely our default capacities for altruism are to atrophy. To the contrary, they will expand in unexpected ways.

And how do we come to know ourselves as beings in situations that call for altruistic conduct? In a variety of ways, of course, many of which we mentioned in chapters four, five, and six, wherein we discussed the ways in which we are *nurtured* to do so. One of the great mysteries of altruistic conduct pertains to spontaneous altruism, those cases in which no lengthy cognitive process can account for the great sacrifice that from time to time takes place in a split second. Consider the case of Petty Officer 2d Class Michael A. Monsoor, a twenty-five-year-old Southern Californian serving in Iraq who saved the lives of fellow officers by throwing himself on a hand grenade tossed into his rooftop hideout, for which he was posthumously awarded the Medal of Honor.[16] It is very similar to the lifesaving action of Wesley Autrey, the fifty-year-old construction worker we discussed in chapter four who, in direct view of his two daughters, aged four and six, jumped down onto subway tracks a few moments before the arrival of a train and saved a young man suffering from a seizure who had fallen onto the tracks at the worst possible time.[17] In both of these examples, the heroic act transpired immediately and resolutely. Both Monsoor and Autrey, like world-class athletes under pressure, displayed the poise of individuals who had benefited from prior preparation for an occasion on which everything was on the line. It would be explanatorily inadequate to suggest that the "first level of nature" alone was responsible for their heroic gestures, for on countless occasions others similarly circumstanced have not acted in kind. By the same token, it does not seem plausible to account for these instances of heroism merely as the result of the heroes' having determined what rules their societies, philosophical frameworks, or religions told them to obey. The sheer reactive character of their actions suggests that "nature" was involved to a far greater degree. Most likely, these altruistic acts were the result of some process of habituation in each altruist, which means that both instinctual drive and reflective introspection played a role in governing their heroic responses. The fine-tuning of the "knobs" of nature, if it is anything, is the repetitive refining of our default moral dispositions. It occurs, quite literally, through moral practice.

Altruists are not all alike and are not distinguished by any one trait.
They employ different means for arriving at the same end.

If nurture impacts even as it extends nature, as we have suggested, then it should not surprise us to learn that differences exist even within the small class of people whom we consider altruists. They display widely varying characteristics and are not all motivated by the same thing. This makes it somewhat tricky to answer the question, "What distinguishes the altruist from the nonaltruist?" Indeed, there is no one trait, or combination of traits, that altruists necessarily possess. What the world generally sees is an end result: the performance of an altruistic deed. Behind the scenes we have the life narratives of each individual altruist, all of which tell different tales. Here it bears mentioning that altruism is not merely a theoretical concept but an action or series of actions having a practical impact on the world. There is no one formula for becoming an altruist. Altruists come from different socioeconomic backgrounds and cultures, practice different religions (or no religion), rely on reason and instinct to varying degrees, are sometimes significantly, sometimes faintly influenced by the norms of their society, and even employ different psychological mechanisms for internalizing the value of selfless conduct. Altruism is sometimes the result of thoughtful, deliberate planning and sometimes completely spontaneous. Complicating matters is the observation that for the most part human beings cannot even be divided into "altruists" and "nonaltruists" in the first place; with very few exceptions, we all have the potential to be both, and likely will be both at one point or another in our lives. (We will talk about the "contingency" of moral goodness in a subsequent conclusion.)

These findings are consistent with our claim about the importance of methodological plurality. Altruism cannot be explained exclusively through one disciplinary approach. Until very recently, "rational actor theory"—the idea that all of human behavior, including moral behavior, can be seen as involving actors who maximize their utility from fixed, clear preferences[18]—has dominated the way in which social scientists of various types have understood the phenomenon of altruism. In *The Heart of Altruism*, Kristen Renwick Monroe establishes the inapplicability of traditional rational actor theory, or any one theory for that matter, to the majority of cases of actual altruism.[19] One of Monroe's points is that theories tend to stress mathematical estimations based on coded entities of evaluation at the expense of attention to real-life face-to-face encounters. Writes Monroe:

When we stress calculation ... we tend to reduce things and people to the calculable, to homogenous units that lose their individuality and distinguishing characteristics. Our study of altruism, if it teaches us anything, reminds us of the importance of seeing the human face, the person needing help, of moving beyond the anonymity of just another nameless victim, one more faceless Jew shipped off to a concentration camp, another child killed in Bosnia or dying from famine in some distant land. . . . I am not suggesting we should not be as objective and analytically rigorous as possible, but we should always remember that in social science we deal with human beings, living and breathing people, and not just numbers or aggregates.[20]

Monroe's contention is not that human behaviors can *never* be approximated by theories that assign high values to key coefficients in order to emphasize certain criteria over others. She is making a broader claim about the power of theories themselves: at best they only ever approximate, particularly when it comes to predicting human behavior. In many instances in which we choose to act one way rather than another, our decision about how to act is not predetermined. It can go one way or another. And while personality by itself cannot transcend the limitations imposed by our genetic makeup, it almost always has something to do with why we do what we do. As Monroe aptly reflects with respect to faith: the "kind of belief that comes only because a clever rational actor deems it prudent to place a Pascal's wager is not really belief at all; it is mere expediency."[21] The same holds for altruism. Monroe's many interviews with altruists reveal that it is with occasions of seeing someone in need—upon *actual experiences* of witnessing a suffering other—that altruists come to feel that they have no choice but to act as they do. From this we should infer that there is no theoretical substitute for the actual, concrete occasion that gives rise to altruistic behavior.

It is for this reason that not all religious believers, thoroughgoing Kantians, and so on, should be expected to be altruistic. The ideology to which we commit is not and never could be the only determining factor in our behavior. There are among us persons engaging in profoundly selfless acts who have no creed, intellectual conviction, or emotional makeup that would seemingly predispose them to be other-regarding. Their altruism remains conspicuously mysterious to us. In the end, there is a residual component to altruistic activity that defies explanation, and that certainly resists being sub-sumed in some grand explanatory theory.

At the same time, as we have argued, to the extent that we *do* discover in ourselves the capacity to be altruistic, and simultaneously discover altruis-tic activity to be conducive to our fulfillment, there are things we can do to become, over time, *more* altruistic than we currently are. Specifically, we can habituate ourselves to being more compassionate. This probably entails committing more deeply to a particular religious way of life that we have already embraced, or adhering more consistently to the norms articulated by the trusted mentors among us in our community (as it did, for instance, for the inhabitants of some European villages in the 1930s and 1940s who sheltered Jews from Hitler's Gestapo).[22] It involves practicing very hard at what has shown already to work in our own case. And, if we have been right in our argument, the effort is worth it. For, while there are many paths, the endpoint to which they all lead is something that, on the balance, is good for us. In this sense we are fortunate, as human beings, to have a multitude of resources available to us.

Altruism is neither a given nor an impossibility for human beings,
but rather an ongoing opportunity in which to participate.
Being more a matter of skill than talent, and therefore largely
the result of hard work, it is something we should regard as contingent
on our moral development.

In the recently published nine-hundred-page *Cambridge Handbook of Exper-tise and Expert Performance*, the psychologist Anders Ericcson and some of his colleagues report their findings from studies involving a number of dis-parate pursuits, from playing soccer, golf, Scrabble, darts, and chess, to per-forming surgery, to piano playing, to engaging in computer software design, to doing exercises involving memory, all in order to answer a simple ques-tion: when someone is able to do something very well, what makes him or her so good?[23] Their conclusion, in a nutshell, is that talent is often given too much credit as an explanation; what makes someone good at something is usually his or her desire to be good at that thing—that combined with prac-tice. Most often, success comes not from the manifestation of a God-given trait but from the always exhausting and sometimes frustrating experience of doing something over and over until the improbable becomes routine. In this book, against the commonsense wisdom, we have suggested that the same is true of matters of morality. Good deeds flow from a good character.

Good character is a matter of habituating oneself to a virtuous life such that when an occasion arises in which a virtuous response is called for, a prospective moral agent will be prepared to act in kind.

Is such a conclusion justified in light of what we have learned about the various disciplinary approaches to understanding the phenomenon of altruism? We think so. We argued in chapters three and four that evolutionary biology gives us both the set of traits that makes other-regard possible and cognitive mechanisms for harnessing such traits, within limits. We then suggested in chapters five and six, in our discussion of the moral and religious traditions that encourage the pursuit of these traits, that we have the means to know ourselves as altruistic beings and that this knowledge, in turn, can serve as the impetus for forming an identity consistent with our potential. As Gandhi famously pointed out, the drive to make our potential a reality at first strikes us an "experiment with the truth." We have no way of knowing for sure how much we can improve upon our natural capacities until we try and then try again.

This trying is, in effect, the process of character development—refining ourselves in order to improve upon how we would otherwise be by default. People do bad and good deeds throughout their lives and, depending on the frequency and intensity of those actions, develop bad or good characters that eventually acquire stability. Whether we end up with a bad or good character is a matter of how we choose to *enhance* the capacities with which we are naturally endowed, as well as a matter of the environment in which we place ourselves (or are placed beyond our control), not the capacities themselves, which differ from one person to another far less initially than after the one who possesses them decides or fails to decide to harness them. Our proximity to those in a position to bring out hitherto underemphasized aspects of ourselves, as well as our own decision to develop these aspects, plays a significant role in who we become; just how significant these environmental factors are, as opposed to sheer genetic disposition, is at present unknown. As Steven Pinker points out, in trying to explain the wide range of characters that human beings display, it is difficult, perhaps impossible, to pinpoint exactly how large a role the "human lottery" plays in assigning us the strengths and weaknesses evident in our personalities. "For example," notes Pinker, "we may all develop a sense of generosity if enough of our friends and neighbors are generous, but the threshold or the multiplier of that function may differ among us genetically or at random: some people need only a few nice neighbors to grow up nice, others need a majority."[24] Almost all of

us, however, have the ability to become *more* generous, and in general to
work on minimizing our weaknesses and maintaining our strengths. Notwithstanding the existence of the rare saint who can do no wrong or the psy-
chopath who cannot be cured,[25] most of us have moral futures that are
unpredictable. We have *enough* influence over our moral futures, in response
to the environments in which we find ourselves, to reach for the far end of
our "genetic" range. By contrast, the vast majority of us could never learn to
throw a fastball at ninety miles an hour. That ability, it would seem, is a matter of sheer, inborn talent.

The idea that altruism is contingent on character rather than on talent
alone is consistent with our personal experience of getting to know and
working with actual altruists in our hometown of Chico, California. For the
last few years, we have had students in the class we co-teach, "What Motivates Altruism?," shadow persons in the community directly engaged in
social advocacy, welfare, and service. These students, serving as "participant
observers," have been charged with the task of following their "altruists"[26] for
a minimum of five hours a week over a fifteen-week semester. In that time,
our students have kept their observations in a journal in order to determine
whether the theories to which they are exposed in the classroom are consistent with what they witness firsthand. One of the things almost all the students noticed was how *ordinary* those whom they shadowed were, a word
the students themselves often chose to characterize their subjects (albeit one
quite consistent with the altruists' own characterization of themselves). One
student reported that her altruist, who ran a homeless shelter in town, lived
a "nonspectacular" life that she could "participate in as easily as she could
praise it from afar." Another remarked in her final paper that the woman she
shadowed claimed that she had to work very hard over several years to want
to create time to counsel socially maladjusted members of the Chico community. Two members of the community that we selected for our students
to observe—Farshad Azad, who participates in several outreach and support
groups in town, including the Basket Brigade, a program he founded in order
to provide Thanksgiving and Christmas dinners to residents undergoing
financial hardship, and Matt Jackson, who launched Chico's Boys and Girls
Club and is known for his tireless contributions to the city council and voluntary work with the NAACP—were recently featured in a *Chico News and
Review* spotlight on Chico's "Local Heroes." In that article, Farshad Azad is
quoted as saying:

This is not charity work. . . . It's a gift from people in the community for people whose lives are tough right now, showing this community truly cares. But there's an expectation. When people say "thank you," I tell them the only way to thank me is when they are in a position of affluence they do the same thing for someone else.[27]

Later in the article, Azad refers to this expectation as the heart of what he calls the "positive ripple effect," a belief that the environment he helps to create will influence others to do the same when they are in a position to do so. Jackson concurs with Azad's claim about the infectious nature of selfless initiative: "This isn't a story about me," says Jackson. "It's a story of very hardworking local citizens committed to youth. I was fortunate enough to have been asked to participate at the beginning. The community took it from there."[28] Both men stress not only that there is little special about them—a self-observation altruists tend to make about which we have remarked more than once in this book—but also that the effort they exert should not be confined to themselves alone. The "work" of becoming altruistic can and should be shouldered by many. Today an article that is written happens to be about them; tomorrow it should be about somebody else.

There is something else that Farshad Azad and Matt Jackson stress, both in the article about them and in person, namely, that there is a difference—as well as a time lapse—between a decision to contribute one's time and resources to others and the habit of coming to do so on a regular basis. The successful performance of moral action requires practice and moral determination, just as making fouls shots and playing musical etudes do. It is an unglamorous, repetitive enterprise, typical of the acquisition of most skills. On the other hand, to know Farshad Azad and Matt Jackson is to know two happy, confident men who, now that they have acquired over time a reliable giving character, have the ability "to practice their moral skills," so to speak, without really practicing. One of the features of developing a stable character is that one can then count on it. Put differently, what was once not part of nature, or existed only as a potential, becomes so. Altruistic dispositions are habituated in this fashion.

Altruism should neither be reduced explanatorily to any one
discipline nor be regarded as an irreducible phenomenon,
understandable only to altruists themselves.

While the testimony of actual altruists like Farshad Azad and Matt Jackson
is useful because it gives scholars and students the opportunity to put a face
behind a hypothesis and lends credibility to the theoretical approaches being
considered, it would be hasty to consider it a "trump" card that has the force
and effect of undermining understandings of altruism that rival the altruist's own self-understanding. As we demonstrated in chapter three, individuals have motives of which they may not be aware, and there is an important
difference between the level of *explanation* of a phenomenon and the prior
level of *description* represented by the self-impressions of the subjects about
whom one is inquiring. Although we have from time to time relied in this
book on the insider testimony of altruists themselves, our primary purpose
has been to provide an interdisciplinary explanation of the nature of and
reasons for altruism. And, particularly in the chapters on the evolutionary
biological and psychological approaches to understanding altruism, we have
noted that there are mechanisms at work in our nature that dispose us to be
altruistic without realizing we are. Thus, for example, while we have in general offered a positive appraisal of Kristen Renwick Monroe's attention to the
narratives of various sorts of altruists, we do take issue with her strong claim
that the unique self-perspective of altruists, which allows them to see the
common link between themselves and all of humanity, is where a valid discussion about altruism ought to *begin*. The impression Monroe gives is that
the canonical expectations of altruists, which include their assumptions
about their connectedness to everyone, everywhere, are independent of the
supposed biological and psychological constraints of human nature, and
thus her hypothesis is immune to critical scrutiny from the perspective of
those (and related) disciplines.

In fact, the canonical expectations of actual altruists, while certainly entailing a view about a "common human identity," are the *result* of the contingent
refinement of a character that develops from resources originally present in
our nature. In merely asserting the fact of their existence, without accounting for their advent, Monroe perhaps unwittingly reinforces the standard
view that some people are simply born with altruistic talents and tendencies,
in contrast to the majority who lack their insight. This impression stands
in tension with other parts of Monroe's argument where she suggests that
people cannot simply be divided into altruists and nonaltruists. To be sure,

she explicitly (and rightly) states that most of us fall somewhere on a contin-uum rather than into one of two categories. But if this is so, then the question of how *universal* resources become differently harnessed into dispositions and actions depending on the *individual* in question also becomes a line of inquiry relevant to her overall project. There is no unifying "theory" account-ing for altruistic behavior that is reducible to the concepts and methodol-ogical apparatus proper to any one discipline, but neither can the sheer phenomenon of an "altruistic perspective" by itself be invoked to explain why altruists see things differently than most of us do. Their self-perspective does not appear to them out of thin air. Like any self-perspective, it is the outcome of the painstaking process of developing the traits one first comes to discover in oneself and then hones or chooses not to hone, depending on one's social environment and individual response to that environment.

At the same time, self-perspective is tremendously valuable in explaining altruistic motivation, and no theoretical analysis should marginalize insider accounts that do not comport with conclusions that the analyst expects his or her approach to yield. So, for example, it is disingenuous to assume that altru-ists who attest that "they are ordinary and do nothing special in engaging in their altruistic actions" are engaging in false modesty because the approach *we* favor leans heavily on a presumption that self-interest is ubiquitous in human behavior, as does, for instance, "rational actor theory." Indeed, it is as a result of the earnest and credible testimony of a wide variety of altruists that we have strong reason to believe that some forms of altruism extend beyond kin selection, reciprocal altruism, and group selection, the only three kinds of altruism that an approach based exclusively on the discipline of evolutionary biology recognizes. An accurate, comprehensive explanation for what moti-vates altruism will make a good-faith effort not to ignore altruists' own under-standings of why they do what they do. Thus, in the final analysis we are not only critical of approaches like Monroe's, which exalt insider testimony at the expense of other insights with which they stand in tension. We are also criti-cal of reductive approaches that dismiss insider testimony entirely, or insights that emerge from rival disciplines, for that matter.

One example of a reductive approach is that advanced in Marc Hauser's recent and widely lauded book, *Moral Minds: How Nature Designed Our Universal Sense of Right and Wrong.*[29] In it, Hauser argues that the biologi-cal and psychological basis for morality is an instinct, or "organ," that humans have evolved that is responsible for all our judgments about what any moral situation calls for at any given time. Hauser postulates that this moral organ is analogous to the "language organ," famously described fifty years ago by the cognitive scientist and linguist Noam Chomsky, which determines our universal grammar and lays out the syntactical rules and constraints within which all languages develop. Hauser claims that our evolved moral organ similarly furnishes us with abstract universal proce-dures for arriving at moral content and sets the limits for adopting cultur-ally specific values. One implication of this claim is that our moral instincts, of which we are not conscious, exist prior to, and are therefore not influ-enced by, the wisdom imparted in philosophical ethical theories and in the moral imperatives handed down in our religious traditions.[30] In other words, the decisive determining factor in our moral decision making occurs at the instinctual, prereflective level, rendering all but irrelevant, in our judgments about right and wrong, the role of tradition and experience coming from teachers, mentors, parents, and secular and religious institutions alike.[31] Our morality is grounded only in our biology.

Hauser's is but one example of a sweeping theory that reduces explana-tions of morality to the presumptions of one discipline and, as critics are now pointing out, as a result does not sufficiently account for the sheer breadth of moral dilemmas that pull us in opposite directions.[32] Hauser dis-misses out of hand the possibility that "nurture," which often does occur at a level of actor consciousness, has much chance of altering the predeter-mined impact of "nature." In fact, people deliberately change for the better and the worse all the time, and in significant ways; they become more altru-istic, for example, as a result of their exposure to, and subsequent decision to become more like, others. Even though the extent to which human beings can change is *limited* by their biology, biology by itself provides at best an estimate of how we will behave. The mechanisms of kin selection, recipro-cal altruism, and group selection do not precisely predict the extent to which humans will follow, fall short of, or exceed, for example, the norm of reci-procity that appears in some versions of the Golden Rule (which, as Hauser does persuasively argue, itself may well turn out to be implied by a human "moral organ").[33] In other words, if a moral organ does exist, it is most appropriately regarded as the starting point for morality. Our philosophical and religious traditions, which themselves contain, with near unanimity, their own versions of the Golden Rule, have disparate narratives for advanc-ing their adherents beyond the moral minimum. This implies that human beings are to a significant degree "genetically unfinished." A moral organ cannot account for all the murky scenarios under which we deliberatively wade through sticky dilemmas, although this is not to say that any viable theory need not at least take into account the influence of our prereflective judgments on moral reasoning. As we pointed out in chapter five, philosophical theories based entirely on moral reasoning are psychologically unrealistic and equally myopic.

In the end, neither social-scientific models based on the presuppositions of rational actor theory nor theories that rely only on biological facts about how we first come to form moral intuitions nor philosophical models or religious traditions that imply that all of morality is the result of following certain rules disclosed by reason or religion nor, finally, what we learn from the first-person testimony of the moral subjects we are investigating can by themselves fully explain the phenomenon of altruism, or morality in general for that matter. Altruism is a complex phenomenon. To account for it requires patience and the scholarly fortitude to piece together partial truths that by themselves do not shed sufficient light on the whole. In the process of researching and writing this book, we have learned to be wary of theorists who deem as insignificant insights that come from some disciplines for the sake of affirming others that come from their own. As the recent wave of scholarship on altruism confirms, there is likely much more overlap than incompatibility among the disciplines with regard to this topic.

We are an "altruistic species"—or at least we can be—
because we have at our disposal the resources, through
nature and nurture, to cultivate our benevolent identity.

In a classic metaphor that invites reflection about human cooperation, a blind man totes a lame man on his shoulders, allowing both men to make their way through the world. As human beings, with human brains, we are clever. Our brains enable us to see how to solve problems together that we wouldn't necessarily be able to handle on our own. Self-interest is not a simple prospect of the self acting alone. It manifests itself in a multitude of subtle ways, some of which can be identified as helping behavior that appears to be "altruistic." In chapter three we discussed numerous examples of cooperative conduct as well as the idea of "reciprocal altruism" that accounts for their prevalence in human behavior. Yet, in this book we have also asked whether these limited forms of helping behavior *fully* account for the phenomenon of altruism, and we have resoundingly answered no. What accounts for the remainder, for those instances of helping behavior that are not readily reducible to helping behavior that has a self-interested payoff?

In short, our answer has been self-regard, which we have at various points sought to distinguish from narrow, "first-order" self-interest. Altruism is not something that confronts the self as a foreign imposition, as a moral directive from the outside. Rather, the seeds for an altruistic disposition are part of our biological machinery, if ones not yet fully developed, and so altruism is, already, an important part of human identity. Since it is part of self-regard to become in our existence what we are in our essence, it behooves us to cultivate our altruistic identity. Not surprisingly, this is precisely what human beings do, in any number of ways: via the formation of psychological self-understandings that follow and complement our biological impulses, through recourse to the demands of moral reason, and by heeding the directives to exhibit compassion issued in various religious traditions. While there is no one bona fide route to becoming an altruist, one of the things altruists do have in common is their self-understanding *as* altruists.

Altruists distinguish themselves most decisively from nonaltruists not because they are essentially different from nonaltruists, but because they have acquired, whereas others have yet to acquire, a proper self-understanding of human nature and (therefore) human purpose in this world. Correct self-understanding precipitates moral virtue. As we explained in chapter four, we are persuaded by the consistency of the testimony of Kristen Monroe's interviewees, all of whom articulated, in one way or another, without prompting, "the idea of being welded together, of belonging to one human family." Trying to get at the "heart" of altruism, Monroe writes:

> I would characterize it as a different way of seeing things; it certainly represents a different way of seeing the world and oneself in relation to others. Altruists have a particular perspective in which all mankind is connected through a common humanity, in which each individual is linked to all others and to a world in which all living beings are entitled to a certain humane treatment merely by virtue of being alive. It is not any mystical blending of the self with another; rather, it is a very simple but deeply felt recognition that we all share certain characteristics and are entitled to certain rights, merely by virtue of our common humanity. It constitutes a powerful statement about what it means to be a human being.[34]

Perhaps the most important remark in this explanation is that altruists are not different from nonaltruists; they *see* things differently. Their perspective is mature. The altruistic outlook represents at once a development beyond and a fulfillment of human nature. Not everyone is so advanced in his or her character development, and so not everyone is as close to self-fulfillment as altruists are. But everyone is, in theory, positioned to move existentially closer to these humanly appropriate states by becoming more benevolent.

This conclusion is consistent with the view that we have presented in this book about the relationship between nature and nurture. In cultivating the loving disposition with which we are provided by our nature—in nurturing our nature—we attend to one of our most "natural" objectives, namely, to become more loving as we spend more time, in the course of our lives, situating ourselves in a human context. Awareness of self and awareness of others go hand in hand. They are the keys to connecting our evolutionarily advantageous proclivities for helping behavior to the psychological mechanisms, rational frameworks, and religious motivations that refine those behaviors into something considerably more robust. The phenomenon of "humanity" itself, quite apart from traits that humans possess, implies a recognition of and identification with others, something that becomes apparent only as we also get to know ourselves. As we discover in ourselves the capacity to love, a capacity that significantly drives our interactions with others even before we are aware of it, we come to realize the use to which this capacity is put and at *that* point begin to take some responsibility for directing it. What this means is that although the many diverse instances of altruism one can identify (many of which we listed in chapter one) are in themselves quite plausibly the product of different motivations, they are nonetheless connected to one another insofar as they represent the various manifested phases of the same maturing trait. This process of trait maturation through self-discovery is not unique to the moral domain. For example, as we age and develop, we recognize in ourselves the inborn predisposition to fight or flee in dangerous situations, a recognition we can then use to begin devising better strategies for protecting ourselves. Likewise, when we discover ourselves as loving, we first wonder why this is so and then, naturally if not easily, begin to take an active role in harnessing that capacity to serve better the end for which it was evolutionarily intended.

Moral development is thus one kind of development within our species. Like other capacities we possess, our capacity to be moral predates but is refined by our consciousness of it. The fulfillment of this capacity may depend upon self-awareness, but the capacity itself does not. So altruism is reflected in both unlearned and learned behavior. This conclusion has implications for how we have evaluated the moral and religious traditions examined in this book. In chapter five we found shortcomings with Kantianism and consequentialism. As we showed, these theories place almost all the emphasis on self-aware, rational deliberation, leaving the impression that morality is an independent constraint on the human agent rather than the natural outgrowth of human flourishing. The Aristotelian alternative to these theories, which itself emphasizes the importance of reason, is a more realistic, organic option, for it takes into account both the preconscious and the rational impetuses for other-regard. Likewise, in chapter six we offered an interpretation of Christian and Buddhist ethics that treats "humanity" as something to be transformed rather than left behind: hence, our decision to call attention to some Christian thinkers who embrace the idea of a grace *fulfilling* nature, rather than to others who subscribe to a notion of grace lifting us out of nature. We are and remain embodied, biological organisms. We are neither trapped by our past nor free from it. Reason and religion, insofar as they are morally useful at all for human beings, must respect this axiom. It follows that an altruistic identity is something we cultivate, not something we can simply or abruptly select for ourselves in response to moral directives handed down to us.

Conclusion: Closing the Moral Gap

Can nature provide an appropriate instruction manual for right conduct? It can, if "nurture" is understood as that offshoot of nature that critiques (and can then go on to correct) itself. We have rejected ethical naturalism, which acknowledges no gap between "is" and "ought," that is, between the default capacity for other-regard with which nature endows us and our incentive (which also implies ability) to refine this capacity as a result of our experience in the world. On the other hand, we have also argued against versions of rational and religious idealism that do acknowledge the is–ought gap but get around it by deeming the default stance irrelevant to the question of morality, considering human nature itself as a mere starting point that can quickly be left behind. Between these two poles, we have tried to carve out a *via media*. There is a "moral gap," we recognize, but that gap is a variable, not a constant, represented by the distance that spans a nature unnurtured and a nature nurtured. Since the very idea of "nurturing" is a process, not a singular event, the distance between "is" and "ought" cannot be determined in any given moment. Over the course of our lifetimes, the gap will shorten, not because our moral demands lessen, but because over time we acquire the skills to be able to meet more of them. What motivates the painstaking desire to acquire these moral skills is, among other things, a proper self-understanding according to which we come to see our welfare and destiny as bound up with that of all others, everywhere, or so we have argued.

This isn't merely a platitude. We really do share not only a common humanity but also a common destiny as a species on this planet. Our collective actions now affect who we become in the future. As organic beings, we exist interdependently with all other beings on earth; and, as never before, we must find a way to address together issues such as looming environmental upheavals, dwindling resources, and outbreaks of violence on ever-grander scales. People in one part of the globe must face the consequences of decisions made in another part. Opting out, as Chris McCandless came to realize, is not a viable choice.

Fortunately, we *do* have the resources and wherewithal to address the problems we will inevitably face. Unlike other animals, we have the ability to reflect on our condition and the consequences of the choices we make. But they are choices, and there are obstacles to overcome, obstacles that themselves are also a product of our nature. There is undeniably a darker side of human existence. Our most recent century was our bloodiest century, and the tribal conflicts, warfare, and genocide occurring all over the planet show little sign of abating. We named this book *The Altruistic Species* not because we are naïve about the baser qualities of human nature; we mean the title to refer to a central part of our identity as a species, a part that can become even more central than it currently is. To be sure, our flourishing, to say nothing of our survival as a species, depends on its becoming more central.

Human beings are a distinctive species insofar as there *is*, for them, an is–ought gap that, in the first place, governs the trajectory of their future interactions with one another and, in the second place, lessens the more these interactions take place. Because of our moral resources—our psychological wherewithal to be self-aware and replicate compassionate behaviors once we recognize them; our ability to reason and thereby perceive the connectedness between ourselves and others outside our kin and clan; and our religious inspirations (fully developed in saints) to come to see our own welfare and that of others as one and the same—we, unlike the other animals, are able to discover just who we naturally are by questioning our natural limitations and exploring our opportunities. The Judaic thinker Abraham Heschel puts this point beautifully in the reflective volume devoted to his theological anthropology, *Who Is Man?* We are different from the animals, Heschel notes, because of our capacity, indeed our imperative, to change over time:

> It is a fatal illusion to assume that to be human is a fact given with human being rather than a goal and an achievement. To the animals, the world is what it is; to man this is a world in the making, and being human means being on the way, striving, waiting, hoping. Neither authenticity of existence nor the qualities of being human are safe properties. They are to be achieved, cultivated, and protected.[35]

According to Heschel, being human is at once always a possibility and a fact. Facticity by itself cannot do justice to human subjectivity. It is in our nature to be in motion, developing, moving toward something. In the moral sphere, this implies, there is no encyclopedia for right conduct that demarcates law from prohibition, the permissible from the proscribed. Sometimes our duty amounts to our discovering, in living, what is required of us. We cannot take for granted what this will be before our encounter with others, much less remain indifferent to new demands that will reveal themselves to us in the future. The distance between "is" and "ought" changes for human individuals throughout the course of their lives and so do the two coordinates that mark these endpoints. The implication in terms of altruism is clear: we perhaps begin held under the sway of simple forms of reciprocity and kin preference, but over time these limited expressions of love expand and find deeper expression across wider gulfs.

Perhaps surprisingly, Charles Darwin believed the same thing. In *The Descent of Man*, Darwin stated:

> As man advances in civilization, and small tribes are united into larger communities, the simplest reason would tell each individual that he ought to extend his social instincts and sympathies to all the members of the same nation, though personally unknown to him. This point being reached, there is only an artificial barrier to prevent his sympathies extending to the men of all nations and races.[36]

According to Darwin, as our inherited traits for sympathy are tested upon manifesting themselves in human environments, the *natural* outcome is for these traits to become more developed. Obstacles to their doing so Darwin regards as "artificial." The point is not, of course, that realities of evolution are not as relevant as we might have thought for determining our moral obligations to one another. Quite to the contrary, as a species we have evolved not to remain static individual organisms throughout our lives.

This observation makes sense in light of the quest of self-realization that many altruists reveal to be autobiographically true. Most altruists reach a point in their lives at which they pause to look back and see what new truths have emerged since an earlier time in which their moral horizons were more limited. Gandhi, a Hindu, *came* to identify with the plight of the harijan (untouchable class) and then with Muslims. Oskar Schindler, initially a profiteer in Hitler's Germany, *came* to see the Jews as deserving of his sympathy and respect. In both cases these "expansions of concern" were somehow environmentally triggered, but could not have been had not at least their latent possibility been programmed within them to begin with. So it is the case with lesser-known altruists-in-the-making around the globe, who are every day arriving at equally fundamental truths about themselves, truths that translate into benevolent acts and, eventually, a benevolent character. This is indeed fulfillment, even if one that never reaches completion.

Notes

INTRODUCTION: SELFISHNESS AND SELFLESSNESS

1. In the months that followed Hurricane Katrina, several newspaper articles appeared substantiating the choice police officers were forced to make between continuing to stand their posts and attending to the needs of their families. See, e.g., "Katrina Made Police Choose Between Duty and Loved Ones," *USA Today*, Feb. 20, 2006, which can also be accessed at www.usatoday.com/news/nation/2006-02-20-neworleanspolice_x.htm.

2. The term "commonsense morality" was given its first explication by Henry Sidgwick. See Sidgwick, *The Methods of Ethics*, 7th ed. (Chicago: Univ. of Chicago Press, 1962), 214–15. Sidgwick's general understanding of the concept, which pertains to common intuitions that the majority of us have about how much morality can come to demand of us, has for the most part remained intact since Sidgwick introduced it, although the concept has spawned scores of subscribers and critics. A classic example of a defender of commonsense morality is J. O. Urmson. See Urmson, "Saints and Heroes," in *Essays in Moral Philosophy*, ed. A. I. Melden (Seattle: Univ. of Washington Press, 1958), 198–216. One of the most notable critics of commonsense morality is Shelly Kagan, whose volume *The Limits of Morality* (Oxford: Oxford Univ. Press, 1989) is a sustained argument for consequentialism.

3. Bernard Gert, *Common Morality: Deciding What to Do* (Oxford: Oxford Univ. Press, 2005), 7ff.

4. Andrew Michael Flescher, *Heroes, Saints, and Ordinary Morality* (Washington, DC: Georgetown Univ. Press, 2003).

5. See especially Kristen Renwick Monroe, *The Heart of Altruism: Perceptions of a Common Humanity* (Princeton: Princeton Univ. Press, 1996), 10ff., 101–5.

6. See, e.g., Gary Becker, *The Economic Approach to Human Behavior* (Chicago: Univ. of Chicago Press, 1976); R. Withrobe, "It Pays to Do Good, but Not More Good Than It Pays," *Journal of Behavior and Organization* 2 (1981): 201–13; Howard Margolis, *Selfishness, Altruism, and Rationality* (New York: Cambridge Univ. Press, 1981); S. C. Kolm, "Altruism and Efficiency," *Ethics* 94 (1983): 18–65; and Robert Axelrod, *The Evolution of Cooperation* (New York: Basic Books, 1985).

7. C. Daniel Batson, *The Altruism Question: Toward a Social-Psychological Answer* (Hillsdale, NJ: Lawrence Elbraum Associates, 1991), 6.

8. Auguste Comte, *A General View of Positivism*, 2d ed., trans. J. H. Bridges (London: Trubner, 1865), 374.

9. The distinction between description and explanation can be found in Wayne Proudfoot, *Religious Experience* (Berkeley: Univ. of California Press, 1985), 69–74.

10. Thomas Hobbes, *Leviathan* (Oxford: Oxford Univ. Press, 1967), 45ff.

11. Axelrod, *Evolution of Cooperation*, 55–69.

12. Richard Dawkins, *The Selfish Gene*, 2nd ed. (Oxford: Oxford Univ. Press, 1989).

13. Monroe, *Heart of Altruism*, 11.

14. Kristen Renwick Monroe, "John Donne's People: Explaining Differences Between Rational Actors and Altruists Through Cognitive Frameworks," *Journal of Politics* 53 (1991): 394–433.

15. Edith Wyschogrod, *Saints and Postmodernism: Revisioning Moral Philosophy* (Chicago: Univ. of Chicago Press, 1990), 147.

16. The phrase is one Martin Luther King Jr. liked to mention. See King, *A Testament of Hope: The Essential Writings and Speeches of Martin Luther King, Jr.*, ed. James M. Washington (San Francisco: HarperSanFrancisco, 1986), 626.

17. Stephen J. Pope, *The Evolution of Altruism and the Ordering of Love* (Washington, DC: Georgetown Univ. Press, 1994), xii.

CHAPTER 1: ALTRUISM DEFINED

1. Albert Camus, *The Plague*, trans. Stuart Gilbert (New York: Vintage Press, 1991), 163.

2. Immanuel Kant, *The Groundwork of the Metaphysics of Morals*, trans. H. J. Paton (New York: Harper & Row, 1964), 63–64.

3. Aristotle, *Nicomachean Ethics*, trans. Terence Irwin (Indianapolis, IN: Hackett, 1985), 1168a28–29.

4. Wyschogrod, *Saints and Postmodernism*, xxiv, 63ff.

5. Neera Kapur Badhwar, "Altruism Versus Self-Interest: Sometimes a False Dichotomy," in *Altruism*, ed. Ellen Frankel Paul, Fred D. Miller Jr., and Jeffrey Paul (Cambridge: Cambridge Univ. Press, 1993), 103.

6. The best of the many articles written about Zell Kravinsky appeared in *New Yorker* magazine August 2, 2004; it can also be accessed at http://facstaff.unca.edu/moseley/zellkravinsky%27skidney.pdf. The article is particularly effective because it leaves the reader ambivalent about how to interpret the donor's actions, simultaneously presenting strong cases for his moral heroism and his irrational lunacy. As a matter of note, Dr. Radi Zaki, who performed the operation, reported that, out of nearly two hundred kidney transplants, he had never before taken a kidney from a living donor and placed it in the body of an unrelated recipient. The recipient, Donnell Reid, was one of almost sixty thousand Americans on the waiting list for a kidney transplant.

7. We distinguish "intent" from "motivation." Intent refers narrowly to the *self-conscious* formation of a motive and implies the influence of some form of reasoning on action, whereas motivation refers to both the self-conscious and the nonconscious motives for doing something. Thus, intent is a species of the larger genus of motivation. This distinction will become significant in part II when we begin to discuss some of the motivations for acting in an other-regarding manner of which we are not necessarily aware.

8. James R. Ozinga, *Altruism* (Westport, CT: Praeger, 1999), xvi.

9. Stephen G. Post et al., "General Introduction," in *Altruism and Altruistic Love: Science, Philosophy, and Religion in Dialogue* (New York: Oxford Univ. Press, 2002), 3.

10. Batson, *Altruism Question*, 6.

11. Richard Dawkins, *The Selfish Gene*, 2d ed. (Oxford: Oxford Univ. Press, 1989), 4.

12. This point seems so counterintuitive that it bears further clarification. We have so far distinguished three things: the ultimate object of other-regard, intention, and consequences. It is the presence of the first of these that, as we will go on to suggest at the end of the chapter, is always indicative of altruism. In the case of Bernie LaPlante, there are bad intentions and good consequences. Are those whom he rescues his "ultimate objects of other-regard"? Given the way the scene transpires, we could make a case that they are. Bernie LaPlante is seemingly transformed through his own actions, despite his initially dubious intentions. One might even argue that his motivations override his intentions, to such a degree that he seems confused at moments by his own conduct.

13. Bernard Williams, "Moral Luck," in *Moral Luck: Philosophical Papers, 1973–1980* (Cambridge: Cambridge Univ. Press, 1981), 18.
14. Anders Nygren, *Agape and Eros*, trans. Philip S. Watson (Philadelphia: Westminster Press, 1953), 722–23.
15. Gene Outka, *Agape: An Ethical Analysis* (New Haven: Yale Univ. Press, 1972), 156ff.
16. Pope, *Evolution of Altruism*, 67–70.
17. Ibid.
18. Mordecai Paldiel, *Sheltering the Jews: Stories of Holocaust Rescuers* (Minneapolis, MN: Fortress Press, 1996), 201.
19. For two volumes that amply confirm this claim, see Samuel P. Oliner and Pearl M. Oliner, *The Altruistic Personality: Rescuers of Jews in Nazi Europe* (New York: Free Press, 1988); and Monroe, *Heart of Altruism*.
20. Kristen Monroe, for example, distinguishes the righteous gentile as the highest sort of altruist within the typology she presents in *The Heart of Altruism*. Beginning with an analysis of entrepreneurs and philanthropists, Monroe's treatment culminates with a consideration of Holocaust rescuers, more morally laudatory even than moral heroes.
21. David Heyd, *Supererogation: Its Status in Ethical Theory* (Cambridge: Cambridge Univ. Press, 1982), 173.
22. Ibid., 273ff. The discussion of Heyd and supererogation offered here is presented at more length in Flescher, *Heroes, Saints, and Ordinary Morality*, 38ff.
23. See, e.g., Monroe, *Heart of Altruism*, 104–5; Oliner and Oliner, *Altruistic Personality*, 113, 228ff.
24. Urmson, "Saints and Heroes," 203.
25. This is how the consequentialist Shelly Kagan characterizes the argument in favor of commonsense morality. See Kagan, *Limits of Morality*, 35.
26. Shelly Kagan makes the distinction between "pale" and "vivid" beliefs in *Limits of Morality*, 283–91.
27. Monroe, *Heart of Altruism*, 11.
28. For a more thorough discussion about interpreting altruists' claim to be doing "nothing out of the ordinary," see Flescher, *Heroes, Saints, and Ordinary Morality*, 139ff.
29. Aristotle, *Nicomachean Ethics*, 1169a6–8.
30. Ibid., 1177b35.
31. Owen Flanagan, *Varieties of Moral Personality: Ethics and Psychological Realism* (Cambridge: Harvard Univ. Press, 1991), 29.
32. It is even conceivable that a "double-effect doctrine" is at work here if it actually turns out to be a form of self-love that motivates love of the other. In this view, once we discover happiness, or a flourishing, in loving ourselves rightly by loving our neighbor, the affirmation that ensues acquires an energy of its own that carries forward and further precipitates altruistic behavior. This process does not reduce altruistic motives to selfishness. To the contrary, it is consistent with the "overlapping Venn diagram" model discussed above. We would like to thank Stephen Post for calling our attention to this observation.

Chapter 2: The Perspective of Psychological Egoism

1. Jack London, *The Sea Wolf* (New York: Bantam Books, 1991).
2. Ibid., 35.
3. Ibid., 55.
4. Ibid.
5. Ibid., 57.
6. Thomas Hobbes, *Leviathan* (London: Andrew Crooke, 1651), in *Hobbes's Leviathan* (London: Oxford Univ. Press, 1967).

7. The individual is likewise explicable by reduction to still smaller quantities, those being the motions of its various parts. This conception of the body as an aggregate of its parts—no different in principle from a complicated machine—is an example of what Edith Wyschogrod disparagingly calls a "Pythagorean body," any version of which cannot possibly, in her view, do justice to the phenomenon of altruism. See Wyschogrod, "Pythagorean Bodies and the Body of Altruism," in *Altruism and Altruistic Love*, ed. Stephen G. Post et al. (Oxford: Oxford Univ. Press, 2002), 29–39.

8. Hobbes, *Leviathan*, 94–95. (Chap. 13, pp. 60–61 in original.)

9. Ibid., 95–96. (Chap. 13, pp. 61–62 in original.)

10. Ibid., 96. (Chap. 13, p. 62 in original.)

11. Ibid., 97. (Chap. 13, p. 62 in original.)

12. Ibid., 98, 99. (Chap. 13, p. 63; chap. 14, p. 64 in original.)

13. Ibid., 100. (Chap. 14, pp. 64–65 in original.)

14. Ibid., 101. (Chap. 14, p. 66 in original.)

15. Ibid., 97. (Chap 13, p. 62 in original.)

16. Thomas Hobbes, *Human Nature*, vol. 4 of *English Works*, ed. W. Molesworth (London: John Bohn, 1839), 49.

17. Hobbes, *Leviathan*, 45. (Chap. 6, p. 27 in original.)

18. Jean-Jacques Rousseau, *Discourse on the Origin of Inequality* (1755), trans. Donald A. Cress (Indianapolis, IN: Hackett, 1992), 19.

19. Ibid.

20. Ibid., 14.

21. Ibid., 38.

22. Ibid., 25–71.

23. Hobbes, *Leviathan*, 97. (Chap. 13, p. 63 in original.)

24. Ibid., 39–41. (Chap. 6, pp. 23–24 in original.)

25. James Rachels, *The Elements of Moral Philosophy*, 2d ed. (New York: McGraw-Hill, 1993), 66–67.

26. See Joel Feinberg, "Psychological Egoism," in *Ethics: History, Theory, and Contemporary Issues*, ed. Stephen M. Cahn and Peter Markie (New York: Oxford Univ. Press, 1998), 559–60.

27. Rachels, *Elements of Moral Philosophy*, 67.

28. Feinberg, "Psychological Egoism," 559.

29. Ibid., 564.

30. Bentham introduced his famous phrase "the greatest happiness divided by the greater number" in 1776. See Jeremy Bentham, *A Fragment on Government* (Cambridge: Cambridge Univ. Press, 1988).

31. For an interesting example of this with pigeons, see Howard Rachlin and Leonard Green, "Commitment, Choice, and Self-Control," *Journal of the Experimental Analysis of Behavior* 17 (1972): 15–22.

32. See, e.g., Kristen Renwick Monroe, *The Heart of Altruism* (Princeton: Princeton Univ. Press, 1996), 104, 105; Samuel P. Oliner and Pearl M. Oliner, *The Altruistic Personality* (New York: Free Press, 1988), 113, 228; and Kristen Renwick Monroe, Michael C. Barton, and Ute Klingemann, "Altruism and the Theory of Rational Action: Rescuers of Jews in Nazi Europe," *Ethics* 101 (Oct. 1990): 103.

33. Joseph Butler, *Fifteen Sermons on Human Nature Preached at the Rolls Chapel* (New York: Robert Carter & Bros., 1860; reprinted as *Fifteen Sermons*, Charlottesville, VA: Lincoln-Rembrandt, 1993).

34. Ibid., 127. This part of Butler's argument is sometimes called "Butler's stone."

35. Ibid., 127–28.

36. Feinberg, "Psychological Egoism," 562.

37. Butler, *Fifteen Sermons*, 128–29.

38. Ibid., 132.
39. Neera Kapur Badhwar, "Altruism Versus Self-Interest: Sometimes a False Dichotomy," in *Altruism*, ed. Ellen Frankel Paul, Fred D. Miller Jr., and Jeffrey Paul (Cambridge: Cambridge Univ. Press, 1993), 90–117.
40. Ibid., 114–15.
41. Ibid., 110–11.
42. Ibid., 111–12.
43. For a moving recounting of these events, see Philip Hallie, *Lest Innocent Blood Be Shed* (New York: Harper & Row, 1979).
44. Originally appeared in the *Springfield* (Illinois) *Monitor,* quoted in Feinberg, "Psychological Egoism," 560–61, and Rachels, *Elements of Moral Philosophy*, 68.
45. Rachels, *Elements of Moral Philosophy*, 68.

Chapter 3: The Perspective of Evolutionary Biology

1. Sigmund Freud, "Introductory Lectures on Psycho-Analysis," in *The Standard Edition of the Complete Psychological Works of Sigmund Freud*, trans. James Strachey (London: Hogarth Press, 1963), 16:284–85.
2. Ibid., 285.
3. Ibid.
4. Stephen J. Gould, "Can We Complete Darwin's Revolution?" in *Dinosaur in a Haystack* (New York: Crown Trade Paperbacks, 1995), 325–34. The metaphor of pedestal-smashing in the preceding paragraph is Gould's.
5. Richard Dawkins, *The Selfish Gene*, 2d ed. (Oxford: Oxford Univ. Press, 1989). Readers should note that a great deal of the content of this chapter is explained by Dawkins in more depth and with greater clarity, wit, and style than we could ever hope to muster. To keep the number of footnotes manageable, we will resist the temptation to footnote every idea that owes something to his body of work.
6. Charles Darwin, *The Origin of Species*, in *"The Origin of Species" and "The Descent of Man"* (New York: World Library, orig. 1859), 374.
7. Gil Ast, "The Alternative Genome," *Scientific American*, April 2005, 60.
8. Dawkins, *Selfish Gene*, 28. Dawkins attributes this definition to George C. Williams.
9. Matt Ridley, *Nature via Nurture: Genes, Experience, and What Makes Us Human* (New York: HarperCollins, 2003), 4.
10. In fact, normal rates of mutation are so high that the genome of any species complex enough to require a fairly large amount of DNA would quickly be randomized (which would be quite fatal to the species) if it did not possess considerable error-correcting machinery. For a fascinating examination of how complex multicellular creatures mitigate the destructive effects of high mutation rates, including how sexual reproduction helps solve the problem of this "mutational meltdown" of the genome, see Mark Ridley, *The Cooperative Gene: How Mendel's Demon Explains the Evolution of Complex Beings* (New York: Free Press, 2001).
11. The general idea of kin selection can be traced all the way back to Darwin, and the idea occurs in the work of the founders of population genetics such as Ronald Fisher, Sewall Wright, and J.B.S. Haldane, but the seminal formal work appears in a pair of papers: William D. Hamilton, "The Genetical Evolution of Social Behavior" (I and II), *Journal of Theoretical Biology* 7 (1964): 1–16; 17–52.
12. Paul W. Sherman, "Nepotism and the Evolution of Alarm Calls," *Science* 197 (1977): 1246–53.
13. Darwin, *Origin of Species*, 204.
14. Robert Axelrod, *The Evolution of Cooperation* (New York: Basic Books, 1985).
15. See Dawkins, *Selfish Gene*, 183.

16. G. S. Wilkinson, "Reciprocal Food-Sharing in the Vampire Bat," *Nature* 308 (1984): 181–84.

17. Charles Darwin, *The Descent of Man*, in *"The Origin of Species" and "The Descent of Man"* (New York: World Library, orig. 1859), 500.

18. V. C. Wynne-Edwards, *Animal Dispersion in Relation to Social Behaviour* (New York: Hafner, 1962).

19. See George C. Williams, *Adaptation and Natural Selection: A Critique of Some Current Evolutionary Thought* (Princeton: Princeton Univ. Press, 1966).

20. Elliott Sober and David Sloan Wilson, *Unto Others: The Evolution and Psychology of Unselfish Behavior* (Cambridge: Harvard Univ. Press, 1998).

21. Ibid., 43–46.

22. Ibid., 23–30.

23. Dawkins, *Selfish Gene*, 4.

24. Lee Dugatkin, *Cheating Monkeys and Citizen Bees* (New York: Free Press, 1999), 18.

25. Dawkins, *Selfish Gene*, 4.

26. Given the present context, we should be clear that Dawkins has argued forcefully that group selection is not a viable evolutionary mechanism (e.g., ibid., 7–11). Considered as a hypothetical possibility, however, group-selected beneficence would meet Dawkins' definitional criteria for altruism.

27. Ibid., 107.

28. Ibid., 6.

Chapter 4: Psychological Perspectives

1. We again want to remind the reader that we are using the term "motivation" considerably more broadly than we have used the term "intent." The latter refers to the self-conscious, deliberate formation of a motive for doing something, while the former refers to a broader class of impetuses of which intent is but one example. This is an important distinction for us because in chapter one we claimed that altruism is likely, but not necessarily, accompanied by other-regarding intent. By contrast, we claimed, when one acts for the sake of others, where their well-being and welfare become the ultimate object of concern, altruism is always present. In the context of this discussion, altruistic motivation essentially means that others are the ultimate objects of concern.

2. For a comprehensive analysis of the fears aroused by the prospect of an innate human nature and why those fears are unwarranted, see Steven Pinker, *The Blank Slate* (New York: Viking Press, 2002).

3. Steven Pinker, *How the Mind Works* (New York: Norton, 1997), 401.

4. This usage of the word *heuristics*, which will be employed throughout this chapter, may seem unusual to those who are unfamiliar with the way it is used in cognitive psychology, where it refers to any of a variety of mental shortcuts (not necessarily implemented consciously) for solving certain classes of problems. Unlike algorithmic problem-solving methods, which guarantee a correct solution if implemented correctly, heuristic strategies apply rules of thumb that are usually, but not always, effective. Heuristic problem-solving strategies offer certain advantages, however; of special note are their execution speed and their applicability to a wide range of problems, the particulars of which may be quite unpredictable. For these reasons, psychological mechanisms much more frequently tend to be of the heuristic rather than the algorithmic sort. Affective states provide a good example; a few emotions can handle an extraordinarily wide range of unpredictable circumstances.

5. Matt Ridley, *Nature via Nurture*, 248.

6. Pinker, *How the Mind Works*, 400–401.

7. Pinker, *Blank Slate*, 247.

8. David Hume, *A Treatise of Human Nature*, ed. L. A. Selby-Bigge and P. H. Nidditch (Oxford: Clarendon Press, 1978), 521.

9. Robert Trivers, "The Evolution of Reciprocal Altruism," *Quarterly Review of Biology* 46 (1971): 35–57.

10. Trivers cites Justin Aronfreed, *Conduct and Conscience: The Socialization of Internalized Control over Behavior* (New York: Academic Press, 1968), in support of this claim. It should be pointed out, though, that greater need is often correlated with greater costs of helping, which can act as a deterrent to helping. For example, in one field experiment, bystanders in a subway were less likely to help a collapsed man if he had blood trickling from his mouth than if there was no blood. See Jane A. Piliavin and Irving M. Piliavin, "Effect of Blood on Reactions to a Victim," *Journal of Personality and Social Psychology* 23 (1972): 353–61.

11. See, e.g., Ernst Fehr and Simon Gächter, "Altruistic Punishment in Humans," *Nature* 415 (2002): 137–40.

12. Joseph Butler, *Fifteen Sermons on Human Nature Preached at the Rolls Chapel* (New York: Robert Carter & Bros., 1860; reprinted as *Fifteen Sermons*, Charlottesville, VA: Lincoln-Rembrandt, 1993), 131. On this topic see also Joel Feinberg, "Psychological Egoism," in *Ethics: History, Theory, and Contemporary Issues*, ed. Stephen M. Cahn and Peter Markie (New York: Oxford Univ. Press, 1998), 561.

13. Pinker, *Blank Slate*, 244.

14. Pinker, *How the Mind Works*, 406.

15. In Batson's usage, "empathy" appears to be a broader construct than "sympathy," with sympathy constituting a key ingredient of empathy when the other is perceived to be in need.

16. For a book-length synopsis of about the first ten years of this line of research, see C. Daniel Batson, *The Altruism Question: Toward a Social-Psychological Answer* (Hillsdale, NJ: Lawrence Erlbaum Associates, 1991).

17. C. Daniel Batson et al., "Is Empathic Emotion a Source of Altruistic Motivation?" *Journal of Personality and Social Psychology* 40 (1981): 290–302. See also Batson, *Altruism Question*, 109–27.

18. See Batson, *Altruism Question*, 149–74, for summaries of these and other experiments showing that empathy is distinct from self-reward seeking.

19. Ibid., 128–48.

20. C. Daniel Batson and Tecia Moran, "Empathy-Induced Altruism in a Prisoner's Dilemma," *European Journal of Social Psychology* 29 (1999): 909–24.

21. C. Daniel Batson and Nadia Ahmad, "Empathy-Induced Altruism in a Prisoner's Dilemma II: What if the Target of Empathy Has Defected?" *European Journal of Social Psychology* 31 (2001): 25–36.

22. See Batson and Moran, "Empathy-Induced Altruism," 913.

23. See Pinker's chapter in *The Blank Slate* called "The Many Roots of Our Suffering" (241–68) for more examples and a more detailed analysis of the societal problems resulting from the mechanisms of altruism.

24. Ibid., 245.

25. Stephen J. Pope, *The Evolution of Altruism and the Ordering of Love* (Washington, DC: Georgetown Univ. Press, 1994), 157.

26. Ibid., 156–57.

27. The description of this incident is based on the story by Warren R. Young, "There's a Girl on the Tracks!" *Reader's Digest*, Feb. 1977, 91–95.

28. Quoted in the *New York Times*, Jan. 3, 2007. For another news report of this incident with links to video clips of interviews with Mr. Autrey, go to http://www.cbsnews.com/stories/2007/01/03/national/main2324961.shtml.

29. Kristen Renwick Monroe, *The Heart of Altruism: Perceptions of a Common Humanity* (Princeton: Princeton Univ. Press, 1996).

30. Samuel P. Oliner and Pearl M. Oliner, *The Altruistic Personality: Rescuers of Jews in Nazi Europe* (New York: Free Press, 1988).

31. Philip Hallie, *Lest Innocent Blood Be Shed: The Story of the Village of Le Chambon and How Goodness Happened There* (New York: Harper & Row, 1979).

32. Monroe, *Heart of Altruism*, 104.

33. Hallie, *Lest Innocent Blood Be Shed*, 20–21.

34. Ibid., 127.

35. Monroe, *Heart of Altruism*, 210–11.

36. Ibid., 234.

37. Dharol Tankersley, C. Jill Stowe, and Scott A. Huettel, "Altruism Is Associated with an Increased Neural Response to Agency," *Nature Neuroscience* 10 (2007): 150–51.

38. For a good recent review, see Nancy Eisenberg and Carlos Valiente, "Parenting and Children's Prosocial and Moral Development," in *Handbook of Parenting*, 2d ed., vol. 5, *Practical Issues in Parenting*, ed. Marc H. Bornstein (Mahwah, NJ: Lawrence Erlbaum Associates, 2002).

39. Oliner and Oliner, *Altruistic Personality*, 179.

40. Jonathan Glover, *Humanity: A Moral History of the Twentieth Century* (New Haven: Yale Univ. Press, 2000).

41. George Orwell, quoted by Glover, *Humanity*, 53.

42. See, e.g., Robert Wright, *The Moral Animal* (New York: Vintage Books, 1994); Frans de Waal, *Good Natured: The Origins of Right and Wrong in Humans and Other Animals* (Cambridge: Harvard Univ. Press, 1996); Matt Ridley, *The Origins of Virtue: Human Instincts and the Evolution of Cooperation* (New York: Penguin Books, 1996); and Marc D. Hauser, *Moral Minds: How Nature Designed Our Universal Sense of Right and Wrong* (New York: HarperCollins, 2006).

43. Hume, *Treatise of Human Nature*, 469.

44. The term is attributed to G. E. Moore, *Principia Ethica* (Cambridge: Cambridge Univ. Press, 1968).

45. Examples of these sorts of behaviors can be found in Scott Forbes, *A Natural History of Families* (Princeton: Princeton Univ. Press, 2005), and Douglas W. Mock, *More Than Kin and Less Than Kind: The Evolution of Family Conflict* (Cambridge, MA: Belknap Press, 2004).

46. Randy Thornhill and Craig T. Palmer, *A Natural History of Rape: Biological Bases of Sexual Coercion* (Cambridge: MIT Press, 2000).

47. Ibid., 144–45.

48. Edward O. Wilson, *On Human Nature* (Cambridge: Harvard Univ. Press, 1978), 195ff.

49. Ibid., 198.

50. Ibid., 198–99.

51. Michael Ruse, "A Darwinian Naturalist's Perspective on Altruism," in *Altruism and Altruistic Love: Science, Philosophy, and Religion in Dialogue*, ed. Stephen G. Post et al. (New York: Oxford Univ. Press, 2002), 151–64.

CHAPTER 5: PHILOSOPHICAL PERSPECTIVES

1. Peter Singer, *The Expanding Circle: Ethics and Sociobiology* (New York: Farrar, Straus & Giroux, 1981), 85ff., 158.

2. Ibid., 139.

3. Ibid., 139–40.

4. Ibid., 140ff.

5. Ibid., 140.

6. Ibid., 109–19.

7. Peter Singer has been at the forefront of those arguing for animal rights for the last thirty years. See, e.g., his pioneering book *Animal Liberation*, 2d ed. (New York: Random House, 1990).

8. Singer, *Expanding Circle*, 125.

9. Ibid., 126.

10. Michael Stocker, "The Schizophrenia of Modern Ethical Theories," in *The Virtues: Contemporary Essays on Moral Character*, ed. Robert B. Kruschwitz and Robert C. Roberts (Belmont, CA: Wadsworth, 1987), 40–41. Stocker is heavily influenced by Elizabeth Anscombe, who launched a version of this criticism in a seminal article that for the first time called into question the popular dominant moral theories of Kantianism and consequentialism in the modern era. See G. E. M. Anscombe, "Modern Moral Philosophy," *Philosophy* 33 (1958): 1–19.

11. Immanuel Kant, *Groundwork of the Metaphysics of Morals*, trans. H. J. Paton (New York: Harper & Row, 1964), 67.

12. Ibid., 68.

13. Ibid., 68–69.

14. Ibid., 91.

15. Ibid.

16. Ibid., 92.

17. Ibid., 59–60.

18. Ibid., 65.

19. Ibid., 97.

20. Thomas Hill Jr., "Beneficence and Self-Love: A Kantian Perspective," in *Altruism*, ed. Ellen Frankel Paul, Fred D. Miller Jr., and Jeffrey Paul (Cambridge: Cambridge Univ. Press, 1993), 13ff.

21. Ibid., 12.

22. Shelly Kagan, *The Limits of Morality* (Oxford: Oxford Univ. Press, 1989), 1–2.

23. Peter Singer, "Famine, Affluence, and Morality," *Philosophy and Public Affairs* 1 (1972): 229.

24. Ibid., 231.

25. James Rachels, "Killing and Starving to Death," *Philosophy* 54 (1979): 162.

26. Ibid., 167.

27. Ibid., 165ff.

28. See, e.g., William James' chapter on saints in *The Varieties of Religious Experience: A Study in Human Nature* (New York: Penguin Books, 1982); Robert Adams, "Saints," *Journal of Philosophy* 81 (1984): 392–401; and Edith Wyschogrod, *Saints and Postmodernism: Revisioning Moral Philosophy* (Chicago: Univ. of Chicago Press, 1990), 3, 146ff. The autobiographies and published reflections of Gandhi, Dorothy Day, and Martin Luther King Jr. are replete with examples of the passionate devotion of these figures to the ones they helped, as well as the suffering and self-reproach they incurred when they felt they failed to do enough. See M. K. Gandhi, *My Varnashrama Dhama* (Bombay: Bharatiya Vidya Bhavan, 1965); Dorothy Day, *The Long Loneliness: The Autobiography of Dorothy Day* (San Francisco: HarperSanFrancisco, 1997); and Martin Luther King Jr., *A Testament of Hope: The Essential Writings and Speeches of Martin Luther King, Jr.*, ed. James M. Washington (San Francisco: HarperSanFrancisco, 1986).

29. Susan Wolf, "Moral Saints," *Journal of Philosophy* 79 (1982): 421ff. In her article, Wolf contrasts the "rational" saint to the "loving" saint. The former listens exclusively to reason and then employs self-discipline to overcome distracting selfish impulses, whereas the latter is somehow effortlessly able to bypass these impulses altogether en route to altruistic sacrifice. Wolf contends that both the rational and the loving saint fail to lead rich or humanly flourishing human lives.

30. Ibid., 439.
31. See, e.g., Stephen G. Post, "Altruism, Happiness, and Health: It's Good to Be Good," *International Journal of Behavioral Medicine* 12, no. 2 (2005): 66–77.
32. William A. Galston, "Cosmopolitan Altruism," in *Altruism*, ed. Paul, Miller, and Paul, 118.
33. King, *Testament of Hope*, 256–57.
34. Obviously, altruists who are influential to a vast number of people cannot, practically speaking, take a personal interest in everyone they help. However, they can get to know many of them personally, and indeed enough of them to ensure that their giving does not remain a project in the abstract but is an appropriate and sensitive response to the actual needs of the ones they are helping. In this sense, the impersonal other can become, if only temporarily, "personal."
35. Stephen G. Post, "Love and the Order of Beneficence," *Soundings* 75 (1992): 505–6.
36. Aristotle, *Nicomachean Ethics*, trans. Terence Irwin (Indianapolis, IN: Hackett, 1985), 1166b33–1167a5.
37. Galston, "Cosmopolitan Altruism," 128–29.
38. In this vein, Dorothy Day's exhortation to "strip ourselves of our possessions" and embrace poverty voluntarily becomes particularly poignant. See Day, *Selected Writings: By Little and by Little*, ed. Robert Ellsberg (New York: Orbis Books, 1992), 109–11.
39. Galston, "Cosmopolitan Altruism," 134.
40. Jean Hampton, "Selflessness and the Loss of Self," in *Altruism*, ed. Paul, Miller, and Paul, 161.
41. Alasdair MacIntyre, *Dependent Rational Animals: Why Human Beings Need the Virtues* (Chicago: Open Court Press, 1999), 71ff.
42. See Julia E. Judish, "Balancing Special Relations with the Ideal of Agape," *Journal of Religious Ethics* 26 (1998): 17–46.
43. Aristotle, *Nicomachean Ethics*, 1155a16–21.
44. Charles H. Kahn, "Aristotle and Altruism," *Mind* 90 (1981): 24.
45. On the point of objectivity in virtue ethics, particularly in the case of Aristotle, see Martha Nussbaum, "Non-relative Virtues: An Aristotelian Approach," in *Midwest Studies in Philosophy* 13, ed. P. French, T. Uehling, and H. Wettstein (Notre Dame, IN: Notre Dame Univ. Press, 1988), 32–53.
46. This account of the thesis of moral development within an Aristotelian ethic is presented in much greater detail in Andrew Michael Flescher, *Heroes, Saints, and Ordinary Morality* (Washington, DC: Georgetown Univ. Press, 2003), 238ff.
47. Here Iris Murdoch's definition of "courage" as indicative of a kind of moral maturity is apt. It is, she explains, "an operation of wisdom and love" that results in "seeing the order of the world in the light of the Good and revisiting the true, or more true, conceptions of that which we formerly misconceived." See Murdoch, *The Sovereignty of Good* (London: Routledge & Kegan Paul, 1970), 95.
48. Aristotle, *Nicomachean Ethics*, 1169a8–11.
49. MacIntyre, *Dependent Rational Animals*, 160 (emphasis ours).
50. Aristotle, *Nicomachean Ethics*, 1169a19–22.

CHAPTER 6: RELIGIOUS PERSPECTIVES

1. St. Augustine, as quoted by John E. Hare, *The Moral Gap: Kantian Ethics, Human Limits, and God's Assistance* (Oxford: Clarendon Press, 1996), 113.
2. Ibid., 113ff. This passage is discussed in Andrew Michael Flescher, *Heroes, Saints, and Ordinary Morality* (Washington, DC: Georgetown Univ. Press, 2003), 45.
3. Jacob Neusner and Bruce D. Chilton, eds., *Altruism in World Religions* (Washington, DC: Georgetown Univ. Press, 2005), vii.

4. For example, as we argued in chapter one, cost to self is not *necessarily* an aspect of all altruistic activity. Furthermore, as we suggest later in this chapter, while saints, the paragons of their religious traditions, do sacrifice themselves for their beneficiaries, they do not necessarily see the acts as sacrifices but rather as self-fulfillment in a larger sense.

5. On the relationship between "worldview" and "ethos" in religious traditions, see Clifford Geertz, "Ethos, World View, and the Analysis of Sacred Symbols," in *The Interpretation of Cultures* (New York: Basic Books, 1973), 126–41.

6. Ernst Troeltsch, *The Christian Faith* (Minneapolis, MN: Fortress Press, 1991), 38.

7. Friedrich Nietzsche, "*Twilight of the Angels*" *and* "*The Antichrist*," trans. R. J. Hollingdale (New York: Penguin Books, 1990), 135.

8. See section nine of William James, "The Will to Believe," in *The Will to Believe and Other Essays in Popular Philosophy* (New York: Dover, 1956), 26.

9. Edith Wyschogrod, *Saints and Postmodernism: Revisioning Moral Philosophy* (Chicago: Univ. of Chicago Press, 1990), 146.

10. H. Richard Niebuhr, *Christ and Culture* (New York: Harper & Row, 1951).

11. For an explanation of this phrase, see Stanley Hauerwas and William H. Willimon, *Resident Aliens: Life in the Christian Colony* (Nashville, TN: Abingdon Press, 1989).

12. This reference comes from Martin Luther King Jr.'s famous 1963 "Letter from Birmingham Jail." See King, *A Testament of Hope: The Essential Writings and Speeches of Martin Luther King, Jr.*, ed. James M. Washington (San Francisco: HarperSanFrancisco, 1986), 300.

13. This is a phrase that Dorothy Day, who appropriated it from St. Thérèse of Lisieux, made famous. See Dorothy Day, *By Little and by Little: Selected Writings of Dorothy Day*, ed. Robert Ellsberg (New York: Orbis Books, 1992).

14. Stephen J. Pope, *The Evolution of Altruism and the Ordering of Love* (Washington, DC: Georgetown Univ. Press, 1994), 153.

15. Thomas Oord, *Science of Love: The Wisdom of Well-Being* (Philadelphia: Templeton Foundation Press, 2004), 84–89. For Oord, love is a relational endeavor, depending always on the connection between giver and recipient, both of whom, in his view, can be human beings as well as God. Love, in other words, is a mutually acknowledged sympathetic response between two parties. In this sense, Oord breaks from traditional interpretations of Christianity that insist on an asymmetrical relation between the giver and the recipient.

16. Pope, *Evolution of Altruism*, xii.

17. For a concise history of the Buddha and an account of the advent of Buddhism, see Walpola Rahula, *What the Buddha Taught* (New York: Grove Press, 1959).

18. We will, in this section, examine aspects of both the Mahayana and the Theravada subtraditions, The two subtraditions are consistent with each other in their understanding of the centrality of the role of altruism in Buddhism.

19. For a clear account of the Eightfold Path, see Rahula, *What the Buddha Taught*, 45.

20. Ibid., 46–47.

21. Ibid.

22. Ibid.

23. Peter Harvey, *An Introduction to Buddhist Ethics* (Cambridge: Cambridge Univ. Press, 2000), 118.

24. *Mahaparinibbana Sutta*, ed. F. Max Mueller, Sacred Books of the East 11 (Oxford: Clarendon Press, 1881).

25. Harvey, *Introduction to Buddhist Ethics*, 36.

26. Ibid., 25–27, 40ff.

27. Ibid., 43.

28. Ibid.

29. Todd Lewis, "Altruism in Classic Buddhism," in *Altruism in World Religions*, ed. Jacob Neusner and Bruce D. Chilton (Washington, DC: Georgetown Univ. Press, 2005), 92.

30. *Samyutta Nikāya*, chapter 1:8, as cited by Lewis, "Altruism in Classic Buddhism," 94.

31. From the *Siksamuccaya*, in *The Buddhist Tradition in India, China and Japan*, ed. Theodore de Bary (New York: Vintage Books, 1972), 85.

32. Harvey, *Introduction to Buddhist Ethics*, 39–40.

33. See Winston King, *In the Hope of Nibbana: Theravada Buddhist Ethics* (La Salle, IL: Open Court Press, 1964), and Melford Spiro, *Buddhism and Society: A Great Tradition and Its Burmese Vicissitudes* (New York: Harper Paperbacks, 1972).

34. Taken from *The Ultimate Light*, as quoted by Harvey B. Aronson, *Love and Sympathy in Theravada Buddhism* (Delhi, India: Motilal Banarsidass, 1986), 63–64.

35. Aronson, *Love and Sympathy*, 24.

36. Ibid., 44.

37. Rahula, *What the Buddha Taught*, 75.

38. Tore Frängsmyr and Irwin Abrams, eds., *Nobel Lectures, Peace 1981–1990* (Singapore: World Scientific Publishing, 1997).

39. John Hick, *An Interpretation of Religion: Human Responses to the Transcendent* (New Haven: Yale Univ. Press, 1989), 307.

40. William James, *The Varieties of Religious Experience: A Study in Human Nature* (New York: Penguin Books, 1982), 358. For a further elaboration of the Jamesian attitude towards saints' relation to ordinary people, see Flescher, *Heroes, Saints, and Ordinary Morality*, 213ff.

41. This and similar quotes that resist the characterization of Dorothy Day as an officially recognized saint appear in Kenneth Woodward, *Making Saints: How the Catholic Church Determines Who Becomes a Saint, Who Doesn't, and Why* (New York: Simon & Schuster, 1990), 32.

42. Robert Inchausti, *The Ignorant Perfection of Ordinary People* (Albany: State Univ. of New York Press, 1991), 70. Also quoted and discussed in Flescher, *Heroes, Saints, and Ordinary Morality*, 197.

43. Wyschogrod, *Saints and Postmodernism*, 150ff.

44. Ibid., 146.

45. Ibid., 147.

46. Ibid.

47. Edith Wyschogrod has been heavily influenced by the ethical philosophy of Emmanuel Levinas, even adopting much of his terminology, such as the "trace" of the other and the "face to face" encounter. See, in particular, Levinas, *Otherwise Than Being or Beyond Essence*, trans. Alphonso Lingus (The Hague: Martinus Nijhoff, 1974).

48. We want to thank John P. Reeder for helping us develop this objection to Wyschogrod.

49. William James, *Varieties of Religious Experience*, 357.

50. Wyschogrod, *Saints and Postmodernism*, 44.

51. A. I. Melden, "Saints and Supererogation," in *Philosophy and Life: Essays on John Wisdom*, ed. Ilham Dilman (The Hague: Martinus Nijhoff, 1984), 77.

52. John A. Coleman, "After Sainthood?" in *Saints and Virtues*, ed. John Stratton Hawley (Berkeley: Univ. of California Press, 1982), 207.

53. For a full discussion of this point, see Flescher, *Heroes, Saints, and Ordinary Morality*, 199ff.

54. King, *Testament of Hope*, 20.

55. James, *Varieties of Religious Experience*, 357.

Chapter 7: Cultivating Our Altruistic Identity

1. As reported in Jon Krakauer, *Into the Wild* (New York: Anchor Books, 1997), 189.

2. Ayn Rand, *Atlas Shrugged* (New York: Penguin Books, 1999).

3. Ibid., pt. 3, chap. 1, sect. 1.
4. Krakauer, *Into the Wild*, 137.
5. Ibid., 135.
6. Stephen G. Post, ed., *Altruism and Health: Perspectives from Empirical Research* (Oxford: Oxford Univ. Press, 2007). Post has also recently published his own companion book summarizing these and similar findings. See Stephen G. Post and Jill Neimark, *Why Good Things Happen to Good People: The Exciting New Research That Proves the Link Between Doing Good and Living a Longer, Healthier, Happier Life* (Louisville, KY: Broadway Books, 2007).
7. Adam S. Hirschfelder and Sabrina L. Reilly, "Rx: Volunteer: A Prescription for Healthy Aging," in *Altruism and Health*, 116–40.
8. Doug Oman, "Does Volunteering Foster Physical Health and Longevity?" in *Altruism and Health*, 26.
9. For example, see Hirschfelder and Reilly, "Rx: Volunteer," 122ff.; and Elizabeth Midlarsky and Eva Kahana, "Altruism, Well-Being, and Mental Health Late in Life," in *Altruism and Health*, 56–69. See also Stephen G. Post, "Altruism, Happiness, and Health: It's Good to Be Good," *International Journal of Behavioral Medicine* 12, 2 no. 2 (2005): 68.
10. Post, "Altruism, Happiness, and Health," 68. The study Post cites was conducted by C. Schwartz, J. B. Meisenhelder, Y. Ma, and G. Reed, "Altruistic Social Interests Behaviors Are Associated with Better Mental Health," *Psychosomatic Medicine* 65 (2003): 778–85.
11. See also Post, "Altruism, Happiness, and Health," 70.
12. King, *Testament of Hope*, 626.
13. F. Warneken and M. Tomasello, "Altruistic Helping in Human Infants and Young Chimpanzees," *Science* 311 (2006): 1301–3.
14. Robert Wright, *The Moral Animal* (New York: Vintage Books, 1994), 9.
15. Ibid.
16. See http://www.msnbc.msn.com/id/15258312/. Since the Civil War nearly thirty-five hundred men and one woman have received the medal awarded for bravery above and beyond the call of duty.
17. As reported in the *New York Times*, Jan. 3, 2007.
18. Gary Becker, *The Economic Approach to Human Behavior* (Chicago: Univ. of Chicago Press, 1976), 284ff.
19. Kristen Renwick Monroe, *The Heart of Altruism: Perceptions of a Common Humanity* (Princeton: Princeton Univ. Press, 1996), 7ff., 159–60, 233ff.
20. Ibid., 236.
21. Ibid.
22. See Philip Hallie, *Lest Innocent Blood Be Shed: The Story of the Village of Le Chambon and How Goodness Happened There* (New York: Harper & Row, 1979).
23. K. Anders Ericcson et al., eds., *The Cambridge Handbook of Expertise and Expert Performance* (Cambridge: Cambridge Univ. Press, 2006).
24. Steven Pinker, *The Blank Slate: The Modern Denial of Human Nature* (New York: Viking Press, 2002), 260.
25. Ibid., 261ff.
26. Since we conceived of this class, many people have asked us how we selected the "altruists" from within our community. Particularly, they are interested in why some did not make the cut. We began with a pool of names recommended by several colleagues, administrators, students, and business leaders responding to our general announcement that we were searching for inspiring community leaders engaged in "social advocacy, service, and welfare efforts." In selecting from this pool we were governed by two limiting criteria. First, we did not include people whose altruistic activity we discovered was accompanied by a monetarily self-serving outcome. So, for example, we did not incorporate into the class people who were paid explicitly for their services (unless, in

rare cases, their contribution dramatically exceeded their compensation). Second, we ruled out those whose contributions to the community were motivated primarily by religious or political objectives. Thus, we did not include a representative of one home-less shelter who made benediction a condition of welfare but included the director of another faith-based organization that did not discriminate with respect to who received food and shelter. Naturally, over a period of the next couple of years, in no small part as a result of reading students' final papers, we arrived at a solid roster of thirty or so citizens from the Chico, California, community whose worthy inclusion on our list of altruists was beyond dispute.

27. As reported in the *Chico News and Review*, Nov. 23, 2006. See http://www.news review.com/chico/Content?oid=oid%3A247844.

28. Ibid.

29. Marc D. Hauser, *Moral Minds: How Nature Designed Our Universal Sense of Right and Wrong* (New York: HarperCollins, 2006).

30. Ibid., 121ff., 421–22.

31. Hauser explicitly says as much in a recent interview in *American Scientist Online*. See http://www.americanscientist.org/template/InterviewTypeDetail/assetid/52880;jses-sionid=aaa5LVFO.

32. See, e.g., Richard Rorty's review of *Moral Minds* in the *New York Times*, Aug. 25, 2006. Rorty makes the interesting point that morality is not analogous to linguistic grammar, the structure of which is arguably rarely ever in doubt. See http:/www.nytimes.com/2006/08/27/books/review/Rorty.t.html?ex=1314331200&en=d7159bc4d0fa6fc7&ei=508 8&partner=rssnyt&emc=rss.

33. Hauser, *Moral Minds*, 163–241.

34. Monroe, *Heart of Altruism*, 206.

35. Abraham J. Heschel, *Who Is Man?* (Stanford, CA: Stanford Univ. Press, 1965), 41.

36. Charles Darwin, *"The Descent of Man" and "Selection in Relation to Sex"* (Princeton, NJ: Princeton Univ. Press, 1981), 1:100–101.

References

Adams, Robert. "Saints." *Journal of Philosophy* 81 (1984): 392–401.

Anscombe, G. E. M. "Modern Moral Philosophy." *Philosophy* 33 (1958): 1–19.

Aristotle. *Nicomachean Ethics.* Translated by Terence Irwin. Indianapolis, IN: Hackett, 1985.

Aronfreed, Justin. *Conduct and Conscience: The Socialization of Internalized Control over Behavior.* New York: Academic Press, 1968.

Aronson, Harvey B. *Love and Sympathy in Theravada Buddhism.* Delhi, India: Motilal Banarsidass, 1986.

Ast, Gil. "The Alternative Genome." *Scientific American,* April 2005, 40–47.

Axelrod, Robert. *The Evolution of Cooperation.* New York: Basic Books, 1985.

Badhwar, Neera Kapur. "Altruism Versus Self-Interest: Sometimes a False Dichotomy." In *Altruism,* edited by Ellen Frankel Paul, Fred D. Miller Jr., and Jeffrey Paul, 90–117. Cambridge: Cambridge Univ. Press, 1993.

Batson, C. Daniel. *The Altruism Question: Toward a Social-Psychological Answer.* Hillsdale, NJ: Lawrence Erlbaum Associates, 1991.

Batson, C. Daniel; Bruce D. Duncan; Paula Ackerman; Teresa Buckley; and Kimberly Birch. "Is Empathic Emotion a Source of Altruistic Motivation?" *Journal of Personality and Social Psychology* 40 (1981): 290–302.

Batson, C. Daniel, and Tecia Moran. "Empathy-Induced Altruism in a Prisoner's Dilemma." *European Journal of Social Psychology* 29 (1999): 909–24.

Batson, C. Daniel, and Nadia Ahmad. "Empathy-Induced Altruism in a Prisoner's Dilemma II: What if the Target of Empathy Has Defected?" *European Journal of Social Psychology* 31 (2001): 25–36.

Becker, Gary. *The Economic Approach to Human Behavior.* Chicago: Univ. of Chicago Press, 1976.

Bentham, Jeremy. *A Fragment on Government.* Cambridge: Cambridge Univ. Press, 1988.

Butler, Joseph. *Fifteen Sermons on Human Nature Preached at the Rolls Chapel.* New York: Robert Carter & Bros., 1860; reprinted as *Fifteen Sermons,* Charlottesville, VA: Lincoln-Rembrandt, 1993.

Camus, Albert. *The Plague.* Translated by Stuart Gilbert. New York: Vintage Press, 1991.

Coleman, John A. "After Sainthood?" In *Saints and Virtues,* edited by John Stratton Hawley, 205–25. Berkeley: Univ. of California Press, 1982.

Comte, Auguste. *A General View of Positivism.* 2d ed. Translated by J. H. Bridges. London: Trubner, 1865.

Darwin, Charles. *"The Origin of Species" and "The Descent of Man."* New York: World Library, orig. 1859.

———. *"The Descent of Man" and "Selection in Relation to Sex."* Vol. 1. Princeton, NJ: Princeton Univ. Press, 1981.

Dawkins, Richard. *The Selfish Gene.* 2d ed. Oxford: Oxford Univ. Press, 1989.

Day, Dorothy. *Selected Writings: By Little and By Little.* Edited by Robert Ellsberg. New York: Orbis Books, 1992.

————. *The Long Loneliness: The Autobiography of Dorothy Day*. San Francisco: HarperSanFrancisco, 1997.

De Bary, Theodore, ed. *The Buddhist Tradition in India, China and Japan*. New York: Vintage Books, 1972.

De Waal, Frans. *Good Natured: The Origins of Right and Wrong in Humans and Other Animals*. Cambridge, MA: Harvard Univ. Press, 1996.

Dugatkin, Lee. *Cheating Monkeys and Citizen Bees*. New York: Free Press, 1999.

Eisenberg, Nancy, and Carlos Valiente. "Parenting and Children's Prosocial and Moral Development." In *Handbook of Parenting*, 2d ed. Vol. 5, *Practical Issues in Parenting*. Edited by Marc H. Bornstein. Mahwah, NJ: Lawrence Erlbaum Associates, 2002.

Ericcson, K. Anders; Neil Charness; Paul Feltovich; and Robert R. Hoffman, eds. *The Cambridge Handbook of Expertise and Expert Performance*. Cambridge: Cambridge Univ. Press, 2006.

Fehr, Ernst, and Simon Gächter. "Altruistic Punishment in Humans." *Nature* 415 (2002): 137–40.

Feinberg, Joel. "Psychological Egoism." In *Ethics: History, Theory, and Contemporary Issues*, edited by Stephen M. Cahn and Peter Markie, 557–65. New York: Oxford Univ. Press, 1998.

Flanagan, Owen. *Varieties of Moral Personality: Ethics and Psychological Realism*. Cambridge, MA: Harvard Univ. Press, 1991.

Flescher, Andrew Michael. *Heroes, Saints, and Ordinary Morality*. Washington, DC: Georgetown Univ. Press, 2003.

Forbes, Scott. *A Natural History of Families*. Princeton, NJ: Princeton Univ. Press, 2005.

Frängsmyr, Tore, and Irwin Abrams, eds. *Nobel Lectures, Peace 1981–1990*. Singapore: World Scientific Publishing, 1997.

Freud, Sigmund. *The Standard Edition of the Complete Psychological Works of Sigmund Freud*. Translated by James Strachey. London: Hogarth Press, 1963.

Galston, William A. "Cosmopolitan Altruism." In *Altruism*, edited by Ellen Frankel Paul, Fred D. Miller Jr., and Jeffrey Paul, 118–34. Cambridge: Cambridge Univ. Press, 1993.

Gandhi, M. K. *My Varnashrama Dhama*. Bombay: Bharatiya Vidya Bhavan, 1965.

Geertz, Clifford. *The Interpretation of Cultures*. New York: Basic Books, 1973.

Gert, Bernard. *Common Morality: Deciding What to Do*. Oxford: Oxford Univ. Press, 2005.

Glover, Jonathan. *Humanity: A Moral History of the Twentieth Century*. New Haven, CT: Yale Univ. Press, 2000.

Gould, Stephen J. "Can We Complete Darwin's Revolution?" In *Dinosaur in a Haystack*, 325–34. New York: Crown Trade Paperbacks, 1995.

Hallie, Philip. *Lest Innocent Blood Be Shed: The Story of the Village of Le Chambon and How Goodness Happened There*. New York: Harper & Row, 1979.

Hamilton, William D. "The Genetical Evolution of Social Behavior" (I and II). *Journal of Theoretical Biology* 7 (1964):1–16; 17–52.

Hampton, Jean. "Selflessness and the Loss of Self." In *Altruism*, edited by Ellen Frankel Paul, Fred D. Miller Jr., and Jeffrey Paul, 135–65. Cambridge: Cambridge Univ. Press, 1993.

Hare, John E. *The Moral Gap: Kantian Ethics, Human Limits, and God's Assistance*. Oxford: Clarendon Press, 1996.

Harvey, Peter. *An Introduction to Buddhist Ethics*. Cambridge: Cambridge Univ. Press, 2000.

Hauerwas, Stanley, and William H. Willimon, *Resident Aliens: Life in the Christian Colony*. Nashville, TN: Abingdon Press, 1989.

Hauser, Marc D. *Moral Minds: How Nature Designed Our Universal Sense of Right and Wrong*. New York: HarperCollins, 2006.

Heschel, Abraham J. *Who Is Man?* Stanford, CA: Stanford Univ. Press, 1965.

Heyd, David. *Supererogation: Its Status in Ethical Theory*. Cambridge: Cambridge Univ. Press, 1982.

Hick, John. *An Interpretation of Religion: Human Responses to the Transcendent*. New Haven, CT: Yale Univ. Press, 1989.

Hill, Thomas, Jr. "Beneficence and Self-Love: A Kantian Perspective." In *Altruism*, edited by Ellen Frankel Paul, Fred D. Miller Jr., and Jeffrey Paul, 1–23. Cambridge: Cambridge Univ. Press, 1993.

Hirschfelder, Adam S., and Sabrina L. Reilly. "Rx: Volunteer: A Prescription for Healthy Aging." In *Altruism and Health: Perspectives from Empirical Research*, edited by Stephen G. Post, 116–40. Oxford: Oxford Univ. Press, 2007.

Hobbes, Thomas. *Human Nature*. Vol. 4 of *English Works*. Edited by W. Molesworth. London: John Bohn, 1839.

———. *Leviathan* (London: Andrew Crooke, 1651), in *Hobbes's Leviathan*. Oxford: Oxford Univ. Press, 1967.

Hume, David. *An Inquiry Concerning the Principles of Morals*. Edited by Charles W. Hendel. New York: Liberal Arts Press, 1957.

———. *A Treatise of Human Nature*. Edited by L. A. Selby-Bigge and P. H. Nidditch. Oxford: Clarendon Press, 1978.

Inchausti, Robert. *The Ignorant Perfection of Ordinary People*. Albany: State Univ. of New York Press, 1991.

James, William. *The Will to Believe and Other Essays in Popular Philosophy*. New York: Dover, 1956.

———. *The Varieties of Religious Experience: A Study in Human Nature*. New York: Penguin Books, 1982.

Judish, Julia E. "Balancing Special Relations with the Ideal of Agape." *Journal of Religious Ethics* 26 (1998): 17–46.

Kagan, Shelly. *The Limits of Morality*. Oxford: Oxford Univ. Press, 1989.

———. *Normative Ethics*. Oxford: Westview Press, 1998.

Kahn, Charles H. "Aristotle and Altruism." *Mind* 90 (1981): 20–40.

Kant, Immanuel. *The Doctrine of Virtue: Part II of the Metaphysics of Morals*. Translated by Mary J. Gregor. Philadelphia: Univ. of Pennsylvania Press, 1964.

———. *Groundwork of the Metaphysics of Morals*. Translated by H. J. Paton. New York: Harper & Row, 1964.

———. *Critique of Practical Reason*. 3d ed. Translated by Lewis White Beck. New York: Macmillan, 1993.

King, Martin Luther, Jr. *A Testament of Hope: The Essential Writings and Speeches of Martin Luther King, Jr.* Edited by James M. Washington. San Francisco: HarperSanFrancisco, 1986.

King, Winston. *In the Hope of Nibbana: Theravada Buddhist Ethics*. La Salle, IL: Open Court Press, 1964.

Kolm, S. C. "Altruism and Efficiency." *Ethics* 94 (Jan. 1983): 18–65.

Krakauer, John. *Into the Wild*. New York: Anchor Books, 1997.

Levinas, Emmanuel. *Otherwise Than Being or Beyond Essence*. Translated by Alphonso Lingus. The Hague: Martinus Nijhoff, 1974.

Lewis, Todd. "Altruism in Classic Buddhism." In *Altruism in World Religions*, edited by Jacob Neusner and Bruce D. Chilton, 88–114. Washington, DC: Georgetown Univ. Press, 2005.

London, Jack. *The Sea Wolf*. New York: Bantam Books, 1991.

MacIntyre, Alasdair. *Dependent Rational Animals: Why Human Beings Need the Virtues*. Chicago: Open Court Press, 1999.

Mahaparinibbana Sutta. Edited by F. Max Mueller. Sacred Books of the East 11. Oxford: Clarendon Press, 1881.

Margolis, Howard. *Selfishness, Altruism, and Rationality*. New York: Cambridge Univ. Press, 1981.

Melden, A. I. "Saints and Supererogation." In *Philosophy and Life: Essays on John Wisdom*, edited by Ilham Dilman, 61–79. The Hague: Martinus Nijhoff, 1984.

Midlarsky, Elizabeth, and Eva Kahana. "Altruism, Well-Being, and Mental Health Late in Life." In *Altruism and Health: Perspectives from Empirical Research*, edited by Stephen G. Post, 56–69. Oxford: Oxford Univ. Press, 2007.

Mock, Douglas W. *More Than Kin and Less Than Kind: The Evolution of Family Conflict*. Cambridge, MA: Belknap Press, 2004.

Monroe, Kristen Renwick. "John Donne's People: Explaining Differences Between Rational Actors and Altruists Through Cognitive Frameworks." *Journal of Politics* 53 (1991): 394–433.

———. *The Heart of Altruism: Perceptions of a Common Humanity*. Princeton, NJ: Princeton Univ. Press, 1996.

Monroe, Kristen Renwick; Michael C. Barton; and Ute Klingemann. "Altruism and the Theory of Rational Action: Rescuers of Jews in Nazi Europe." *Ethics* 101 (Oct. 1990): 103–22.

Moore, G. E. *Principia Ethica*. Cambridge: Cambridge Univ. Press, 1968.

Murdoch, Iris. *The Sovereignty of Good*. London: Routledge & Kegan Paul, 1970.

Neusner, Jacob, and Bruce D. Chilton, eds. *Altruism in World Religions*. Washington, DC: Georgetown Univ. Press, 2005.

Niebuhr, H. Richard. *Christ and Culture*. New York: Harper & Row, 1951.

Nietzsche, Friedrich. *"Twilight of the Idols" and "The Antichrist."* Translated by R. J. Hollingdale. New York: Penguin Books, 1990.

Nussbaum, Martha. "Non-relative Virtues: An Aristotelian Approach." In *Midwest Studies in Philosophy* 13, edited by P. French, T. Uehling, and H. Wettstein, 32–53. Notre Dame, IN: Notre Dame Univ. Press, 1988.

Nygren, Anders. *Agape and Eros*. Translated by Philip S. Watson. Philadelphia: Westminster Press, 1953.

Oliner, Samuel P., and Pearl M. Oliner. *The Altruistic Personality: Rescuers of Jews in Nazi Europe*. New York: Free Press, 1988.

Oman, Doug. "Does Volunteering Foster Physical Health and Longevity?" In *Altruism and Health: Perspectives from Empirical Research*, edited by Stephen G. Post, 15–32. Oxford: Oxford Univ. Press, 2007.

Oord, Thomas. *Science of Love: The Wisdom of Well-Being*. Philadelphia: Templeton Foundation Press, 2004.

Outka, Gene. *Agape: An Ethical Analysis*. New Haven, CT: Yale Univ. Press, 1972.

Ozinga, James R. *Altruism*. Westport, CT: Praeger, 1999.

Paldiel, Mordecai. *Sheltering the Jews: Stories of Holocaust Rescuers*. Minneapolis, MN: Fortress Press, 1996.

Paul, Ellen Frankel; Fred D. Miller Jr.; and Jeffrey Paul, eds. *Altruism*. Cambridge: Cambridge Univ. Press, 1993.

Piliavin, Jane A., and Irving M. Piliavin. "Effect of Blood on Reactions to a Victim." *Journal of Personality and Social Psychology* 23 (1972): 353–61.

Pinker, Steven. *How the Mind Works*. New York: Norton, 1997.

———. *The Blank Slate: The Modern Denial of Human Nature*. New York: Viking Press, 2002.

Pope, Stephen J. *The Evolution of Altruism and the Ordering of Love*. Washington, DC: Georgetown Univ. Press, 1994.

Post, Stephen G. "Love and the Order of Beneficence." *Soundings* 75 (1992): 503–15.

———. "Altruism, Happiness, and Health: It's Good to Be Good." *International Journal of Behavioral Medicine* 12 (2005): 66–77.

———, ed. *Altruism and Health: Perspectives from Empirical Research*. Oxford: Oxford Univ. Press, 2007.

Post, Stephen G., and Jill Neimark. *Why Good Things Happen to Good People: The Exciting New Research That Proves the Link Between Doing Good and Living a Longer, Healthier, Happier Life*. New York: Broadway Books, 2007.

Post, Stephen G.; Lynn G. Underwood; Jeffrey P. Schloss; and William B. Hurlbut. *Altruism and Altruistic Love: Science, Philosophy, and Religion in Dialogue.* New York: Oxford Univ. Press, 2002.

Proudfoot, Wayne. *Religious Experience.* Berkeley: Univ. of California Press, 1985.

Rachels, James. "Killing and Starving to Death." *Philosophy* 54 (1979): 159–71.

———. *The Elements of Moral Philosophy.* 2d ed. New York: McGraw-Hill, 1993.

Rachlin, Howard, and Leonard Green. "Commitment, Choice, and Self-Control." *Journal of the Experimental Analysis of Behavior* 17 (1972): 15–22.

Rahula, Walpola. *What the Buddha Taught.* New York: Grove Press, 1959.

Rand, Ayn. *Atlas Shrugged.* New York: Penguin Books, 1999.

Ridley, Mark. *The Cooperative Gene: How Mendel's Demon Explains the Evolution of Complex Beings.* New York: Free Press, 2001.

Ridley, Matt. *The Origins of Virtue: Human Instincts and the Evolution of Cooperation.* New York: Penguin Books, 1996.

———. *Nature via Nurture: Genes, Experience, and What Makes Us Human.* New York: HarperCollins, 2003.

Rousseau, Jean-Jacques. *Discourse on the Origin of Inequality.* Translated by Donald A. Cress. Indianapolis, IN: Hackett, 1992.

Ruse, Michael. "A Darwinian Naturalist's Perspective on Altruism." In *Altruism and Altruistic Love: Science, Philosophy, and Religion in Dialogue*, edited by Stephen G. Post, Lynn G. Underwood, Jeffrey P. Schloss, and William B. Hurlbut, 151–67. New York: Oxford Univ. Press, 2002.

Sherman, Paul W. "Nepotism and the Evolution of Alarm Calls." *Science* 197 (1977): 1246–53.

Sidgwick, Henry. *The Methods of Ethics.* 7th ed. Chicago: Univ. of Chicago Press, 1962.

Singer, Peter. "Famine, Affluence, and Morality," *Philosophy and Public Affairs* 1 (1972): 229–243

———. *The Expanding Circle: Ethics and Sociobiology.* New York: Farrar, Straus & Giroux, 1981.

———. *Animal Liberation.* 2d ed. New York: Random House, 1990.

Sober, Elliott, and David Sloan Wilson. *Unto Others: The Evolution and Psychology of Unselfish Behavior.* Cambridge, MA: Harvard Univ. Press, 1998.

Spiro, Melford. *Buddhism and Society: A Great Tradition and Its Burmese Vicissitudes.* New York: Harper Paperbacks, 1972.

Stocker, Michael. "The Schizophrenia of Modern Ethical Theories." In *The Virtues: Contemporary Essays on Moral Character*, edited by Robert B. Kruschwitz and Robert C. Roberts, 36-45. Belmont, CA: Wadsworth, 1987.

Tankersley, Dharol; Jill C. Stowe; and Scott A. Huettel. "Altruism Is Associated with an Increased Neural Response to Agency." *Nature Neuroscience* 10 (2007): 150–51.

Thornhill, Randy, and Craig T. Palmer. *A Natural History of Rape: Biological Bases of Sexual Coercion.* Cambridge, MA: MIT Press, 2000.

Trivers, Robert. "The Evolution of Reciprocal Altruism." *Quarterly Review of Biology* 46 (1971): 35–57.

Troeltsch, Ernst. *The Christian Faith.* Minneapolis, MN: Fortress Press, 1991.

Urmson, J. O. "Saints and Heroes." In *Essays in Moral Philosophy*, edited by A. I. Melden, 198–216. Seattle: Univ. of Washington Press, 1958.

Warneken, F., and M. Tomasello. "Altruistic Helping in Human Infants and Young Chimpanzees." *Science* 311 (2006): 1301–3.

Wilkinson, G. S. "Reciprocal Food-Sharing in the Vampire Bat." *Nature* 308 (1984): 181–84.

Williams, Bernard. "Moral Luck." In *Moral Luck: Philosophical Papers, 1973–1980*, edited by Bernard Williams. Cambridge: Cambridge Univ. Press, 1981.

Williams, George C. *Adaptation and Natural Selection: A Critique of Some Current Evolutionary Thought.* Princeton, NJ: Princeton Univ. Press, 1966.

Wilson, Edward O. *On Human Nature.* Cambridge, MA: Harvard Univ. Press, 1978.

Withrobe, R. "It Pays to Do Good, but Not More Good Than It Pays." *Journal of Behavior and Organization* 2 (1981): 201–13.

Wolf, Susan. "Moral Saints." *Journal of Philosophy* 79 (1982): 419–39.

Woodward, Kenneth. *Making Saints: How the Catholic Church Determines Who Becomes a Saint, Who Doesn't, and Why.* New York: Simon & Schuster, 1990.

Wright, Robert. *The Moral Animal.* New York: Vintage Books, 1994.

Wynne-Edwards, V. C. *Animal Dispersion in Relation to Social Behaviour.* New York: Hafner, 1962.

Wyschogrod, Edith. *Saints and Postmodernism: Revisioning Moral Philosophy.* Chicago: Univ. of Chicago Press, 1990.

———. "Pythagorean Bodies and the Body of Altruism." In *Altruism and Altruistic Love,* edited by Stephen G. Post, Lynn G. Underwood, Jeffrey P. Schloss, and William B. Hurlbut, 29–39. Oxford: Oxford Univ. Press, 2002.

Young, Warren R. "There's a Girl on the Tracks!" *Reader's Digest,* Feb. 1977, 91–95.

Index